The Philosophy of Creative Solitudes

Also available from Bloomsbury

On the Feminist Philosophy of Gillian Howie, edited by Victoria Browne and
Daniel Whistler
Aesthetic Marx, edited by Samir Gandesha and Johan Hartle
The Subject of Rosi Braidotti, edited by Bolette Blaagaard and Iris van der Tuin
The Sea, David Farrell Krell

The Philosophy of Creative Solitudes

Edited by David Jones
Kennesaw State University, USA

BLOOMSBURY ACADEMIC
LONDON • NEW YORK • OXFORD • NEW DELHI • SYDNEY

BLOOMSBURY ACADEMIC
Bloomsbury Publishing Plc
50 Bedford Square, London, WC1B 3DP, UK
1385 Broadway, New York, NY 10018, USA

BLOOMSBURY, BLOOMSBURY ACADEMIC and the Diana logo are trademarks of
Bloomsbury Publishing Plc

First published in Great Britain 2019

Copyright © David Jones and contributors, 2019

David Jones has asserted his right under the Copyright, Designs and Patents Act,
1988, to be identified as Editor of this work.

Cover design: Eleanor Rose
Cover image © David Farrell Krell

Bloomsbury Publishing Plc does not have any control over, or responsibility for, any
third-party websites referred to or in this book. All internet addresses given in this
book were correct at the time of going to press. The author and publisher regret any
inconvenience caused if addresses have changed or sites have ceased to exist, but can
accept no responsibility for any such changes.

A catalogue record for this book is available from the British Library.

A catalog record for this book is available from the Library of Congress.

ISBN: HB: 978-1-3500-7785-0
ePDF: 978-1-3500-7786-7
eBook: 978-1-3500-7787-4

Typeset by Newgen KnowledgeWorks Pvt. Ltd., Chennai, India
Printed and bound in Great Britain

To find out more about our authors and books visit www.bloomsbury.com
and sign up for our newsletters.

Contents

Contributors

Peg Birmingham is Professor of Philosophy at DePaul University. She is the author of *Hannah Arendt and Human Rights: The Predicament of Common Responsibility* (Indiana University Press, 2006), coeditor (with Philippe van Haute) of *Dissensus Communis: Between Ethics and Politics* (Koros, 1996), and coeditor (with Anna Yeatman) of *The Aporia of Rights: Citizenship in an Era of Human Rights* (Bloomsbury, 2014). She is the editor of *Philosophy Today*.

Walter Brogan is a member of the philosophy department at Villanova University and of the College of Fellows at Western Sydney University. He is on the board of directors of the Collegium Phaenomenologicum in Italy. Dr. Brogan is a past member of the executive committee of the American Philosophical Association and the Society for Phenomenology and Existential Philosophy. He is the cofounder of the Ancient Philosophy Society and a past editor of *Epoché: A Journal for the History of Philosophy*. His publications include a book on Heidegger and Aristotle, several edited volumes, and an array of articles on ancient philosophy and contemporary continental philosophy.

Françoise Dastur taught philosophy at the University of Paris I (1969–1995), the University of Paris XII (1995–1999), and the University of Nice-Sophia Antipolis (1999–2003). She was a visiting professor at the Universities of Mannheim, Rio de Janeiro, Caracas, Warwick, Essex, DePaul, Northwestern, and Boston College. She was, as honorary Professor of Philosophy, attached to the Husserl Archives of Paris (ENS Ulm), a research unit affiliated to the French National Center for Research (CNRS), until June 2017. She was one of the founding members in 1993 and the president until 2003 of the École Française de Daseinsanalyse, of which she is now honorary president. She has published many articles in French, English, and German on Husserl, Heidegger, Merleau-Ponty, Ricoeur, Derrida, Levinas, and is the author of several books in French, from which five have been translated into English: *Heidegger and the Question of Time* (Humanities Press, 1998); *Telling Time, Sketch of a Phenomenological Chronology* (Athlone Press, 2000); *Death, An Essay on Finitude* (Athlone Press, 1996); *How Are We to Confront Death? An Introduction to Philosophy*, translated by Robert Vallier with a foreword by David Farrell Krell (Fordham University Press, 2012); and *Questions of Phenomenology, Language, Alterity, Temporality, Finitude*, translated by Robert Vallier (Perspective in Continental Philosophy, Fordham University

Press, 2017). Her latest publications in French include *Déconstruction et phénoménologie. Derrida en débat avec Husserl et Heidegger* (« Le Bel Aujourd'hui » collection, Paris, Hermann, 2016); *Leçons sur la Genèse de la pensée dialectique, Schelling, Hölderlin, Hegel* (« Cours de Philosophie » collection, Paris, Ellipses, 2016); and *Figures du néant et de la négation entre Orient et Occident* (Les Belles Lettres, Paris, Encre Marine, 2018).

David Jones is University Distinguished Professor and Professor of Philosophy at Kennesaw State University in Atlanta. He is Editor of *Comparative and Continental Philosophy* (Taylor and Francis) and has been Visiting Professor of Confucian Classics at Emory and Visiting Scholar in 2013 and 2015 at the Institute for Advanced Studies in Humanities and Social Science at National Taiwan University. His *The Fractal Self: Science, Philosophy, and the Evolution of Human Cooperation* with John L. Culliney is published by the University of Hawai'i Press (2017), and edited books include *The Humanist Spirit of Daoism* by Chen Guying with Sarah Flavel (Brill Academic, 2018); *Confucianism: Its Roots and Global Significance*, Ming-huei Lee, edited and annotated (University of Hawai'i Press, 2017); *On the True Sense of Art: A Critical Companion to the Transfigurements of John Sallis* (Northwestern, 2016) with Jason M. Wirth and Michael Schwartz; *Emerging Patterns within the Supreme Polarity: Returning to Zhu Xi* with He Jinli (SUNY Press, 2015); *The Dynamics of Cultural Counterpoint in Asian Studies* (SUNY Press, 2014) with Michele Marion; *The Gift of Logos: Essays in Continental Philosophy* (Cambridge Scholars, 2010) with Jason M. Wirth and Michael Schwartz; *Asian Texts—Asian Contexts: Encountering the Philosophies and Religions of Asia* with Ellen Klein (SUNY Press, 2009); *Confucius Now: Contemporary Encounters with the Analects* (Open Court, 2008); and *Buddha Nature and Animality* (Jain, 2007).

David Farrell Krell is Emeritus Professor of Philosophy at DePaul University, Chicago, and Brauer Distinguished Visiting Professor of German Studies at Brown University, Providence. His philosophical work focuses on the areas of early Greek thought, German Romanticism and Idealism, and contemporary European thought and literature. His most recent scholarly books include *The Sea: A Philosophical Encounter* (Bloomsbury, 2018) and *The Cudgel and the Caress: Reflections on Cruelty and Tenderness* (SUNY Press, 2019). He has also published a number of short stories and three novels.

Alphonso Lingis is Professor of Philosophy Emeritus at the Pennsylvania State University. Among his books published are *The Community of Those Who Have Nothing in Common, Abuses, The Imperative, Dangerous Emotions, Trust, The First Person Singular, Contact, Violence and Splendor, Irrevocable,* and *The Alphonso Lingis Reader.*

Dawne McCance is a Distinguished Professor at the University of Manitoba, Canada. She has published six books and many journal essays and book chapters in disability studies, critical animal studies, and on the work of Jacques Derrida. She is the author of *The Reproduction of Life Death: Derrida's La vie la mort* (Fordham University Press, Spring 2019).

Jill Marsden is Senior Lecturer in The School of the Arts at The University of Bolton, UK. She is the author of *After Nietzsche: Notes Towards a Philosophy of Ecstasy* (Palgrave, 2002) and a range of other writings on Nietzsche, modernism, and continental philosophy. Jill was a student of David Krell's at the University of Essex in the 1980s, and her approach to philosophy has been greatly inspired by him. She is currently working on the concept of literary thinking.

Michael Naas is Professor of Philosophy at DePaul University. He works in the areas of ancient Greek philosophy and contemporary French philosophy. His most recent books include *The End of the World and Other Teachable Moments: Jacques Derrida's Final Seminar* (Fordham, 2014) and *Plato and the Invention of Life* (Fordham, 2018). He also coedits the *Oxford Literary Review*.

William McNeill is Professor of Philosophy at DePaul University. He is the author of *The Time of Life: Heidegger and Ēthos* (SUNY Press, 2006) and *The Glance of the Eye: Heidegger, Aristotle, and the Ends of Theory* (SUNY Press, 1999). He has translated numerous works by Heidegger, most recently his lectures on Hölderlin's Hymn "Remembrance" (co-translated with Julia Ireland [Indiana University Press, 2018]).

Angelica Nuzzo is Professor of Philosophy at the Graduate Center and Brooklyn College (City University of New York). Among her books are *Approaching Hegel's Logic, Obliquely: Melville, Molière, Beckett* (SUNY Press, 2018); *Memory, History, Justice in Hegel*, (Macmillan, 2012); *Ideal Embodiment: Kant's Theory of Sensibility* (Indiana University Press, 2008); and *Kant and the Unity of Reason* (Purdue University Press, 2005).

John Sallis is currently the Frederick J. Adelmann Professor of Philosophy at Boston College. Previously he held chairs at Pennsylvania State University, Vanderbilt University, Loyola University of Chicago, and Duquesne University. He has published more than twenty books, his books have been translated into more than a dozen languages. He has also served as Editor of many publications. Indiana University Press has announced the project of publishing his *Collected Writings*; this edition will run to more than forty volumes. He has lectures extensively in Europe, Asia, and North and South America.

Charles E. Scott is Professor of Philosophy, Penn State University; and Distinguished Professor of Philosophy Emeritus and Research Professor of Philosophy, Vanderbilt University. His publications include *Living with Indifference* (Indiana University Press, 2007); *The Lives of Things* (Indiana University Press, 2002); *The Time of Memory* (SUNY Press, 1999); *On the*

Advantages and Disadvantages of Ethics and Politics (Indiana University Press, 1996); *The Question of Ethics: Nietzsche, Foucault, Heidegger* (Indiana University Press, 1990); *The Language of Difference* (Humanities Press International, 1987); and *Boundaries in Mind: A Study of Immediate Awareness Based in Psychotherapy* (Crossroads, 1982). In addition to his service to the profession as chair and interim head of philosophy at Vanderbilt and Penn State, Charles E. Scott served as Director of the Mellon Regional Faculty Development Program at Vanderbilt University from 1979 to 1987, Founding Director of the Robert Penn Warren Center for the Humanities at Vanderbilt University from 1987 to 1993, and in 2005 returned to Vanderbilt to serve as Founding Director of the Vanderbilt University Center for Ethics.

H. Peter Steeves is Professor of Philosophy and Director of the Humanities Center at DePaul University, where he specializes in phenomenology, ethics, and philosophy of science. Steeves is the author of eight books, including *Beautiful, Bright, and Blinding: Phenomenological Aesthetics and the Life of Art* (SUNY Press, 2017) and the forthcoming *Being and Showtime* (Northwestern, 2020). His current research focuses primarily on cosmology and astrobiology—on the origin events of both the cosmos and life.

Jason M. Wirth is Professor of Philosophy at Seattle University and works and teaches in the areas of Continental philosophy, Buddhist philosophy, aesthetics, environmental philosophy, and Africana philosophy. His recent books include *Mountains, Rivers, and the Great Earth: Reading Gary Snyder and Dōgen in an Age of Ecological Crisis* (SUNY Press, 2017), a monograph on Milan Kundera (*Commiserating with Devastated Things*, Fordham University Press, 2015), *Schelling's Practice of the Wild* (SUNY Press, 2015), *The Conspiracy of Life: Meditations on Schelling and His Time* (SUNY Press, 2003), a translation of the third draft of *The Ages of the World* (SUNY Press, 2000), the edited volume *Schelling Now* (Indiana University Press, 2004), the coedited volume (with Bret Davis and Brian Schroeder) *Japanese and Continental Philosophy: Conversations with the Kyoto School* (Indiana University Press, 2011), and *The Barbarian Principle: Merleau-Ponty, Schelling, and the Question of Nature* (SUNY Press, 2013). He is the associate editor and book review editor of the journal *Comparative and Continental Philosophy*. His forthcoming manuscript is called *Nietzsche and Other Buddhas* (Indiana University Press, 2019), and he is currently completing a manuscript on the cinema of Terrence Malick.

David Wood is W. Alton Jones Professor of Philosophy at Vanderbilt, where he teaches continental philosophy and environmental philosophy. He is the author and editor of numerous books including *Time After Time*; *Eco-Deconstruction: Derrida and Environmental Ethics* (coedited with Matthias

Fritsch and Philippe Lynes) (Fordham University Press, 2018); *Deep Time, Dark Times: On Being Geologically Human* (Fordham University Press, 2018); *Reoccupy Earth: Notes toward an Other Beginning* (Fordham University Press, 2019); and *Thinking Plant Animal Man* (Fordham University Press, 2019). He is also an earth artist and director of Yellow Bird Art Farm in Woodbury, TN.

Introduction

This book celebrates and engages the play found between the hard and vigorous work exhibited in philosophy, its related challenges of translation and textual interpretation, and the creative passion that such work can bring to the philosopher. This volume includes some of the best Continental philosophers and is inspired by David Farrell Krell's lead essay from which the book derives its title. Krell, a philosopher of the sublime, intimately realizes philosophy's passion when it takes its creative turn. As an author of fiction, as well as a virtuosic philosopher and a superb translator of a number of philosophical and poetic texts, Krell's essay was used as a prompt for authors to respond to his essay "Creative Solitudes."

This request was met in a variety of ways. Some chose to respond in their own creative ways and create more fictional philosophical narratives. These authors include H. Peter Steeves's *The Abandonment of the Circus Horses* and the introduction to the volume, *You Lonely* Farang: *Hiatus in Inducing an Introduction*. Others chose reflective philosophical responses alighting on the prospects of creative solitudes through a more singularly direct engagement either with Krell's work on the topics of solitudes and creativity or other thinkers such as Heidegger or Hölderlin. We see a number of chapters engaged directly with Krell's chapter in light of some of his other work. These chapters are by Walter Brogan (*David Farrell Krell: The Impossible Voicing of Philosophy's Double*), Peg Birmingham ("*An Incarnation Openly Bearing Its Emptiness*": *Life, Animal, Fiction, and Solitude in the Work of David Farrell Krell*), and Michael Naas (*Withdrawal Symptoms: David Farrell Krell and the Solitude of a Body Born of Chaos*). The undertaking was met differently by others to take the opportunity to reflect on the philosophy of solitude by looking into traditional philosophy's role in relation to creativity. Examples of this approach are: Angelica Nuzzo's *A Creativity to Sustain, A Solitude to Endure*; Charles E. Scott's *Solitude, Creativity, Delinquency*; Alphonso Lingis's

Reticence, Solitude; William McNeill's *An Enigmatic Solitude*; Jason Wirth's *Solitude and Other Crowds*; and *Sounion* by John Sallis. Françoise Dastur's *Hölderlin's Solitude* is also an illustration of this type of response when she turns to the philosophical dimensions of Hölderlin's philosophical poetry. Remaining authors delve into the experiential nature that our solitudes bestow. David Wood's *Off the Beaten Track*, Jill Marsden's *Landscapes of Solitude: Some Reflections on the Free Spirit*, and *Cabin Solitudes* by Dawne McCance embark on the book's mission more in this way. The book, however, has been organized to offer readers a more holistic approach to its contents and is divided into four sections: Creative Solitudes, Imagining Solitude, Imagining Krell's Solitudes, and Solitudes. There are a number of photographic images throughout the book. When not specified, they are David Farrell Krell's photographs of his own place of creative solitudes.

Our solitudes are always in the plural, not only in the differences between ourselves, but even in the singularity of our own selves because we are always a multiplicity of voices ruminating, listening, and contending with each other among ourselves and within. Our solitudes change, transform, and return to other times and their imaginings. In appropriate form and expression, this volume of companions and responders to Krell's insights to creative solitudes bears its words in degrees between the thresholds of the extremes of the philosophical-poetic and poetic-philosophical, with some authors offering fictional stories or creative narratives and others tendering the verges of what constitutes the finest of Continental philosophical musings on the topic of solitudes and its accompanying creativity. By its nature, this book will present challenges to those readers who only desire a rigid philosophy devoid of feeling and absent of the humanness that made philosophy the love of wisdom for our ancient forebears. Likewise, those seeking only literary cleverness without the engagement of measured thinking will find themselves tested by the philosophical richness contained in all of the book's chapters. For David Farrell Krell, our inspiration for *The Philosophy of Creative Solitudes*, the truth is in the fiction, and there is fiction in truth.

The superlative cast of Walter Brogan, Angelica Nuzzo, Charles E. Scott, Peg Birmingham, William McNeill, John Sallis, Michael Naas, Françoise Dastur, David Wood, Alphonso Lingis, Jill Marsden, Dawne McCance, Jason Wirth, and H. Peter Steeves practices this truth and rehearses this fiction in their own ways of creative solitudes. The play of truth in fiction and fiction in truth awaiting readers is the sublime and critical responses of the authors' own creative solitudes prompted without any intentional inducing, except by the unfolding of the soul of this rare friend of wisdom and lover of life.

This book is dedicated to David Farrell Krell in appreciation of his creative musings, prodigious philosophical work, contributions to the philosophical profession, and the friendship emerging from his own *creative solitudes*.

—David Jones

You Lonely *Farang*: Hiatus in Inducing an Introduction

His hand began slipping away from her and hung limp by his side. She thought nothing of this, but the vacant look in his eyes made her pause. He fell from his stool to the hard-tiled pavement hitting his head. She looked in disbelief as she had done earlier that morning when she encountered the dead bird on the typically uneven Thai sidewalk. She remembered the brief passing conversation she had with the *Farang*. She sidestepped the bird and stared at its lifeless body with its feet in the air and broken wing. The *Farang* had said to her, "We should do something about it, perhaps bury it." She turned, and he saw her beautiful face as it broke into a smile that brought even greater radiance to the bright morning that promised to be a hot day. She replied to the foreign man that "She would take care." He smiled warmly and replied, "Yes, you take care," realizing she would not understand the double entendre of his reply. He was pleased nevertheless to let her know he cared, even if she didn't understand. The foreign man continued walking along the *soi* looking for his son, and she took care of the dead bird.

As his son lay on the tiles convulsing, his eyes searching the dark emptiness of their sockets, he frothed from his mouth, a hypostasis of sorts, in this his first epileptic seizure. His body went as rigid as the dead bird's, but he moved without his own volition, for there was no control, no intentionality, no nothing from his point of view except the abject nothingness of this between state of being alive, but being absent. She bent over him and held his head in her bronze hands with long slender fingers and brightly painted nails until his rigid body slowly began to relax some. Normal breathing returned to the young man and slowly his consciousness of the world started to seep into him with its thick and maddening reality. It all annoyed him for some reason to be returning from his newly found dark place and its submissive nothingness. For her, it all seemed as if an eternity had elapsed for him to awaken, especially since in her village many would think him to be possessed by wretched spirits of the underworld—those demonic disenchanted ones reaching out with their tentacles to snatch the unsuspecting and unfortunate ones above. She didn't really know if he was possessed or not—she had yet to completely forfeit her beliefs—but she did sense something special about this young man whom she held with her lovely hands, from this young man she hoped would buy some of her time.

His eyes opened, he had no idea where he was, who he was, or even the sound of his name. She remembered his name; it was part of her job to make customers feel like they mattered. So many men came to Thailand in hopes of healing, and to escape from something back home—a divorce, memories of the war crimes they witnessed or committed in the name of freedom, or from their just plain and simply disenchanted lives. In some sense, her life was not so much different, and she realized this as she prayed for her own healing, or the occasional intimacy that was somehow disallowed to her by a culture where many men felt their wives were possessions, and that somehow happened—not all the time—but on occasion, with these *Farang* men from faraway places with lots of money.

She stroked his black hair; he could be Thai, she thought, but she knew he wasn't. He was darker than his father, the Filipino in him, and as she spoke Thai to him he had no understanding what she was saying, but it felt soothing; Thai wasn't one of the several languages he learned to speak, and even his closest language, English, went by without any understanding as she attempted to reach into his darkness and pull him back into the light. And slowly as he recovered, regaining some sense of the reality around him, he understood her words for the first time. "Mano, Mano, you okay?" He nodded with his eyes, for he couldn't even smile yet as she helped him to his feet and took him into the shade and yelled out for some water.

All of this was being observed by others in the outdoor bar. Other girls were coming to work and stopped to pay homage to the Buddha by holding their hands together in the mudra of prayer or *wai*. They too had hopes of a healing for this possessed young man and prayed for their own protection from the underworld ghosts that might creep through his spirit and into theirs. Another observer sat expressionless, taking it all in as if in some kind of omniscient way. This man had been appearing to his father in a number of other places—first in Hawai'i, then China, Taiwan, and now here in Thailand as his father sat listening to music and drinking a beer in another place far from the epileptic young man and his Avalokiteśvara, his *bodhisattva* of compassion. This other place, not wanting to erupt but destined to, as polling day came nearer. His father would be there when it came and would witness several of these strategically placed protests to "Shutdown Bangkok—Restart Thailand." On polling day, the father listened to the music and the speeches in Thai, understanding only the feeling behind the words, those feelings that drove their words of frustration, anger, and hope, and the lingering residue of those feelings that also drives them into being.

It was on an earlier day that this man walked by the father, tall, thin in an athletic way, long black hair with some occasional grey strands, and a bit of a straggly beard. He smiled and the seated man nodded and after he passed by, the father realized the connection seemed to go back to other places. He wondered about this passing man, always and only Asian, who appeared to be Thai in Thailand, Chinese in China and Taiwan, and one of those wonderful Hawaiian blends that make for such striking varietal beings in Hawai'i. The thought passed along with the strange man as the music ended when the father wanted it to continue. It was familiar music from the days when he protested against the war in Vietnam—that war that left some names on the Wall for him, that war that would always somehow define his life and being. His time in Vietnam was different from theirs; it came later, but he, too, went there to make some kind of peace with the people, the place, and himself. Some peace did come to him, but was an easier kind, a more fortunate kind of peace than those before him ever could be.

And there this man with long black hair and some occasional grey strands was witnessing his son coming back from wherever he would now forever go for the rest of his life, and his return came this day in the arms of an enchanting bar girl with a heart of compassion. His son would later learn her name, but his father never would. She had an evening of money to make and the young *Farang* was costing her wages. Like most of the young women, she would send money back to her family in Isaan, home to most of the working girls in Thailand. It was the same story: money for the family and the child now cared for by the mother as her daughter worked in the city where the *Farang* came. The father was either dead, worked to death by life's hardships or by cancer, or was selfishly irresponsible. It seemed to be the same story, over and over again, but many times it was about hardworking fathers whose bodies succumbed to the strains and mandates of labor. Isaan is a poor region. The people of Isaan are in many ways more Lao in their local languages and customs than Thai. Even though accepted in Thai culture by other Thais, they are the farmers living far from the influences of the "higher" culture of the cities. They always worked hard to make food grow in the dry region and learned to be inventive in eating what the land could provide. The man's son would learn later to eat grasshoppers and beetles and even come to think of them as delicacies. His mother, if she ever knew, would be abhorred at the thought. They both wanted to find him in their own and different ways. She and her former husband wanted him back, back like he used to be. They were, the father guessed, still a family of sorts, but their son would never come back.

She gently and sympathetically stroked his hand and arm until he had fully regained himself. He told her he was tired, and she said, "I take care you." An evening of possible wages from other *Farang* from their distant places wanting her attentions, her company, would be lost—a portion of her cut from the inflated prices of "lady drinks," bar fines to free her from the bar, and the time charged if she decided to go out for "short-time" or "long-time." All of these possibilities would be lost this evening when she became his Buddha of Compassion. She watched him breathe in and out more easily as he slept into the evening and night in her simple home. She was used to staying awake late for the *Farang* who came to her for their healing. She grew to be grateful to them and wished for their arrival every night because occasionally they brought her something close enough to love, even sometimes they genuinely did bring their love to her, and she gave them something in return, something she was just now beginning to understand, something that resembled love. This browner *Farang* still slept on her hard Thai bed and would only awaken the next day. She felt close to him for some reason, perhaps because he had chosen to have his seizure with her. This lovely woman then crawled in beside him and held him throughout the night. Somewhere deep inside he must have felt safe with her. Finally, she slept too.

The father, not knowing how close he was to his son at that time, would sit at the same bar later in the week and buy her an overpriced drink. There was something special about her he noticed, a softness and gentleness for life and a sadness hidden only by the pervasive happiness that seems to fill Thai life in spite of the harshness of its realities. This is, he would later realize, their remedy for suffering. How many times had the *Farang* heard the words, "I just want you happy." These foreigners loved hearing this, because life was all about them, their happiness, but behind the remedy was the most profound acknowledgement of suffering—the Buddha's First Noble Truth.

He sat with her, they joked some, and she asked if he had a hotel room, but she left out the "a" that often prefaces our nouns in English. Such a strange word this "a" is, he thought, and how it has multiple uses—an indefinite article, preposition, and even on occasion a noun, and it once was a verb in its archaic form. No wonder it's not understood by other language speakers; we don't even understand it ourselves. These thoughts visited him as he looked into her deep brown eyes. "Of course," he replied. "I come with you," she stated in question form. The *Farang* man reached out and gently touched her hand with the long thin fingers and long, painted nails—gentle hands they were, in spite of working in the fields until she came of age. He smiled and replied, "Thank you, you're most lovely, but I'm here looking for my son." She looked at his face and saw its sadness and heard it in his tone. She recognized his loneliness coming through the slightly sunburned skin on his nose and cheeks, all the places that stand out to catch just a little more from the over-rich star that makes this planet inhabitable.

"Oh, so sorry your son lost." "I hope you find him." Her words were spoken with such feeling. He realized she actually meant them, and he was authentically touched by her empathic susceptibility to his pain—he realized she could experience his pain. Her moist eyes glistened with the reflection from the neon lights that were overhead casting their glow on everything. But her glow was steady to him, not blinking like the lights, and shined its way toward him. His hand was still on hers he realized. He had gotten lost in the moment of her caring, but she grasped it more tightly. "I sorry." "You kind man." "Maybe you find your son somewhere." She could read him like the books he wrote, or the ones he wanted to write. It seems she knew he was searching, had always been searching throughout his life, for something that was even unknown to him. It was his curse like so many others that afflicted him because there was nothing to find, except the magic of another being to understand. Perhaps it was this way for her as well he wondered. He wouldn't ever know; or could ever know. This was his abject nothingness. "I go now," he said to break her spell and as he thought in his mind, "before I ask you to marry me." This brought a smile to his face, for that's the only way it could happen at this age, he thought.

As he walked down the narrow *soi*, he paused and looked back expecting to see her pursuing the next *Farang* for the evening. But she just sat there, not knowing that this white man's son was the young man she had nursed and brought back to a new life. She sat there thinking of the suffering of the young man at home and the old man who had just left and how theirs were the same as her suffering. How could she know that the *Farang*'s lost son wasn't white like him? That the *Farang* was so close to finding his son Mano, an endearment he had given him and that his son would use when he wanted to withhold his real identity. She sighed and smiled, knowing it was time to be happy again and she returned to the work that was hers.

The next day, the searching father returned to his hotel in Bangkok and sat at the occupied corner, which is normally the busiest corner in the city. The tall, musician-looking man with long black hair streaked with some grey walked by and caught his eye again. He smiled and hurried along his way with the flow of people trying to get to work around the demonstrators who had been camped there for weeks. The tall man disappeared into the abyss of the crowded street. As the father freely obliged himself of the hotel's happy hour, David Farrell Krell came to his mind. How odd to think of him in a place such as this, a place so antithetical to everything Krell is and for which he stands. Not solitude, but massive ongoing flows of people; not silence and sounds of nature, but the constant noise of motor scooters, cars, trucks, overhead trains railing across the skyway; not the smell of flowers after a rain being delivered by gentle cool mountain breezes, but the smell of diesel, the occasional waft of a sewer punctuated by street food vendors frying fish or chicken in fish oil, and the cigarette smoke from those *Farang* from faraway places between their boisterous laughter that proclaims they own this place.

And this is where David decides to come to the man! Does he come to tell him to find a creative solitude elsewhere, or does he come to assure him that our creative solitudes take many forms and that even amid all these people one can find oneself alone, and in solitude. As he begins his piece in this volume of creative solitudes of companions for the DFK, he hears Krell's words ring out clearly above the ambient noise. "Clearly, by 'creative solitudes' I do not mean isolation and self-absorption. To languish in narcissism, whether dreamily or wretchedly, is not creative but destructive—we all know that. Yet I suspect that aloneness and loneliness are essential components of creative solitudes. They may be self-inflicted wounds, but they are not accidents and mere options."

But was not the searching father here by accident? Has not everything in his life been accidental—even his self-inflicted wounds of searching for that which is not there, that which never was there in the first place? "But my poor man," Krell might say to the writer of this saga of searching, "Are you not languishing in your own self-made narcissism?" "It's not very creative you know" so the man imagined Krell's voice speaking to him inside his head. Then listening to his own voice of self-reflection, he heard himself say, "Always in my head, even after years of meditation!" As this internal dialogue unfolded, he pondered why Krell would mindfully come to him now and here in Bangkok, and why in the voice of his own superego. He knew Krell surely would have helped him search for his son—and he knew this in his soul—and that Krell would never assume the sound of his own guilt for taking so long to find inspiration and to call on whatever talents he had. Krell's voice was his own summoning to let the muses enter into and possess him right there on this occupied corner in Bangkok. And with this thought, he felt a smile coming to his face, and something in him was able to feel it spreading and transforming into laughter as he was sitting there alone amid all the others—being happy in this Happy Hour, for David Farrell Krell was coming to him as a mythic muse to set afire his imagination and urging him to get started, finally.

And he began to type—began to write—about how he felt his life was just a series of unplanned events that had congealed and crystallized into this unexpected moment of being in Bangkok during the occupation to "Shut Down Bangkok—Restart Thailand." This day when he started writing, soldiers joined the riot police, helicopters flew just over the tops of the skyscrapers, and the protestors continued their singing and praying. He was now alone, at least for a while, and felt lonely not noticing the others as he finally began working without isolation and self-absorption.

The fortuitous occasions of all of our births seem to make all the difference. As Enrique Dussel, one of Latin America's most poignant philosophers, reminds us:

> European philosophy has given almost exclusive preponderance to temporality .... The "where-I-was-born" is the predetermination of all other determinations. To be born among pygmies in Africa or in a Fifth Avenue neighborhood in New York City . . . is to be born into another world; it is to be born spatially into a world that predetermines—radically, though not absolutely—the orientation of one's future *proyecto*. (Dussel, *Philosophy of Liberation* [Eugene, OR: Wipf and Stock, 2003], 24–25)

Yes, our plans, projects—even this one, a hiatus in inducing an introduction, which has languished for far too long—have accidental dimensions. And the man supposed that it is accidental that he would be given the honor of editing this book instead of another. Others wondered too, he realized. Surely, he had the idea, but it never meant that he would somehow become the one attached to the delivery of the idea. His idea was to honor David Farrell Krell in a new series with Northwestern, and then, through the strange forces of life that had brought David and him together, here he was; he was learning to love his fate, but it came with such trials and troubles. From another perspective, it was just his *karma* acting up again. The karma that had taken him Eastward, taken him to places he understood better than the culture of his own country, from his own hill in Pittsburgh. Could Nietzsche have meant something like karma with his *amor fati*?

Dussel is one of our greatest thinkers. His perspective is an important one for us to realize. Life is different for those who were colonized and had their cultures stolen from them, leaving them only with the culture of the colonizer. How to decolonize oneself in a postcolonial time is a great challenge. Sadly, this is the fate of too many people. But it is a fate that must be affirmed and not allow a preponderance of hierarchy imposed upon being one rather than being another. To be born a Buddhist, to accept the particularity of one's incarnation, is to affirm the givenness of our arrival either as a dog animal or a human animal, as a pygmy in Africa, or a millionaire on Fifth Avenue. In many ways, the impoverished lives of those who dwell on Fifth Avenue are no different from those of a man looking for his son in Thailand, a place where his son has never been. For David Farrell Krell, the call to creative solitudes is about freedom, a freedom from suffering and a freedom to and for the celebration of life. This call is about finding our creative solitudes amid all that surrounds us, and often what encircles us is waste, pain, suffering, and loss.

This book is an extraordinary book for and on the work of an extraordinary man written by a chosen group of extraordinary philosophers and writers. The echo here is intended, notwithstanding that such echoes can be seen as examples of poor writing, for "extraordinary" takes us beyond the ordinary, yet positions us amid the everyday with the challenge of how to accept it and make every single day extraordinary through unexpected outbursts of creative responses stemming from our solitudes. One remarkable feature of David Farrell Krell's oeuvre is the play found between the hard work of the philosopher and the creative passion of the poet, like the play between the mutability and force of water as it finds its way along to its destination of either conformity or creativity and destruction. This volume of companions to Krell's oeuvre also finds its play between the Dionysian and Apollonian, between the philosophical and poetic. But in all of the authors' contributions, their words bear the philosophical-poetic and poetic-philosophical in degrees between the thresholds of either extreme, with some offering fictional stories or creative narratives and others tendering the verges of what constitutes the best of Continental philosophical musings.

This movement is the most appropriate recognition for David Farrell Krell, one of the best philosophers of the twentieth and twenty-first centuries, most significant translators of our day, and most talented writers of fiction and fictional biographies of some of the deepest thinkers of the West.

The cast of characters of *The Philosophy of Creative Solitudes* includes Walter Brogan, Angelica Nuzzo, Charles E. Scott, Peg Birmingham, William McNeill, John Sallis, Michael Naas, Françoise Dastur, David Wood, Alphonso Lingis, Jill Marsden, Dawne McCance, Jason Wirth, and H. Peter Steeves, and begins with David Farrell Krell's own *Creative Solitudes*. Each author offers reflections on the creative solitudes composing standpoints of their lives in response to the impetus of the protagonist of this volume, while some respond more directly to him. In arranging the book, I have sought to combine pieces that go together in content and flow together in style. This does not mean, however, that the combination necessarily reflects all of the fictional fragments of creative solitudes merely being lumped together, nor does it reflect the placement of the more direct pieces of philosophical panache into one section. The blending of these reflections on solitudes was the aim. If this aim has missed its mark, the selections of this volume stand on their own merits in tribute to one of the very best.

And it was here that he happened to hear the waitress say:

"I think you lonely."

"I'm just alone," was his reply.

She smiled, as only the Thai can smile, as only Thai women can smile at *Farang* men—as if they harbor some hidden truth of happiness, or if they want something from the *Farang*.

The *Farang* sat enjoying the beer that was very cold—not very good, but cold. He sat as many foreigners—the *Farang*—do in Thailand. Just sitting there, these men staring outward, looking somewhere in some kind of subversive meditative way. He was an expert in this form of meditation.

The man had been coming to Thailand for some time now, looking for something that wasn't ready at hand at home. As he sat, he remembered Heidegger's distinction between present-at-hand and ready-at-hand, and he pondered how many *Farang* saw Thai women as being simultaneously as *ready-to-hand*, that is, available for some purpose and *present-at-hand*, as simply an object of gratification. They were just like tools for the purpose of pleasure or power for many foreigners. Although each of these ways of "seeing" is different, in Thailand they somehow collapsed together in one "standing reserve" when they came to women, he thought. The thought brought a frown to his forehead as he sipped on his icy beer; the objectification of people, especially of women, or anything breathing for that matter, was abhorrent and something that saddened him.

"You mad now," she asked with apparent concern in her voice.

"No, no" he replied, "Not at you, at least."

"Not good to be mad," she responded.

"I'm just perturbed about why people are mistreated."

"Oh, me too, I guess. But then I just think of something else."

The *Farang* replied, "Yours is a better way, I think," and then he smiled warmly for her.

But, he continued to think, this is why he comes to Thailand, in search of the ability to respond creatively to the sufferings that constitute his life. "What would Krell say to him now—more self-indulgence?" he thought with a mind that kept coming back to the introduction that just somehow would not write itself. He knew it wasn't "writers' block," whatever that is, because he was able to write other things. He let the thought go, because it often accompanied him, and maybe in this place, the place that brought him in search of his son and everything that he stood for in the *Farang*'s life, would become a writing place—one of those places that opens the soul.

Staying in place often, but always wandering around—sometimes with destination, sometimes without—this was his mood today, a prevailing mood like a fog that never seems to lift. He realized he was looking for something, but after all, he had been looking for something all of his life. But what could it be for him, this *Farang* who sat in his subversive meditation on this day in this place? It wasn't the woman who had just spoken his loneliness with such forthrightness, but sometimes it could have been, and often it was. This wandering man who often stayed in place valued and respected this about Thais—their honesty and willingness to accept the conditional truth of circumstance; just acceptance, not victimization, nor punishment, just *karma*. "What's the problem?" he asked himself. And then, "Why's there always got to be a fucking problem?"

He was feeling alone, not lonely, in spite of the astuteness of her perceptive wisdom. He realized she was wise, possessed a wisdom that came naturally to her, unlike his own; he had to work at it, like all philosophers. "Why am I a philosopher; of all things to be, why a philosopher?" He was tired of trying to achieve this thing called wisdom, as if it were actually attainable—an object to be attained, a state to be reached, some kind of teleological place of which to emigrate. He just didn't care anymore about this kind of wisdom, or even about its Asian counterpart, enlightenment, especially the kind that would spirit him away to where no one needed to be, really wanted to be if they knew any better, or should ever aspire to be if they were sensitive enough to what it means to always be with, the *being-with* of Heidegger. It was clear enough to him that he had at least arrived at the stand-point of Nietzsche's insight into life that he too, like Nietzsche, found folly in wisdom and the perennial search for it as life evaporated around the seekers of life's meaning.

"Does the sun bother you?" she asked as she was about to obstruct his view by lowering the shade in the outside bar overlooking the street, the bar that sat on the sidewalk.

"Oh no, please don't. The sun feels good; it won't last long," he said and then thought to himself the "warmth of light never lasts long enough, only the dismal eternal darkness of the nothing that awaits everything alive seems always present."

Even in Chiang Mai in the winter the sun was warm, but it did not feel as discernably damaging as in Bangkok or Phuket, Pattaya, or Koh Samui and other places farther south. The air was cooler here and the sun felt warming; it accompanied him as he sat in his meditative posture taking it all in as life passed along the thoroughfare that was life here—the place that he was in and the time that pervaded it. So, he sat, sipping the coldness of the beer, celebrating the glow of the warm sun and the occasional backdoor breath of the *tuk tuk* sputtering by trying to interrupt his meditation. All of this along with the caressing breeze coming from the mountain where the monastery looked down upon the city and him—the necessary counterpoint that makes everything in the world so perfect. The wat was just a little beyond the halfway point up the mountain where it sat alone in its own meditative state as only buildings can, by itself, never lonely, only alone, because it was surrounded by the beauty of the earth's vibrant crease that reached to touch the sky from the flatness of the plain on which Chiang Mai sits. Perched midway up the mountain, it felt no suffering whatsoever.

Wats are everywhere in Thailand, the most Buddhist country in the world. In fact, there was a wat on this busy little street lined with bars, massage parlors, and numerous shops selling overpriced wares but nevertheless bargains to the unexpected; those non-expecting ones would bargain down in self-fulfilling ways and still, nevertheless, get ripped off and, in turn, inflate prices for locals. The overweight *Farang* from Russia and Germany were now completing what the Americans had started after the Vietnam War.

He sat alone for the early happy hour meditation before the louder, obnoxious other *Farang* would come and interpose on his daily meditation with their boisterous behavior of holiday entitlement that brought disrespect, oftentimes unintentional but always hurtful and never completely understood by the residents of this special land.

As he turned toward her activity, she sensed his question and answered, "For Buddha, he get hungry too you know! And he like whiskey too!" She smiled as she made her proclamation as if it would offer her a better incarnation next time around. But that was his thought, not hers.

The wanderer always sensed that the Buddha must have enjoyed the libations that dissolved the border regions between self and other. But he realized the Buddha's alcoholic enjoyment likely did not possess an addictive quality like his own. How else could it be, for the Buddha was the unattached one? So he smiled at his insight and said, "Yes, the Buddha is hungry and thirsty too."

And that was the way it was in Thailand. One must feed and give drink to the Buddha. Not a god beyond desires, needs, and believability, but a god with all the same desires, needs, and wishes for perfection as our seated wanderer. But this god, this Lord Buddha, wasn't attached and could see beyond the perpetuation and acceleration of all of what the rest of us felt. "Yes, feed the Buddha, so he will not need to sit hungry and thirsty in meditation," he said to her without saying, "Make love to this Buddha who is your Buddha, so he won't have the desires I have when a Thai woman like you smiles back at me!" He didn't say these words aloud and let them remain in the loud silence of his mind where most of our thoughts thankfully stay. She liked it when he smiled; she smiled back, not needing to know the thought that brought the smile to her customer's face.

She placed the offering as so many shop owners do on the sidewalk off to the side somewhere and in the alley where her bar was situated beside the wat. "Temples and bars, what better combination is there!" he thought. The bar is a temple as the Irish so well know—"ah, what he would do for a good pint of Irish brew now!" he daydreamed.

As she placed her offerings in their profane place in this profane world next to the profane spot where the man sat in his profane meditation, the birds immediately flocked, seemingly coming from nowhere, hungry and in need of libation like our man—like our *Farang* wanderer in the bar on the sidewalk by the busy street in some place in Thailand, the most Buddhist country in the world.

The pigeons came, big and fat, well-fed like the Hoi-tai Buddha, but all of a sudden hungry as they strutted in dance cooing for their meal. There they consumed the Buddha's food and spilled his drink, mixing it with the sticky rice, vegetables, and likely some pork.

"Didn't the Buddha die of rancid pork?" He thought of the irony the situation posed and how Thais would not even consider this to be an ironic matter in the least. They would just accept it at its face value—as the life, and the death, of the Lord Buddha. The pigeons came into the bar and strutted their dance around his bare feet that he had slipped out of his sandals to be cooler; they strutted as if he had something to offer them, cooing as they came and went. He sat there watching without judgment. "Looking for more sustenance in this world of craving," he thought to himself, "They share this with all other species, and yes, they share this with me, and I with them." He would often tell his Japanese-American-with-a-little-Filipino-in-him son that he was working on his own Hoi-tai Buddha belly in observance of this sacred tradition. This son of his who, by this time, had completely disappeared with all traces turning cold in the hot sun of Thailand. The wandering *Farang*, this sitting man we are considering for the moment, continued his meditation amid male cooing and strutting with their bellies inflated from the offering to the Buddha; they now strutted after their female counterparts after satiating themselves on the Buddha's food and drink. Yes, his son had disappeared, losing his substantiality in this world of flocking and strutting Buddhas.

His meditation was interrupted by her laughter, "Birds hungry too. Hungry just like Buddha!" He looked at her without surprise, or even with anything that resembled anticipation, and said, "But you feed the Buddha and the birds eat his food, and look they're drunk just like me now!" As he uttered these words, his laughter came deep from his stomach, a place where authentic laughter originates. All laughter should come from here, not from its more frequent throaty expressions, or so he would later reflect. Perhaps he was finally learning a little without realizing and finally, if only momentarily, just *being-here*; this laughter made him grateful for being alive, and it often came to him here, in this place, for some reason—this most Buddhist place in the world.

She laughed even harder accepting his contagion, "I still think you lonely *Farang*!"

He smiled at her and felt the warmth the smile brought to his face; he let it spread without any encouragement to satisfy him; it spread throughout his body as the sun dipped and disappeared behind the buildings and the mountain where the monastery sat midway up its rise, shedding its intensity and leaving only its refracting glow.

"Check please," he asked turning toward her again with the smile still lingering, not yet beginning to fade with the sun's light.

After a quick nod, a formal bow in this temple bar, his check soon arrived, and he left the required baht rounding off the amount without a tip, which was the custom before the Americans, Germans, and Russians came.

As he left and walked out into the street alone just as he had entered, she yelled out to him expecting no answer. "Come back again."

And no answer ever came.

He never would return to her, her Buddha temple with its craving pigeons. From her vantage point, he soon disappeared into the passing flow, and she immediately forgot him, forever, for, to her, he was like all the others. As he moved along the uneven pavement, a thin tall man off to the side in the wat aimed his Mamiya RB-67 camera with its 105 mm traditional macro lens with a fixed focal length at the *Farang* and snapped a picture at the slowest of shutter speeds. Holding his camera absolutely steady, he eventually captured the passing *Farang*'s image. Without expression, the man ran his hand through his long black hair streaked with some grey, after returning his equipment to its case. He stepped out from his hiding place behind a statue of Ganesha, the elephant god that removes obstacles, at the wat's back alley entrance and was noticed by no one, especially this time not by the man whose image he had just seditiously seized and captured.

When her customer had completely faded into the world around her wat, she spoke out loud to no one but herself, the always hungry pigeons, and to the Buddha.

"I think you lonely *Farang*."

He often thought that somewhere in Thailand just might be the place for him to enter that place of nothingness, that place where he might finally reunite with his son. He may not ever be alone then, or even lonely, if he too could find his Buddha of Compassion, his Avalokiteśvara.

For David Farrell Krell with respect, admiration, and love.

—David Jones

Part One

Creative Solitudes

1

Creative Solitudes

David Farrell Krell

When David Jones first proposed this volume to me I was both grateful and surprised. He had heard me deliver a lecture entitled "Creative Solitudes" at Kennesaw State University in 2005. The lecture was originally written for the Cortelyou-Lowery Award ceremony at DePaul University in 1997, then revised and presented at a number of colleges and universities over the next few years. Wherever I have given the lecture the reaction has been the same: faculty and students seem to agree with much of what I am saying, and some are enthusiastic about it, whereas administrators generally hate the whole thing. I take that as a good sign.

A number of years ago, David sent this paper to a group of philosophers with the request that they respond with an essay on their own experiences of creative solitudes. Some chose to examine various books and essays of mine, while others went in the direction of their own research and reflection. In both cases, the theme was solitude in our creative and scholarly lives, and not my own work. Not even Paul Auster claims to have "invented" solitude. Everyone who reads and writes does so under the auspices of solitude. Is it safe to say that both reading and writing are endangered species in a culture whose very first axiom when it comes to "mental health" and "social adjustment" is that solitude be assiduously avoided? If that seems too alarmist, we may nevertheless agree that ours is a good time to think about the pains and the gains of solitude, and not by way of "tweets."

I have taken the liberty of cutting portions of the original lecture in order to make space for some remarks on more recent work of mine. I regret the resulting patchwork and the autobiography, but it seemed necessary to say what I am using or abusing my "creative solitudes" for these days. My gratitude to all the contributors to this volume and to David Jones. And I am still surprised.

"Creative solitudes." What a splendid title! Both Ralph Waldo Emerson and Henry David Thoreau, and perhaps even William James, would have written stirring essays on it. Well, then, that makes it a quaint nineteenth-century topic, both edifying and obsolete. Besides, no one has ever cracked the code of creativity, although much empirical-psychological ink has been spilled over it. And solitude? No one has ever been able to distinguish it properly from aloneness or loneliness, even though we know that these states or conditions are far from identical. Clearly, by "creative solitudes" I do not mean isolation and self-absorption. To languish in narcissism, whether dreamily or wretchedly, is not creative but destructive—we all know that. Yet I suspect that aloneness and loneliness are essential components of creative solitudes. They may be self-inflicted wounds, but they are not accidents.

I have two questions to pose concerning creative solitudes. First, what is the relation of such solitudes to teaching and learning, especially in our colleges and universities? Second, what will be the fate of creative solitudes in the age of information technology, electronic mass communication, and social media? Are there any resources that may help us to avoid the worst potholes on the information highway down which we are tearing, roaring along so confidently in the direction of ignorance, ugliness, and mean-spiritedness? My complaints about information technology (and, believe it or not, my main example will be email) are three: first, that it invades our creative solitudes in a particularly pernicious way; second, that it subverts our language and our thought processes; and third, that it encourages our most rancorous side—the side that loves gossip and slander. What I am worried about, in a word, is that information technology is invidious to both creativity and civility, both solitude and community. The celebrated global village is a village stripped of its sense of creativity *and* fair play. Perhaps it is silly of me to be nostalgic about these things, and perhaps I am merely being paranoid about what is everywhere touted as an exciting and useful tool of communication and community. We shall see.

However, on the way to the question concerning the effect of information technology on creative solitudes, let me not forget to ask about the importance of such solitudes for college and university teachers—indeed, for teachers and learners generally. Important they are, and yet in some way they are also menacing. Part of the poignancy of solitary reading and writing is the momentary realization of how much of life we are missing. Thoreau says of the act of writing, "I know not whether it was the dumps or a budding ecstasy."[1] We do have to be comfortable (if not ecstatic) when we work, but a terrible aloneness also has to subtend the comfort. Such isolation is hard on the others who are close to us—this need for aloneness, this need to forego something of life—and it is hard on us. If there were an easier and more gregarious path, we would walk it and talk it. Creative solitudes may not have to be mournful, but whenever we are caught up in them we do have to notice that something is missing, something is in default. Time may seem to stop in such solitudes, but it stops merely in order to gesture toward the transience of things, the very passing of time, the deaths of parents and friends and lovers—along with the demise of ideas, feelings, and sensations—as we write. We must clear a space at the writing table for ghosts, if only because specters too are vulnerable, ephemeral, and, if the ancients are to be believed, wretchedly lonely. The French playwright Hélène Cixous tells her students that when they write plays they must bring the dead onto the stage, since otherwise—apart from our dreams about them—the dead do not stand a chance. Perhaps, then, every creative solitude entertains ghosts. We are always writing with them and for them, even when we are writing against them. No matter how joyous and exhilarating our solitudes may be, they are always haunted. We may feel at home in them, yet our being-at-home is riddled with uncanny, unhomelike sensations.[2]

It may be objected that the haunted solitude demanded by philosophical or literary work is too taxing a standard for our everyday academic work. Yet the populations of the night—that is, of both our everyday sorts of nights and of what Maurice Blanchot calls the "other" night[3]—probably do touch our work of the day, at least if there is anything at all creative about it. And our desire to forget or turn a deaf ear to those populations (for who wants to entertain ghosts, who wants to be lugubrious?) perhaps explains our willingness to surrender creative solitudes to just about anything. Without creative solitudes, however, we cannot read or write or teach, and to a college or university professor, and to teachers in general, that is a disadvantage.

I cannot say, as Thoreau does, that I have "never felt lonesome or in the least oppressed by a sense of solitude" (W 99). Emerson's journal entry for October 27, 1851, makes more sense to me, and it exposes Thoreau's braggadocio for what it is. Emerson writes: "It would be hard to recall the rambles of last night's talk with H. T. [i.e., Henry Thoreau]. But we stated over again, to sadness, almost, the eternal loneliness . . . How insular and pathetically solitary, are all the people we know."[4] Pathetically solitary? Perhaps. Yet sometimes also heroically so. Herman Melville, in *Pierre or The Ambiguities*, describes the blank sheet of paper on which his hero is trying to write in the following way: "If man must wrestle, perhaps it is well that it should be on the nakedest possible plain."[5]

Something else about creative solitudes, however, something more mundane than ghosts, frightens us. A university administrator once said to me, "You know, creative solitudes are wasted on some people," and all I could reply was that often I am one of them. I ought to have added that I am in good company. When Gustav Mahler was at his summer cottage in Maiernigg, working on the *Adagietto* movement of his Fifth Symphony, he felt he might be one of them; so did the young W. E. B. Du Bois while he was studying economics in Berlin, if only because he was aiming so high on behalf of so many; so did Hannah Arendt feel it when she was writing a lecture in New York and Ticino on what she called, with some trepidation and even embarrassment, *thoughtfulness*, mere thoughtfulness, as the only effective response to the banality of evil. To be thoughtful, to be creative in thinking, is to be never cocksure. When the German poet Hölderlin was twenty-five, he wrote to Schiller, who at that time was a kind of foster-father to him: "I am living a very solitary life, and I believe it is good for me."[6] Six incredibly creative years later, he was less sure. He wrote to his friend Christian Landauer: "Tell me, this being solitary—is it a blessing or a curse? My nature determines me to it, and the more purposefully I choose my state with a view to finding out who I am, the more irresistibly I am forced back into it again and again—this being lonely" (CHV 2:896).

Maurice Blanchot writes of the "essential solitude" of the work of art or literature. His model solitary is Franz Kafka.[7] Blanchot describes essential solitude in terms of a night that is more nocturnal than the nights of all our days. The fruits of such a night, in which we are intimate with writing and reading alone, while intoxicating, are meager. For both writer and reader are fascinated and are on automatic pilot, as it were, rapt to mere words—to what Sartre, in *Les mots,* calls "the rigorous succession of words."[8] Rapt, seized, and very much alone. Blanchot writes: "To write is to enter into the affirmation of solitude, where fascination menaces us" (EL 27). Why should fascination menace? Blanchot is thinking of a letter Kafka writes to Milena Jesenská. (Twenty years after Kafka's death in Prague due to tuberculosis, Milena died of kidney failure at the concentration camp in Ravensbrück; she had been imprisoned there because she was a socialist and had married a Jew.) One can hear in this letter to Milena echoes of Kafka's subversive tale of desperate loneliness, *Der Bau,* "The Burrow." On September 14, 1920, Kafka writes to Milena:

> It is something like this: I, an animal of the forest, was at that time barely in
> the forest; I lay somewhere in a muddy hollow (muddy only as a consequence
> of my being there, naturally); and then I saw you out there in the open, the

most wonderful thing I had ever seen; I forgot everything, forgot myself totally; I got up, came closer, anxious to be secure in this freedom that was new though familiar; I approached even closer, came to you, you were so good, I huddled near you, as though I had the right, I placed my face in your hand; I was so happy, so proud, so free, so powerful, so much at home; always and again it was this: so much at home;—and yet, at bottom, I was only the animal; I had always belonged to the forest alone, and if I was living here in the open it was only by your grace; without knowing it (because of course I had forgotten everything), I read my destiny in your eyes. It could not last. Even if you stroked me with your favoring hand, it was inevitable that you would observe my singularities, all of which bespoke the forest, this origin of mine, my real homeland; the necessary words ensued, about my "anxiety," necessarily they were repeated, about the anxiety that tormented me (as it did you, albeit innocently), until my nerves screeched; the realization grew in me, I saw more and more clearly what a sordid pest, what a clumsy obstacle I was for you in every respect . . . I recalled who I was; in your eyes I read the end of illusion; I experienced the fright that is in dreams (acting as though one were at home in a place where one did not belong); I had that fright in reality itself; I had to return to the darkness, could not bear the sun any longer; I was desperate, really, like a stray animal, I began to run breathlessly; constantly the thought, "If only I could take her with me!" and the counterthought, "Is it ever dark where she is?"

You ask how I live: that is how I live.[9]

The loneliness of the love life and of the life of writing mirror one another. Kafka pictures himself writing through the night "in the innermost space of a vast, sealed cellar," a place underground where it is always night, Blanchot's "other" night. He pauses only long enough to rise and shuffle "beneath all the vaults of the cellar" to the "outermost portal," where some unidentified keeper has left some food for him. Why live this way? Because, he writes, one "cannot be sufficiently alone when writing; . . . never enough silence around oneself when writing; the night itself is still too little night. . . ."[10]

What I would add to Kafka's and Blanchot's haunting descriptions of essential solitude is an ignominious and perhaps banal consequence of the fascination with words: one cannot dedicate oneself to reading and writing without also committing oneself to what will be an extravagant waste of time, or, at the very least, a maddening inefficiency. Perhaps that explains why we are losing the capacity and the courage to read and write. And even if we are not wasting time when we engage with words, time is wasting us. No piety of the *sub specie aeternitatis* type will rescue us any longer from this squandering. It will be clear not only to outsiders, nor merely to managers and efficiency experts, nor only to those for whom the fascination has flagged, but also to those who find themselves on the crest of the creative wave, that time is a-wasting. It is at best a desperate sort of feeling, the sense that one belongs to a very foolish subspecies of mortality. During the winter, Melville used to begin his days—before striking out for the nakedest possible plain of writing—by feeding pumpkins to his cow. As the cow began to ruminate, so did he. No doubt he was grateful that the cow blessed his silence and absurdity. She gave him the time he needed to waste.

—Now go and write, she said to him after a few mouthfuls. I'll see you at four.

How rare this bovine wisdom is among us pushy humans, who goad one another to get busy and be as productive as possible. Cows know that there are no calculable guarantees concerning "outcomes" and that it takes time for time to "do its thing." We others, with our human wisdom, will persist in calling creative solitudes a "waste of time."

Yet this dark romanza of reading and writing seems quite remote from much of what goes on in our institutions of higher learning. Keyboarding lecture notes or a book review, writing up the results of an experiment or a grant proposal or a committee report, or, *horribile dictu,* typing up data for yet another entirely useless departmental review—surely these kinds of writing are circumscribed in advance. They are meant to be and will be read by few or none; they constitute a document rather than a text or a work. And if the exercise has boredom as its end, then boredom—and not fascination—will accompany it every step of the way. The only problem is that some things at college are meant to be not boring. Teaching, for example.

We so often oppose teaching to research, reading, and writing that we forget a terrible truth: although reading and writing are incapable by themselves of fashioning a skillful teacher, no one can teach who has not been able to sustain the creative solitudes of reading, research, reflection, meditation, and writing. It is necessary to repeat this truism concerning the importance of all these lonely activities for teaching at a time when disapproval of solitude has been institutionalized. In spite of the endless talk among professors, administrators, and professional educators about teaching, very little thought is given to the day-to-day encounters that teaching entails. We are told it is better to spend endless hours at workshops, chatting earnestly and most often in bad faith about course "inputs" and "assessed learning outcomes." It is taken as a given that there will be sufficient time and energy for the creative solitudes of reading—*thoughtful* reading—and class preparation, even though every teacher reading these words of mine is disturbed, I believe, by the increasing number of classes we all have had to teach on the wing.

Who can protect teachers against the institutionalized war on creative solitudes? No one. Nor should we expect understanding on this point from persons who no longer teach much. One of my most distinguished professors back in graduate school once said to me, "Don't expect anyone to protect the time for your work. No one will ever do that for you. And, by the way, never paint your house." Stephen Dedalus invoked the cunning old artificer who was his namesake to help him create, whereas Hegel no doubt counted on the cunning of reason, but no cunning and calculating efficiency expert will ever lend a sympathetic ear to a teacher, not even if it is the case that without the creative solitudes of reading and writing the life of a school, college, or university is doomed.

We talk endlessly about how to "improve" our teaching, but a large part of this talk is an exercise in what Nietzsche calls "active forgetfulness." We tend to forget who our own great teachers were and why they were great. We hope we can pick up the knack from the chatter in a faculty chat room. Yet our great teachers were not full of chat; they were not "personalities," and certainly not song-and-dance performers or talk-show hosts. Rather, they spoke well about what they had read and contemplated well; they brought something of their solitary reading and thinking and writing with them when they entered a classroom. It was not a marketing trick they learned at a meeting or in a workshop; it was something that happened to them—many times over—when there was no one there to observe.

Moreover, solitude must accompany both teacher and learner throughout the teaching encounter. Garrulity is never enough, and it is often too much. We are losing the sense of what learners—such as ourselves—need to do alone. We are reminded of it when a beginning student comes up to us after class in order to say how strange and difficult they have found the assigned reading, and could it really be saying *this*, and after we listen to their struggles we smile and say, without flattery, "You are right on track, you are reading well, keep it up." True, those words of support have to be spoken. Yet they must be spoken discreetly, and that means they must be communicated from one solitude to another; otherwise they are simply vacuous "validations," mere manipulations. We teachers usually overestimate ourselves as catalysts of learning. In our effort to be not boring, we go glib or even apoplectic. In our fervor to be active and even proactive, we forget the higher form of passivity that all teaching and learning require, passivity in the sense of *releasement* or *letting be*, Meister Eckhart's *Gelassenheit*. One of the great teachers of the twentieth century said that what teaching calls for is "letting learn":

Indeed, the proper teacher lets nothing else be learned than—learning. His or her conduct, therefore, often produces the impression that we are really learning nothing from them, if by "learning" we now automatically understand the mere procurement of useful information. Teachers are ahead of their apprentices in this alone, that they still have far more to learn than the apprentices. For teachers have to learn to let them learn.[11]

My guess is that this mysterious *letting* learn, which is neither uncaring abandonment nor overzealous intervention, has to do with creative solitudes. Creative solitudes on both parts, as teachers demand of their students what they demand of themselves, namely, cultivation of those forms of fascination and even rapture that let us learn.

Among the threats to the creative solitudes of reading, writing, thinking, and teaching- by-letting-learn, none is so full of promise as the World Wide Web and email. It is perhaps still too early to assess the advantages and disadvantages— the promise and the threat—of the cybernetic and information revolutions for creative solitudes. These are heady days, however, and a word of caution may be in order. We often forget that most electronically stored "information" is quite accurately designated by that familiar icon to which we most often drag it: it is Trash. Now, I do not wish to bash trash in order to glorify the creative process. Sifting through trash is all we mortals ever do when we create. Remember that even Plato's Demiurge does not create out of nothing—he needs Necessity, or Ananke, who rules over the chaos of becoming. All the more reason, however, that the quality and quantity of *our* trash be scrutinized. The talents required for such scrutiny, however, cannot themselves be nurtured on-line. There is the cybernetic rub. When a student downloads someone else's paper for a course assignment, he or she cannot see what trash it is—they believe that the downloaded trash is better than the miserable scraps they themselves have failed to cobble together. Yet their hope is misplaced. They would have done better to cobble. The task before us, then, is to hone the skills that will enable them to see that they cannot lose by being original—the available materials are that bad! We have to teach them confidence by default, as it were. Socrates assures us that the only thing we can know is that we do *not* know. There are teeth in that realization. The internet is just another incarnation of those self-proclaimed "experts" of ancient Athens whom Socrates dialectically dismantles. It is doubtless faster than prior purveyors of knowledge, but it is every bit as bemused.

As for electronic communication and the social media, computers and smartphones put us in ever closer touch with one another—touch at a distance—through email and text-messaging. They therefore enable us to interrupt one another's creative solitudes with ever greater speed and impact. Yet the sad truth is that the interruptions occur on the inside: we do it to ourselves. With so many new messages in our little mailboxes we must be more important than we thought we were while being defeated by some difficult book or by the attempt to scribble a few ragged lines of our own. To be at the others' electronic beck and call is the wish-fulfillment dream of those for whom the fascination has flagged. Some of our colleagues have given up entirely on creative solitudes; their supreme need is to interrupt those who have not yet succumbed. Misery loves emails calling for yet another committee meeting. Such misery will find its best allies in us, however, in our own most vulnerable moments.

What lies at the root of the problem? I do not know. Perhaps it is harder than ever to be alone for any reason. Creative solitudes never looked so lonely, and their libidinal source never seemed so suspect, especially at a time when libido has been identified as nothing more than grounds for sanctions or a lawsuit. No wonder we who are increasingly out of touch with touch (except when it comes to touch pads) are secretly grateful for those avenues of escape, the websites and chat rooms and the new messages in our mailbox that trap us for hours, the committee meetings convened for an entire afternoon—all of them welcome postponements of yet another bout of solitude. We yearn for hours and days when we will not have to face another struggle on that nakedest possible plain. The blank sheet of paper resists our efforts more than a blank screen does; it will not be calendared as readily as a meeting that exhausts an entire afternoon, an afternoon we sacrifice with a pristine conscience. The writing desk will not support that sterile sociality that seems to compensate us for the people and the intimacy we have lost in this age of relentless competition, litigation, and aggression.

Let me return to the more general theme of creative solitudes by raising a final suspicion. Is all this nostalgia for solitude merely an echo of Western egoism, rugged individualism, self-reliance, and solipsism? Solipsism—indeed, an *existential* solipsism—is where a number of great thinkers in the century recently past say we have to be, are condemned to be. We are not alone at birth: like John Lennon's "Bungalow Bill" we always take our mothers with us. We do die alone, however, no matter who is in attendance. Nevertheless, I am suspicious of such claims concerning the inevitability of existential solipsism, which seem to be in a direct line of descent from the skull-gazing tradition of the *memento mori*. I am suspicious of the putative singularity of the *solus ipse* and of the emphatic egocentricity that seems to derive from the metaphysics and morals of both late antiquity and European modernity since Descartes. For such singularity of self—the rational self in solitude, cogitating to beat the band—has more to do with disciplining the self, that is, with producing a self for purposes of disciplining, than with anything either altruistic or creative. I confess I admire those theories of selfhood that remember how much of other persons each human being internalizes, from the cooing of the mother and the no-and-yes-saying of the father to all the subsequent voices each human existence carries with itself. I admire most of all the thought elaborated by Pierre Klossowski in response to Nietzsche's uncanny notion of the eternal recurrence of the same. Klossowski, noting the *elation* that accompanies the thought of eternal recurrence *each time we think it*—as though we were forever thinking it *for the very first time*—argues that human beings must be living out a recurrence of multiple selves on a cycle of amnesia and anamnesis, periodically forgetting and remembering who they might be. For a time we forget virtually everything about who we are and what sustains us, but then we suddenly find ourselves swimming against the current of Lethe toward the farther shore of our many selves, the selves which we will never come to know fully but which we must affirm if our solitudes are to be creative.[12]

That is my image of Arendt in New York and Ticino, Du Bois in Berlin and Atlanta, and Mahler in Vienna and Maiernigg. Without his summer solitudes in 1901 and 1902, Mahler would not have concluded the *Adagietto* movement with those infinitely descending final notes; without his solitudes at the University of Berlin, Du Bois would not have written for us those insights into the veil and our national double consciousness when it comes to the color line; without her solitudes in Berlin and New York and Ticino, Hannah Arendt would not have given us her lucid and worldly-wise "thoughtfulness." The terrible truth, however, is that each of these solitudes could have ended badly: Mahler could have been frightened off by those notes in the bass that are so deep they leave us nothing to stand on; Du Bois could have admitted defeat, when so many wanted the black man not to aim at such *intellectual* achievement; Arendt could have vacillated and joined the choruses of condemnation. Results are always the result of retrospective illusion. As long as Mahler, Du Bois, and Arendt were caught up in their creative solitudes, those solitudes were desperately lonely. Even their promise was unpromising. Someone was always there to tell them they were wasting their time, and that someone was none other than one of the selves they carried with themselves. Luckily, it was not their most solitary self, not the self that rallies the others in the night when hope seems absurd, the self that affirms even tragedy.

My own call to creative solitudes wants to be a call to this society of selves each of us is. The purpose of the call is not to announce *I think I am . . . sufficient to myself.* The purpose is rather to suggest that all our selves need to listen harder to the *creative others* who are without and within, whether they are dead or living— that in our solitudes we need to be rapt to these others to the point of rapture. And so, this final affirmation: creative solitudes do not have to be shattered by every interruption. A friend can drop by and ask you what you are writing; you show it to him, he nods slowly, and either he lets you get on with it or he stays and tells a story that will help you get on with it.

I was very near the end of a novel called *Son of Spirit*, which is about the short unhappy life of Hegel's first son—an illegitimate child, Louis Fischer, eventually named after his mother—when a friend, Dr. Kevin Miles, came to visit. He asked to see what I was writing, and I handed him the notebook, reluctantly. It was too new, too fresh, too vulnerable. He read for some time, then avoided direct comment by telling me stories of other illegitimate children, stories that were important to his own life as a writer and thinker. Among them was the story of the natural supernatural son of Io, Epaphos, whose name means "touched by Zeus." Epaphos, according to an ancient story (picked up by Aeschylus), fathered the peoples of Africa. Miles referred also to the story of Ishmael, the son of Hagar and Abraham, or, it may be, the child of Hagar and Herman Melville. Finally, he recounted the story of Adeodatus, "given *by* or *to* God," the illegitimate son of Augustine and a slave who was sent back to Africa by Augustine's pious, relentless mother. Miles was absorbed by these stories, and he absorbed me into them. After he left, I sat down and wrote one of the sections I love best in the novel, a section that manages—thanks to the stories brought to me by a friend— to gather Epaphos, Ishmael, and Adeodatus into a kind of posthumous family album for Louis Fischer, the solitary son of spirit.

Visitors, then, bring us bouquets of stories, and no creative solitude dare be churlish and inhospitable towards them. For their own multiple selves often invite the best of our selves into the vaulted cellar of creative solitudes. They are the keepers who bring the writer sustenance. And yet what would become of creative solitudes if everyone who wanted to interrupt them had the instantaneous electronic means to do so? Worse, what would happen if we ourselves, fleeing that struggle on the nakedest possible plain, succumbed to the chattiness of the chat room and the reassuring somebody-out-there-loves-me- or-at-least-can-use-me feeling that radiates from a stuffed mailbox? Our creative solitudes would be driven to distraction in all that white noise.

"Creative solitudes are wasted on some people," says the administrator, and he or she is surely right. Have I become one of these? When I decided to write the Nietzsche novel back in 1988, I vowed to myself that I would "waste" my entire sabbatical year on it, and from a scholarly point of view that is exactly what I did. By now things have deteriorated to such an extent that I am often writing books that could hardly be called "scholarly"; furthermore, I do not hesitate now to try my hand at fiction writing whenever an idea for a story presents itself. I seem to be more solitary in this respect than ever—even if more and more colleagues find themselves desiring new directions and new instruments for their thinking and writing, Zarathustra's "new lyre." Indeed, Robert Musil says that the "normal career" of an academic philosopher can be summarized in this way: "taking up a teaching position, patiently bearing the boring tasks of an assistant professor, intellectual participation in the transformations taking place in psychology and philosophy—and then, after being satiated with all that, a natural decline and the attempt to make a transition into literature."[13]

Be that as it may, what use am I making of my solitudes? What do I ask of them? Some astute person once defined golf as a good way to spoil a pleasant walk. I love to walk, but I am no good at golf. I am not very good at philosophy, either, as my more analytically inclined colleagues have always insisted. To be sure, I hate arguments, which seem to me another way to spoil a walk. I often find it both difficult and bootless to follow the thread of a thesis for more than a minute or two. As for serious scholarship, it takes more patience, thoroughness, and conceptual skill than I perhaps ever possessed. I do have the reputation of being a good translator of philosophical and literary texts, but that is a rumor I started myself. I make up for being a fair-to-middlin' translator by wearing out the pages of my thesaurus. This will sound like false modesty to some readers, as I hope, and false modesty, fishing for compliments, is a more despicable sport than even golf. Yet as far as I can tell, what I am saying is true. The publication a decade ago of my translation of Hölderlin's *Der Tod des Empedokles* gives me hope, however, and with luck, I will continue to do some translating. Yet why fiction?

I recall a conversation with David Wood somewhere near a pond in Umbria, a conversation in which he remarked that the difference between us, philosophically speaking, was that whereas he always felt constrained to come down on the side of the light, I invariably came down on the side of darkness. He was right. Obscurities have always attracted me more than enlightenments. When Herman Melville read Nathaniel Hawthorne's *Mosses from an Old Manse*, he felt encouraged to add a larger dose of the "blackness of darkness," "mystical blackness," "darkness," and even "tragicalness" to his own story of the white whale, which was under way at the time. I have always felt that both Hawthorne and Melville were talking to me. More darkness! More tragicalness! Hawthorne and Melville, of course, were writing fiction. I had not noticed at the time. Now I believe I have.

I have to admit that I am uncertain, more so recently than ever before, about whether I am any better at fiction than philosophy. Until quite recently things were looking bleak. I certainly cannot plot and I have scant imagination for situation. As for characters, where are *my* circus animals? What's keeping them? Occasionally they do show up, and then my solitudes are a delight: I love writing when the characters themselves approach and tell me the words they have always meant to say, the deeds they have always wanted to perform, and the sufferings they have always feared most. And so I plan to persist. Aristotle says, or at least suggests, if I remember well, that every being is good *at* something, or good *for* something: the point is to keep on searching. To date I have published only two of my short stories; a stage play, based on the life of Grete Trakl, although rewritten a dozen times, is not being produced; my film scripts attract dust instead of production companies—and that is probably for the best. Yet it is a pleasure for me to labor on these things.

Pleasure? you may say, a bit archly. Why not? I reply, only slightly defensively. And you never know, I may get good at one or other of these very different sorts of writing, each new genre an adventure for me, each incredibly challenging.

What exactly do I want from fiction writing? I dream of producing a *work*. I mean by this not some grand contraption that moves world and earth, but a minuscule cosmos all its own, a tiny gem, not precious, a mere stone, but cleanly cut and ably set. My models for such a work are almost always musical: a nocturne by Chopin, any one you like—if you are undecided, then opus 27 number 2. Or, if I may dream in the direction of some of my favorite stories, then something approaching Joyce's "Araby," maybe even "The Dead." Or how about Hemingway's perfect story, "The Capital of the World," or Melville's outrageous "Cock-A-Doodle-Doo!" Why not dream extravagantly?

Yet by now I realize that it is not a matter of leaving philosophy and nonfiction writing behind. I have recently completed two books on philosophical themes, one a meditation on the sea, the other a study of tenderness and cruelty—more precisely, of the German words *Zärtlichkeit* and *Grausamkeit*. A few years ago, I published a book on the poetry of Georg Trakl and another on what Heidegger calls "ecstatic temporality." Most recently, I completed a trip retracing Hölderlin's journey—over a thousand kilometers by foot and by post-coach—from

Nürtingen (near Stuttgart) to Bordeaux, and then back home again, another thousand-plus kilometers. The journey there took him through the northern part of the Black Forest to Strasbourg, and from Strasbourg to Lyon, Clermont-Ferrand, and over the snow-laden Auvergne to Limoges and Périgueux to Bordeaux and the Gironde. His walk took two months to complete: he left Nürtingen around December 6 or 10, 1801, and arrived in Bordeaux on January 28, 1802. Astonishingly, in May of that same year, he walked back home, this time by way of Paris. (I confess that I did not *walk* in his footsteps—had I tried to walk I would still be lost and snowbound somewhere in the northern Schwarzwald.) At the moment, I am trying to write about these exacting journeys of Hölderlin's, to and from Bordeaux, journeys of unimaginable aloneness. They were solitudes that proved to be both creative and destructive. When Hölderlin arrived home, he was in such a state that even his old friends failed to recognize him. Yet in the months that followed he was still able to compose many of his most memorable poems and hymns, among them, "Bread and Wine," "Half of Life," "Patmos," "Mnemosyne," and "Remembrance."

I have no way of knowing whether I will be able to recount these journeys, his and my own, which will have had their own solitudes. But then, readers may ask, why not be satisfied with such nonfiction work, which is gripping enough? And why not be content with *philosophical* writing? My response to the second question is that, to put it negatively, it has become clear to me that I am not driven by a pervasive and impelling philosophical *question*—for example, the question of being or the question of the trace, or even the question of the question—not compelled by a singular question or affirmation that would inspire a philosophical project worthy of the name. As for serious scholarship, it inspires footnotes, and that is another way to spoil a pleasant walk. Yet there is a more positive reply to the question. The work I feel most compelled or called to do involves persons and personae rather than ideas or philosophical systems. The philosopher Schelling long ago reminded me that whatever is *known* has to be *recounted* or *narrated*. Such narration, with all its masks, has always been the crucial matter for me—not as a theoretical matter for an aesthetics but as a practice and a way of life.

No one, it seems to me, not even Musil, would or should begrudge me this chance (however slight) to produce a work, a well-wrought tale or two. Whatever my earlier or even current philosophical work has to contribute to the writing of fiction it will contribute; the rest will fall away, or has already done so, and I hope that no one is or will be the worse for it. "The most innocent of occupations," Hölderlin said of creative writing (CHV 2:638). Innocent it may be, but it is also full of ruses. This same Hölderlin calls language itself "the most dangerous of gifts" (CHV 1:265).

It turns out that I have been making my way toward ruse-ridden fiction for a long time. Recently I discovered a journal that I had misplaced for many years and had considered lost, and so I looked into it. (Otherwise I never read my journals. What do we keep them for, anyway? For eventual but highly unlikely autobiography? For an uninterested posterity? For the repetition compulsion?) Allow me to cite one entry, made on October 15, which is Nietzsche's birthday, in the year 1969, which is now some fifty years ago. I wrote, near Seehausen in Oberbayern:

> I've been reading Hemingway's *A Movable Feast*, about his early years in Paris and his efforts there at writing . . . I gobble up what the writer writes about writing . . . But it is all a matter of how we devote our time. What I have so far written is quite bad, if only because I expect to get what I want as soon as I sit down at the desk. One who will not waste time won't write. I must free myself from my schooling.

That was a year before I completed my dissertation—if not my "schooling." Looking back, it seems as though philosophy was the long detour that eventually had to return me to the main road, fiction. I recall that during my earliest years, even before elementary school, I was forever telling stories, "performing" embellished fairy tales for parent-groups. I even performed such stories for a university class on one occasion; perhaps it was a class in abnormal psychology, I do not know. I must have been pretty good at it, though.

In later years, my mother thought I was good at philosophy, but she had her own reasons for hoping so. She wrote me on the occasion of my fiftieth birthday, two years before she died: "To my son David, who renounced a promising career as a juvenile delinquent and became a sober philosopher instead—while retaining still the *joie de vivre* of a ten-year-old!" Well, then, from here on out, let it be the joy of life, with a dash of delinquency—and that sounds pretty much like fiction writing. I hope to make it all the way back to my tenth year.

Several years ago, I was trying to write a story about a second-grader, an eight-year-old who has to give a speech in front of the class: she opens her mouth, but in her terror all that comes out is a spit bubble. I could see that bubble plainly, but I found it impossible to describe it in such a way that readers would not laugh at it but see and feel in it a reflection of the girl's terror. I discovered that words for being are as easy (or as difficult) as *dynamis* and *energeia*, whereas words for bubble are utterly elusive. Some will find my turn to saliva risible, an absurdly ontic undertaking. All I can say is that according to Heidegger ontology is founded upon and grounded in the ontic—or, if it's not, it isn't worth spit.

Hemingway, in the preface to his *First Forty-Nine Stories* (imagine that: his *first* forty-nine!) asks for nothing more than a stretch of time to spin out three more novels and twenty-five more stories. His justification? "I know some pretty good ones," he says. I am not sure I can say that just yet. After I round up my prodigal circus animals and round off my bubbles, bubbles for being, I will let you know.

Again, my thanks to David Jones and to all who have written here. The best thing about creative solitudes is that they allow you to surround yourself with such wonderful people. Finally, my thanks to readers of the present volume, who will have devoted moments of their own very precious time to engage with the theme of creative solitudes. The contributors to the present volume, I am certain, will give them good courage.

Notes

1 Henry David Thoreau, *Walden*, in *Walden and Civil Disobedience: The Variorum Editions*, ed. Walter Harding (New York: Washington Square Press, 1968), 171. Cited henceforth as W with page number.

2 This is the uncanny claim of Jean Genet in *The Studio of Alberto Giacometti*: "I understand badly what in art they call an innovator. Should a work be understood by future generations? But why? And what would that signify? That they could use it? For what? I do not see. But I see much better—even though very darkly—that every work of art, if it wishes to attain the most grandiose proportions, must, with an infinite patience and application from the moments of its elaboration, descend the millennia, and rejoin, if it can, the immemorial night peopled by the dead, who are going to recognize themselves in this work." Jacques Derrida cites Genet in *Glas* (Paris: Galilée, 1976), at 93B.

3 Maurice Blanchot, *Espace littéraire* (Paris: Gallimard, 1955), 223–24. Cited henceforth as EL with page number.

4 Ralph Waldo Emerson, *Selected Writings*, ed. William H. Gilman (New York: New American Library, 1965), 153–54.

5 Herman Melville, *Pierre or The Ambiguities*, ed. Harrison Hayford et al. (Evanston, IL, and Chicago: Northwestern University Press and The Newberry Library, 1971), 297.

6 Friedrich Hölderlin, *Sämtliche Werke und Briefe*, 3 vols., ed. Michael Knaupp (Munich: Carl Hanser, 1992), 2:590. Cited henceforth as CHV with volume and page.

7   Many (though not all) of Blanchot's essays on Kafka are gathered in Maurice Blanchot, *De Kafka à Kafka* (Paris: Gallimard, 1981).

8   Jean-Paul Sartre, *Les mots* (Paris: Gallimard, 1964), 36.

9   Franz Kafka, *Briefe an Milena*, expanded edition by Jürgen Born and Michael Müller (Frankfurt am Main: Fischer, 1986), 262–63.

10 Franz Kafka, *Briefe an Felice*, ed. Erich Heller and Jürgen Born (Frankfurt am Main: Fischer, 1976), 250.

11 Martin Heidegger, *Basic Writings*, 2nd edn (San Francisco: HarperCollins, 1993), 379–80.

12 See Pierre Klossowski, *Nietzsche et le cercle vicieux*, revised edn (Paris: Mercure de France, 1969), esp. chapter 3.

13 Robert Musil, "Sketches Toward an Autobiography (1937)," in Musil, *Drei Frauen* (Reinbek bei Hamburg: Rowohlt Taschenbuch, 1954), 132.

Part Two

Imagining Solitude

2

David Farrell Krell: The Impossible Voicing of Philosophy's Double

Walter Brogan

It is incredibly difficult to condense into a short presentation a worthy representation of the scholarly work of such an original, impactful, and prolific author as David Farrell Krell. I will not even pretend to do this. It is equally difficult to contain any commentary on the scholarly work of this philosopher simply to the field of philosophy, since Krell is not only one of America's greatest living philosophers but also an incomparable translator of philosophy and literature and an accomplished literary figure who has written some amazing works of fiction, some incredibly powerful short stories, and a number of plays. Let me begin with a comment on this last aspect of Krell's work.

I believe Krell is of two heads. He knows how significant his philosophy work is. But he is also an artist and aspires to the kind of success in literature that would parallel the influence his work in philosophy has had. He even sometimes intends, I think, to stop doing philosophy so that he can concentrate on literature and, so to speak, devote himself fully to this pursuit. Yet, at least to date, and thank goodness, he has been unsuccessful in severing his connection to philosophy. He continues to do it and has in fact produced in the last five years what I consider to be his most important philosophical work to date, for example, his book *The Tragic Absolute*, which appeared in 2005. So, I would like to address, first of all, this aspect of Krell's work, that is, the impossibility of separating his work as an artist from his work as a philosopher and his desire, nevertheless, to do so. It is this difficult joining of philosophy and art that I think Krell is experiencing and that we experience in all of his writing, whether literary or philosophical per se. And I think this recalcitrant joining of the two is what echoes in most of his recent work and perhaps even provides its impetus.

Two of Krell's novels are titled *Nietzsche: A Novel* and *Son of Spirit: A Novel*. The simple fact that these "novels" are about Nietzsche and Hegel would seem to offer, on the most surface level, evidence to this thesis about Krell's double-headedness. But are these even novels? Are they not rather letters, or biographies, or fictional autobiographies, or simply anecdotal shards of insight into these two great thinkers? Not only the fact that these novels are about Nietzsche and Hegel but also the style of these works blurs the borders between philosophy and literature, truth and fiction, fact and memory, imagination and concepts in provocative ways that are obviously intentional. For me, Krell is saying and showing in these novels something that can only be revealed on the frontier between philosophy and literature, something essential to any understanding or experience of Hegel or Nietzsche. This border insight that belongs to neither philosophy nor literature, an insight that also crosses and transgresses the border and crosses it out, is captured in one of the letters Krell translated in the Nietzsche novel and that Nietzsche wrote to Elizabeth in 1885:

> The feeling that there is something utterly remote and foreign about me, that my words take on different hues in the mouths of others, that there is a great deal of colorful foreground in me which deceives—precisely this feeling, corroborated recently on various fronts, is really the very sharpest degree of "understanding" that I have found up to now. Everything I have written prior to this is foreground; for me it all starts with the hiatuses. (*Nietzsche: A Novel*, 362)

Krell's novel, though scrupulously researched and carefully documented, demands of the reader a suspension of the distinction between the fictional and imaginary words of Nietzsche and those he actually said, a suspension of the distinction between what Krell authors and what Nietzsche says. Krell intentionally blurs this distinction while at the same time rigorously marking it.

Both of these novels are celebrations of the hiatus, those inexplicable interruption periods and periods of madness, those sudden insertions into the flow of the story line that give trouble to the pretense to completion and comprehension in which philosophy so often disguises itself. But not only philosophy. The modern novel has all too often adopted precisely this very same disguise, and Krell's novels will have none of it. What he wants to say and show does not occur in the holistic vision of uninterrupted philosophical and systematic thinking but only in the crevices opened up by what interrupts these stories. For example, in *Son of Spirit*, Krell tells the story of Hegel's bastard son Ludwig, the son of spirit. It is hard to capture how poignant are the passages that depict the voice of Hegel's son and it is difficult to choose an example among so many that, by virtue of giving a voice to this son, Hegel's vision of absolute spirit is so devastated and disrupted. But this is a book of non-dialectical dialogues between father and son, sister and brother, husband and wife, and between lovers, and it is precisely this "between" that Krell is going for in his novels, a between, I think, that needs both philosophy and literature, truth and fiction, in juxtaposition. Toward the end of this novel, the son of spirit says, presumably to spirit, and Ludwig says to Hegel:

> He needed me for one thing alone. He needed me for oblivion. He needed me to obliterate the memory of me—the fortuitous accident, the gratuitous contingency, the stain on the linens—and so he tried to extirpate my memory of him. For my remembering, my distant mourning, could only have been an offense to his memory, the ironic consolation prize of survival. He needed me to forget him, and so he tried to forget me. Yet in order to forget fully he needed for me never to have been. And yet I was. Never to have been is best, ancient wisemen say, yet he could get but second best, for me to turn away. As soon as possible, into remote distances. To recede into the infinite oceans of time and tide. Which I did. However, I procrastinated. I littered a few sad documents beneath the archivist's table, something to stumble over, something to be lost and found in the shuffle. (*Son of Spirit: A Novel*, 170–71)

This is surely literature on the verge of philosophy. I will dare risk saying about another text of Krell's, unfairly excluding the encompassing scope of this other work that traces the philosophical history of memory from Plato through Descartes and Hobbes and from Freud to Nietzsche, Heidegger, and Derrida; I will dare risk saying that in these few sentences of the son of spirit from his novel, so much is captured of what Krell thematizes in this book *Of Memory, Reminiscence, and Writing: On the Verge*, which is also so much about forgetting, mourning, and death. *On the Verge* concludes by saying, "The 'ambiguity of memory' expresses the ultimate failure of interiorizing remembrance. Whether one chases *Erinnerung* or champions *Gedächtnis*, the result is 'rupture, heterogeneity, disjunction' [Derrida], rather than dialectical resolution or speculative reconciliation" (*On the Verge*, 292). Krell's novels follow, as only literature can do, these disjunctions and breakdowns, these bastard, doubling voices that are repressed in but energize the ordinary discourse of philosophy. Krell makes clear that philosophy needs literature and makes this point persistently in all of his recent work. In the beginning of *Lunar Voices*, Krell says,

> What are men and women anyway? Thinking things said one thinker, speaking on behalf of many thinkers before and after him, although of course, if the

bulk of human time and experience were taken into account, the answer would be: things that think they think. That gently ironic fold, doubling, or duplicity of thinking is literature. Literature is philosophy's duplicitous twin. (*Lunar Voices*, xi)

In commenting on this passage in an interview for *Mosaic* that David did with Dawne McCance, he writes of the way literature has always been seen as troubling philosophy and how philosophy has persistently attempted to tame it or banish it as something dirty in order to preserve philosophy's commitment to the One. Then he says, "Literature, even the literature of the monologue and the soliloquy, is always doubling over on itself, always opening onto its other and the otherwise. It seems to me [he says] that there can't be literature without engagement with this trouble, the welcoming of this trouble, double trouble" (*Mosaic*, March 2006). Krell inhabits this troubling space of the double between philosophy and literature, like a love affair of sorts, one that, I'm sure he sometimes feels, will tear him apart, but one that he risks as any good lover would. Krell loves the fact that literature, especially in the eyes of philosophy, is dirty and impure; he is willing to risk this contamination and this distinguishes his relationship to philosophy from that of many others.

I think Krell calls *Nietzsche* and *Son of Spirit* novels, even though neither of them falls easily into any single category of either literature or philosophy, because it is only within works of literature that he is able to express a basic philosophical insight that philosophy would otherwise repress. Both novels shout loudly, even ferociously, at least to me, about the impossibility of separating philosophy and literature or at least about the tragic outcome of any attempt to do so. The Nietzsche novel portrays the madness one risks by staring into the abyss of this division; the Hegel novel portrays the tragic loss of one who stridently avoids doing so.

In one of his short stories, one that particularly moves me, "Glaciers in January Are Not the Place to Be," the character Sepp says, "There is no trick to getting up onto a glacier if you are smart enough to avoid the face of it, its forbidding 'portal.'" Thus begins the story of the tragic deaths of Walter Spohr and Ernst Koslan who died on January 22, 1910, on the Hüfi Glacier in the Swiss Alps. As they plummet into the gap that had opened up in a crevice of the glacier, David writes, or, perhaps better, the narrator says,

What remains incontrovertibly true, however outrageous it may seem, is the fact that they did not know they were falling as they were indeed falling, and, further, that their not knowing the fact had no effect whatsoever on the fall. For a gargantuan gap in a glacier in January is not an object of knowledge . . . [much is known, of course, both scientifically and theoretically, as the narrator points out, about these gaps in the glacier heights. But the narrator continues]. What is not known, however, among the infinite number of things in the universe not known, is why a gap of two meters will open precisely here, why it will have jagged teeth and narrow lateral crevices precisely there, why it will run through the depth granted by ten or twenty or a hundred winters, or why not all things but only some things are swallowed and then regurgitated, compelled to rise through the refrozen ablations of summers and winters over decades of snowstorm and melt and freeze—these things are not known, not by Leibniz's *Characteristica* and calculus, nor by Novalis's thaumaturgic logarithms nor even by surfing on the internet. No, these things are not known. Not even by a would-be omniscient narrator.

The rest of the story is about the intimacy of particular memories and the tenderness of insignificant moments, the very things that matter most and escape the grasp of knowledge precisely because of their utter specificity. This is what transpired, according to the narrator's rendition of it, in the thoughts of these two hikers during those final "brittle hours of eternity." These thoughts "on the way down" are crossings between memories and dreams, on the border between now and then, on the frontier between imagination and sense, always particular, always not so much thoughts of the past as the recurrence of feelings that had sunk into oblivion, frozen in time and buried in the abyss of the deepest subterranean shafts that can be encountered only when one has lost one's grip. In *On the Verge*, in a chapter titled "Of Pits and Pyramids," Krell says,

> Hegel's thought remains a matter of the grasp, of production and technique— mechanical dialectic mining the depths rather than freely exploring them without a thought to reserves. His is a philosophy of the granite presupposition, all seed ensconced in the protective husk and hull of the absolute. It does not peer patiently down the shaft, much less overcome all prohibitions and inhibitions and descend into it. And what it does not condescend to see it cannot remember. (*On the Verge*, 230)

In Krell's short story, "Glaciers in January," Walter Spohr and Ernst Koslan undergo this abysmal descent into impossible memories, recovering feelings that perhaps were not even known or acknowledged at the time the incidents remembered had occurred, feelings that occur between friends, between fathers and sons, between lovers. As these feelings mix with the sensuality of dying that melts the frozen heights of the glacier and opens the infinite abyss that it has contained at so heavy a price, as the memories of touch and taste mix with the pain of splintered legs and crushed bodies, Ernst struggles to remember if he confessed to Walter that he loved Walter's wife Wilhelmine:

> Had he been able to describe the emptiness he felt before her touch the ache when her touch was potential but not yet actual and the soaring flight the leap the catapulting of his already airborne body when at last she did touch him? And where? Did he go so far as to talk of her taste, of the freshness of her, of her melting morning snows transported to evening tropics? Was he able to tell Walter of the shame and the shattered nerves they shared and the intensity of their capitulation their terror over and over and over again?

Krell's philosophical work has been preoccupied throughout with these intimations of mortality, not just those about which Heidegger writes but even more so those that Schelling, Hölderlin, Novalis, and Nietzsche address. In Krell's short stories, these intimations and feelings of mortal being gain a powerful voice, a tragic voice. In his philosophical writings, Krell writes always in the direction and towards the verge of this tragic voice, tragic not because it is sad or unfulfilled, though this may be true, but tragic because it cannot be heard in philosophy alone and is the other of philosophy's voice, its duplicitous twin, the Echo of its Narcissus. I would like to turn with some final remarks to one of Krell's works that especially thematizes this tragic dimension at the edge of philosophy, namely, *The Tragic Absolute*. In this book, Krell is at home among a group of figures who do not shrink from the chiasmic, cataclysmic, and chaotic crossing of philosophy and literature and who celebrate all of the titanic force of an erotic sensuality unleashed by an untamed divinity that arises out of the ashes of an absolute that has entered into the undergoing of mortality.

Among these figures, none stands out as closer to the heart of Krell than Nietzsche, and it is with Nietzsche that Krell ends this book. It is Nietzsche who, for Krell, enters the furthest and with the fullest intensity into the tragedy of the Absolute. Krell writes in *Postponements*:

> According to Nietzsche, the Apollinian dream-world of Olympus serves as a mirror by which the Hellenic world is able to confront an archaic, violent nature; confront and overcome it, subduing the Erinnyes, placating the Moirai, decapitating Medusa, arrogating the Gorgo. These figures, all of them female, provide our first curious glimpse of the mother(s) of tragedy. Yet at a certain point in the history of Hellenism the Apollinian mirror cracks, the measure of the Apollinian style falters, and the gods of Olympus themselves grow livid at the wisdom of Silenus. (*Postponements*, 35)

It is Nietzsche, even more so than Novalis, Schelling, and Hölderlin—although Krell pushes each of these figures to the extreme of their insights into the divine character of tragedy through his peripheral readings of these authors—still it is Nietzsche who announces finally what Krell shows to be the direction of German Romanticism, namely the dying of god, the undergoing of mortality that is the culminating truth and final victory of the absolute. One of the major accomplishments of this incredibly original and erudite book is to show—even in the face of Nietzsche's justified resistance to the ambiguity of the German romanticist's yearning for an absolute that remains pure and uncontaminated—the lineage that can be traced from Novalis, Schelling, and Hölderlin to Nietzsche. Krell writes:

> Nietzsche regrets having confused in his early work the ancient pessimism of strength with "the most modern things" (KSA 1:20), things such as the Wagner of the collective artwork. He regrets the language of consolation and redemption.... He wishes that the language of *Zarathustra* had been available to him, wishes he were more poet than genealogist, wishes that he had *sung*, or even better, that he had obeyed Zarathustra's injunction and fashioned a new lyre. Yet the fact that the god is *redeemed* rather than redeemer, and redeemed *in the world*, the world of *suffering*, sets Nietzsche in proximity to Novalis, Schelling, and Hölderlin in their most radical moments. (*The Tragic Absolute*, 420)

Krell addresses the question of the role of the absolute in Nietzsche's thinking and acknowledges that the trajectory of Nietzsche's philosophy is antithetical to a philosophy of the absolute in anything like the Hegelian sense. But then he adds: "Yet would it not be enlightening to see his work, from *The Birth of Tragedy*, through *Thus Spoke Zarathustra* and *Beyond Good and Evil* (especially the final pages on "Dionysos philosophos"), up to *Twilight of the Idols*, as an extended essay in tragic thinking—a thinking that elevates tragedy to absolute significance, and thinks the absolute as tragic?" (*The Tragic Absolute*, 420–21). In my understanding, Krell sees Nietzsche's success in thinking the absolute as tragedy as a question of style. Nietzsche's style crosses the border between philosophy and literature. For Krell, the site of this crossing is multiple: poetic myth, tragic drama, and most of all, the satyr-play of Dionysian, bodily music and of festival and dance. Krell says, "Schelling therefore opens a question that Schopenhauer and Nietzsche will not fail to pursue, namely, the question of the absolute tragedy that absolute music initiates" (*The Tragic Absolute*, 7). In Krell's reading, following Schelling and Nietzsche, it is music that initiates and underlies tragedy, and for this reason one can perhaps say that absolute music is more absolute than tragedy in that it gives birth to words. This is not to say that music comes before words in some *a priori* state before literature or philosophy. It is rather to say that music is the site of the giving birth of tragic language, which is the language of the gods and the language of the downfall of the gods; it is the language of their mimetic fecundity and rebirthing, that is, the language that enacts and performs what otherwise the gods could not have, namely, birth and love and ecstatic transport outside themselves. Music is the sound and rhythm of the divisive force that unites and couples gods and humans, as well as nature and art. It is thus also what originates the connection between nature and literature; tragic literature is a literature of nature, of *physis*. But precisely this question of origin, this originary contamination of the gods with matters of *eros* and the pulsating rhythm of fecundity, this absolutely unavoidable tonality and dispersing materiality of the divine, this complicity of the primal imaging of the song of the gods with the textuality of tragic myth, this coupling of necessity and contingency is the complex story of what Krell calls the tragic absolute. It is an absolute that belongs to gods who are infected with temporality and who are saturated with the desire for the other from whom they are absolutely separated and to whom they belong by virtue of this absolute separation. The tragic absolute is an absolute that is originally divided and torn apart. This sundering of the absolute belongs to its doubling unity.

Krell traces the doubling of the absolute—the infection of the absolute with duality—to three aspects of the absolute uncovered respectively by Schelling, Hölderlin, and Novalis, namely, inhibition, separation, and density. Schelling, Krell tells us, "would love to promote a monistic system of infinite activity as the sole possible system of reason, and yet he is compelled ever and again to posit a dualism of the traditional sort, nature vs. freedom, matter vs. spirit, becoming vs. being, the ideal vs. the real" (*The Tragic Absolute*, 48). The problem is that natural things are and yet come to be through sexual opposition and through relationship to illness and death. How can there be such an interruption of the pure, seamless, infinite activity of the absolute that stays with itself, such that it gives rise to a being that belongs to becoming, unless it, too, is able to be infected by deviation and the otherness of sexual difference? Schelling gradually comes to realize that this "trauma of the absolute," God's trauma, lies in its incapacity to hold itself apart from this heterogeneity, and even further that the godhead desires and yearns precisely for this *Hemmung*, this inhibition to its infinite activity, this being other to itself that occurs as conception, gestation, and birth.

The desire for itself that sustains infinite activity and the eternal absolute that moves solely within its own orbit is always already infected with otherness and difference.

For Hölderlin, in turn, the *aporia* of the absolute lies in the impossibility of separation, which nevertheless is necessary for it to be. The absolute's absolute unity with itself, its inviolability, its absolute identity, is always only posited as an absolute unity of the whole that surpasses the division of subject and object and the division into parts. The absolute strives to contain and surpass all that is other than itself so that its unity holds itself apart from all that would sully it with its negative and negating power. But this excessive unity that would consume in itself all being and hold separate from itself all difference, this principle of separation that infects the absolute incorporates within the absolute the very materiality and negation that it would deny. It is thus that "the divine unity of intellectual intuition is brought to tragic separation and dissolution," and the absolute suffers the debility that is produced by its own strength. For the gods must descend to the earth and join themselves to the earth in order to incorporate the earth into their heavenly orbit, becoming bodily. Thus, the gods, in order to be gods, need to stand in the greatest proximity to death, mortality, and otherness. The infinite activity that abides nothing to be outside of itself demands this proximity to that force which would unravel it in its apartness and open it to love, lest it substitute for its genuinely godly separation a merely "catatonic isolation and absolute autism" that would, in the end, close it off from itself so that it would cease to be.

The third principle that belongs to the absolute and causes the pretension to purity and self-possession of the absolute to dissolve is discovered by Novalis. Krell takes this up briefly in *The Tragic Absolute* and more extensively in *Contagion*. Novalis points out that density, absolute density, must be one of the principal characteristics of the absolute. For Novalis, the infinite activity of the absolute, thought thinking itself, can occur only in resistance to what would oppose its action. Though contradictory, matter and spirit are mutually grounding and thus contaminate one another. Everything stands in relation to another, whether this relation be absolute as in contradictory relations or relative as among contraries. Everything, even the absolute, is dichotomous. Being *is* as not nonbeing. The absolutely absolute, an absolute without relation, is impossible. Yet there is on the part of thought this drive to think the absolutely absolute. As Krell says, for Novalis, "the absolute is our absolute inability to think or act in conformity with an absolute. Whence, then, our drive to think and act on the horizon of such impossible absolutes? . . . [Novalis replies:] 'We seek the unconditioned in every nook and cranny, and all we ever find are [conditioned] things'" (*The Tragic Absolute*, 63). At best, then, we can approximate the absolute. To achieve the absolute would be to achieve the impossibility of absolute density, which would destroy the oxidation that breathes life into spirit. The absolutely absolute cannot live because it extinguishes the fire and the negativity of destruction that is needed by life. The absolutely absolute in its absolute, impervious density is death.

It is, I would like to suggest, by way of conclusion, precisely because the philosopher's dream to approximate the absolute is in danger of suffocating life by positing an ideal absolute that is so ethereal as to be without air (and, thus, ironically, the attempt to posit an absolute without earth ends up suffocating without air) and without the combustion that makes life possible, that literature is necessary. Tragic literature depicts the drama of the drive of the universal and the absolute, and the tragic danger of denying these transcendent forces in our lives. But, as Krell points out, these dramas occur in a small number of houses, those, for example, of Oedipus and Agamemnon; and these dramas are played out in the face of the full force of the individuality and situatedness of the characters that are portrayed. Literature lets us keep our yearning for the absolute in touch with particularity and allows us to keep our desire for the universal and the necessary in connection with the contingent and with our sensual being. For this reason, philosophy needs literature. In turn, the yearning for the excess of the absolute that characterizes philosophy contributes to the power of literature. Literature that forgets or represses the demand that it gives voice to this absolute necessity becomes merely contingent and hackneyed. Perhaps that is why literature needs philosophy and why Krell cannot silence the need for philosophy even as he pursues his amazing talent in writing literature.

The Tragic Absolute is a book about heroes and heroines. In commenting on Schelling's notion of human freedom, Krell says, "Freedom asserts itself as downgoing, welcoming the punishment that honors the hero with an uncanny obsequy: *You were destined to fail in the face of a higher power, but even so you struggled—in vain! In freedom!* For the hero and heroine there is only an imperfect freedom, a freedom that can reply only thus: *By this you see that I, the defeated one, was free. I had freedom . . . to burn!*" (*The Tragic Absolute*, 187). I think of David Krell as such a hero; this is not to say that he has failed or will fail as a writer; we all know that this is not true. But it is not true because greatness, tragic greatness, does not flee in the face of failure and weakness; this willingness to embrace one's impotency in the face of godly pursuits is a sign of a great writer **and** a great philosopher.

References

Krell, David Farrell. 1986. *Intimations of Mortality: Time, Truth and Finitude in Heidegger's Thinking of Being*. University Park: Pennsylvania State University Press.

Krell, David Farrell. 1986. *Postponements: Woman, Sensuality and Death in Nietzsche*. Bloomington: Indiana University Press.

Krell, David Farrell. 1990. *Of Memory, Reminiscence, and Writing: On the Verge*. Bloomington: Indiana University Press.

Krell, David Farrell. 1995. *Lunar Voices of Tragedy, Poetry, Fiction, and Thought*. Chicago: University of Chicago Press.

Krell, David Farrell. 1996. *Nietzsche: A Novel*. Albany: State University of New York Press.

Krell, David Farrell. 1997. *Son of Spirit: A Novel*. Albany: State University of New York Press.

Krell, David Farrell. 1998. *Contagion: Sexuality, Disease and Death in German Idealism and Romanticism*. Bloomington: Indiana University Press.

Krell, David Farrell. 2005. *The Tragic Absolute: German Idealism and the Languishing of God*. Bloomington, Indiana University Press.

Krell, David Farrell. "Glaciers in January Are Not the Place to Be." A yet-to-be-published short story.

McCance, Dawne. 2006. "Crossings: An Interview with David Farrell Krell." *Mosaic*, vol. 39, no. 1, March 2006.

3

A Creativity to Sustain, A Solitude to Endure

Angelica Nuzzo

The Question: Creative Solitude, the Process

I first heard David Farrell Krell's lecture "Creative Solitudes" when it was delivered in occasion of the Cortelyou-Lowery Award ceremony at DePaul University in 1997. I was then at the beginning of my time at this university, lucky to have David Krell as a colleague and friend. The lecture left me full of admiration for him and surprisingly elated from the sense of guilt that, now I realized, had always accompanied my efforts at creating and protecting those precious moments of undisturbed work, which now I knew had a name by which I could proudly call them—"creative solitudes." To be sure, it was already a surprise for me to realize, perhaps for the first time, how much I had always labored—and labored secretly or covertly because of that sense of guilt—to make that space for myself; and it was a surprise to acknowledge that heretofore I had taken the necessity of those efforts as unavoidable—it was, in a certain way, part of the job, no need to speak about it, useless to hope that someone could ever relieve me of it. But now, at last, this was the topic of a lucid, eye-opening, public reflection.

After many years, I encounter this essay again at the beginning of 2011, reading it this time. I have had this text for quite a while, but I always saved it for a moment of concentrated solitude (hopefully, a creative one). Fearing that otherwise its message would be lost, I wanted to let it speak to me at a time in which I would be able to hear, to really hear what it had to say so as to be able to respond to it. Solitude is indeed the condition for true dialogue. Since its first presentation in 1997, David Krell's assessment of the external factors conjuring up against creative solitudes and his prediction concerning a worsening situation to come has been unfortunately fulfilled. Things only seem to get progressively worse on all fronts. Web technology has exponentially multiplied its weapons of distraction increasingly promising to reduce creative solitude to a myth of the past, utterly unknown and meaningless to the younger generations deft at Twitter and Facebook but unable to even approach anything sounding like "creative solitude" (loneliness certainly, solitude doubtfully, creative solitude certainly not); administrators, on their part, are triumphant in their battle against creativity, while our desperate efforts to conquer precious solitary moments are matched only by the efforts spent to defend those moments in the rare occurrences in which they are granted.

Since my first attending the Cortelyou lecture at DePaul University, I have followed (and in brief, particularly fortunate moments, even participated in) the varied, multiform process through which David Krell has consistently continued to live and explore the path of creativity—in philosophy and literature. The body of work that he has produced is known to many, has influenced many, is admired and celebrated by many. But what intrigues and fascinates me even more than the produced work is the *process* in which that work has happened—the process that has made that work happen in the first place. It is on such process, I take it, that David Krell reflects in his essay. What captures my attention of that process is, more particularly, its persistence and sustained course. For, more than an isolate "state," creative solitude is an enduring process—perhaps a lifelong process—to be valued for what it is even independently of the results it produces. To be sure, more than the condition for creation (of works), creative solitude is itself a precious creation. It is indeed a curious process, difficult to pinpoint in its specificity: it is something that we (voluntarily) do but also something that simply happens to us (in a moment of passivity or *Gelassenheit*, as Krell suggests), something in the midst of which we find ourselves; it is something that we can (and we do) plan for, but then only to a certain extent as contingency seems the true cipher of its happening; it is a process that we never know when and how it will begin and end, both dreading and desiring that beginning and that end.

Moreover, way too often we are so taken by the results (the Book, the Novel, the Work), which are much easier to circumscribe and analyze, that we omit, forget, neglect the process that has led to them. Productivity takes the spotlight away from creativity or is confused with it. Solitude is so easily shattered by the noise of always too many discussions that it is as if it had never existed. Although the focus on the results may be entirely justified in many cases, it is, yet again, David Krell's merit to have brought to the foreground the importance of creative solitude as an unfolding process over and above the results that it yields. Creative solitude is not the same as productivity. This, in any case, is the point to which my rereading of the essay "Creative Solitudes" leads me today. This is the topic that I would like to address in the following reflections.

If I consider David Farrell Krell an exemplar of creativity (of scholarly as well as artistic creativity), it is not only because of the quality and quantity of his philosophical and literary work but first and foremost because he has shown throughout the years the courage of the sustained, continuing, persistent movement of the solitary process of creativity. He has persistently fed this process and made it continue. Truly, he is a *maestro* of creative solitudes.

What is worth exploring, I submit, is not only the punctual act of creation and its concrete results but also the extended process through which creativity is sustained throughout a life and how it is allowed to have a duration and an endurance through time and obstacles (albeit, way too often, a fragile endurance), thereby becoming itself the cipher of a life and the precious center of its value. Creative solitude is a sort of poetic Aristotelian *eudaemonia*: it is truly there if and only if it passes the test of time, that is, if it consistently occupies an entire life. For, in this case only, as Aristotle says, it cannot be easily taken away from its possessor.[1] But how is such endurance possible? How do we achieve such duration? In fact, creative solitudes in this sense are a rare and fortunate occurrence.

Here I want to pursue the suggestion that "creative solitude" does not indicate an existential *state* but the effort to sustain a process, a transformative process that must be taken independently from the works it produces and whose secret is precisely its duration and endurance—a duration that is up to us to nourish and encourage. This is the true lesson that we should learn from Krell's own creative solitudes. What is really remarkable is not to create in solitude but to keep creative solitude going, to make it last. The ambiguity that characterizes the idea of solitude—the distance between longed-for solitude and dreaded loneliness—carries over to the idea that creative solitude as creativity is itself a multifaceted concept, an act that is both welcome, pleasurable, as it were, and fearful. Perhaps framing the creativity of solitude and the solitary nature of creativity in terms of the duration and the trajectory of a process can help us put that double ambiguity into focus. Thus, I want to raise the following questions: How does creative solitude maintain itself? Where does it find the energy of its own renewal, the force that keeps it going? What is it that allows creativity to sustain its effort and not plunge into a sterile loneliness? In effect, this is a double question. What is it that sustains solitude through its duration, making it last despite the vertigo that we encounter in it but also even with its many external interruptions? And what is it that keeps creativity going beyond its results and in spite of its results?

In the following reflections, I will not give answers but only attempt to progressively articulate these questions. They are questions that I direct to David Farrell Krell as the teacher of creative solitudes who he has become for me not only through his many books but particularly through the process that he has endured for many years. Through the path of creative solitudes that he has persisted in traveling, he has thereby shown that the poietic *eudaemonia* of creative solitude is for us a real possibility and a value worth pursuing. I take his 1997 lecture—its enduring truth and willful repetition throughout the years—as a testimony precisely of such a process, as a message to all of us that creative solitude can and indeed must endure, can and indeed must be kept up despite the increasingly hostile environment in which we work, and even more so because of it.

Whose Solitude is Creative? Discursive Thinking and Intellectual Intuition

My suggestion is that the chief question of creativity, its "mystery" as it were, is the same as the chief question of solitude: not how to begin but rather how to move on, how to maintain what has already begun not as a still, unmoved, sclerotic moment to be cherished and preserved, but as a dynamic process in which ongoing transformation is central. So central is this that we are constantly on the verge of losing the continuity of the process in which we find ourselves (or of losing ourselves in it). In other words, I maintain that the white sheet that faces the writer as she begins writing is far less threatening (although far more glamorous) than the second blank page that is expected to follow the first if the first is to make sense and be justified precisely as a first. The power of creativity, I submit, should be measured by the capacity to take the second step, that is, by the courage to advance the process.

I shall articulate this point by asking, *What kind of thinking needs creative solitude?* This question is implicit in the argument of Krell's 1997–2009 essay. His answer is that not only Mahler, Thoreau, Kafka, and Hölderlin, among others, certainly needed creative solitude (they were conscious of their need and did not "waste" their creative solitudes) but that all of us—teachers, philosophers, writers of many kinds and aspirations—need it (although we are not always aware of it and chances are we may "waste it").[2] Administrators and technocrats, by contrast, definitely do not need it, but then they also do not want it.

My answer pursues a different, more abstract connection (which, however, eventually rejoins Krell's point). I suggest that creative solitude is the element and the living process of *discursive thinking*, not that of *intellectual intuition*. It is only our human, embodied, finite thinking and not a divine, disembodied intellectual intuition that creates in solitude, that needs and longs for solitude to create, and that is able to alight its solitude through creativity. Intellectual intuition simply and unconditionally creates; its action is a first that can be followed by no second (hence, properly, is not even a first). It begins and ends in an individual instantaneous act out of time and out of space, an act that knows of no process and of no possible development.

By contrast, our thinking—the only thinking that is in need of creative solitude and is challenged by creative solitude as an enduring process—is necessarily discursive and thereby proceeds and unfolds in time and space. It is articulated in discrete unities (concepts, representations, images, or sounds) that follow one another, whatever the logic (or nonlogic) of what this following may be, whatever the obstacles, the interruptions, the hiatuses, and the revolutions that the process must go through in order to actually proceed. All human creative thinking is discursive thinking—not philosophical thinking alone but also literature (to bring up the duplicity of Krell's work which, in my view, is not so duplicitous after all) as well as artistic and scientific thinking.[3] Along with intellectual intuition, at the opposite extreme of the spectrum, I would exclude from the realm of human creativity any form of thinking that may resemble the noncreative functioning of a computer—to this I associate the reasoning of administrators and technocrats of all kinds.

As I shall argue below, common to all forms of discursive thinking is the need to tell stories. Stories are its peculiar creations. They are complex developments that come out of creative solitude and populate its course. Stories unfold and proceed with the same rhythm that characterizes the process that creative solitude itself is. Just as creative solitudes tell stories (through narratives and arguments, through words and sounds, concepts and images), they also articulate (each of them) their own (existential) story—a story of struggle and endurance, of success or wasted time.

And yet, not every form of human thinking is discursive. Intellectual intuition is not the exclusive province of the divine. In the short story "Solitude" (1884), Guy de Maupassant offers a counterexample of the view of creative solitude as discursive process that I am proposing. Solitude is for the protagonist of Maupassant's story a sterile existential loneliness and fundamental human incommunicability. Creativity, on the other hand, is the instantaneous intuition of truth that, unable to sustain itself and immediately shutting down as truth is revealed, achieves very meager results indeed. It is a process paralyzed and killed in its very inception, immediately reabsorbed back in the loneliness from which it has arisen. Just as intellectual intuition, this kind of thinking does not "need" creative solitude because, properly, it cannot create as it cannot endure the duration of a process. Walking up to the Champs-Élysées at night, the lonely protagonist confesses to his companion: "Je ne sais pourquoi, je respire mieux ici, la nuit, que partout ailleurs. Il me semble que ma pensée s'y élargit. J'ai, par moments, ces espèces de lueurs dans l'esprit qui font croire, pendant une seconde, qu'on va découvrir le divin secret des choses. *Puis la fenetre se refêrme. C'est fini.*"[4] The intuition of truth is revoked in the very moment it is made present by the elation and incipient enthusiasm that announce it to our spirit. Herein solitude and creativity remain inexorably disjoined, yet another proof that intellectual intuition has no place in the human world. The instantaneous intuition of truth that immediately vanishes and cannot maintain itself in the duration of a process is not a creative act. While it arises indeed in solitude, it also plunges back into incommunicable loneliness. Solitude is a vacuum that cannot sustain itself and is utterly meaningless. *C'est fini.*

The problem of discursive thinking, by contrast, the condition of its meaningfulness, is the problem of weaving its discourse as a sustained narrative or, alternatively, as a sustained argument.[5] And this is the problem of how thinking can go on thinking, creatively thinking, *thinking through*—through things and events and ideas and obstacles, and through the many imaginative and real possibilities to which thinking must be open even (and in particular) in its solitude. The point is that it is not enough to secure the beginning— the uninterrupted, secluded peace of solitude—in order to have secured the advancement of the creative process. At stake is not the success of such a process, but the contingency of the fact that a process takes place at all—the fact that the window does not shut in the very same moment in which it opens, the fact that a second page does follow the first one, and that, contrariwise, it is immaterial whether the blank page remains blank or is filled at all. Everyone who has attempted this knows it. If our thinking were intuitive, this would indeed be all there is to it: a creation exhausted in the instant or in the point of its very inception, without a story to tell and without a trace left behind.[6] The real issue for our discursive thinking is instead how to keep the creative process going as a process and how to remain in that solitude and dwell in it creatively or meaningfully. (It is at this point that the self-inflicted doubt, which only echoes the administrator's certainty, surfaces: "I am wasting my time," and menaces to extinguish the process in its inception.)

Thus, the touchstone of thinking's creativity is its ability to sustain its solitude in the unfolding of a movement in which risks are taken, the new is encountered, disappointments and seeming dead ends need to be overcome, and, yes, the pleasure and enthusiasm of discovery are also occasionally met. Ultimately, the process of thinking's creativity—its discursivity—is the cipher of its inexorable finitude, materiality, and embodiment. Creative solitude is the movement of a kind of thinking that is anchored in and nourished by time and space—it is neither the solitude of the pure void nor that of the immaterial nothingness, just as it is not the purely immanent and self-sufficient creativity of a pure intuition. It is a solitude that makes its way advancing in time and space, recreating its own time and its own space—as the time and space of discourse, argument, musical composition, fiction, or artistic object—giving to time and space the configuration of a new life and a new order (or lack thereof). Such is the peculiar creativity of discursive thinking in opposition to the instantaneous, immaterial happening of intellectual intuition.

Pitched against the immateriality of intellectual intuition, discursive thinking is Plato's "light dove" that as condition for its free flight needs the resistance offered by that very same materiality, which constitutes its finitude. In taking up Plato's image in the opening of the *Critique of Pure Reason*, Kant's effort is to convert the limitation associated to that finitude into a positive sign of distinction.[7] There may be one thing for which discursive thinking should not envy intellectual intuition after all. And this is the capacity to dwell in creative solitudes.

Creative Solitude: What It Takes to Tell a Story

I have argued so far that the chief difference separating discursive from intuitive thinking is that while the latter consumes itself in the punctuality of the instant, the former is creative in a developmental process that stretches through time and space and engages the preexisting materiality of the world that surrounds and sustains it. This process, I suggested, is our thinking's creative solitude—the creative solitude of human finite embodied thinking. Another way to construe this difference is to claim that for our thinking, because of its discursive character, sense and meaning necessarily unfold in a process that is the narrative of a story (articulated by words, material images, sounds, and so forth) or the structure of an argument. Discursive meaning is neither revealed by the first word on a page, nor by an isolated sound, nor by the first premise of a syllogism. It is rather to be found *in the connection* to a following second word or sound, in the unfolding of a phrase or of a melody, in the movement to a second premise and in the inference to a conclusion. By such connections, a story is generated. Intellectual intuition, by contrast, knows no story and tells none. Now, how does the telling of a story or the weaving of an argument illuminate the process-like nature of creative solitude?

> It happens like this: a kind of languor;
> A ceaseless striking of a clock is heard.
> Far off, a dying peal of thunder.
> I somehow sense the groaning and the sorrows
> Of unrecognized voices,
> A kind of secret circle narrows.
> But in the abyss of whispers and ringing
> Rises one triumphant sound.
> Such an absolute silence surrounds it
> That one can hear the grass growing in the woods
> [. . .]
> But now words are beginning to be heard
> And the signaling chimes of light rhymes—
> Then I begin to comprehend,
> And the simply dictated lines
> Lie down in place on the snow-white page.[8]

This is the extraordinary way in which Anna Achmatova condenses the process of poetic creation in the poem "Creation." That is, in speaking of creative solitude, the poem reenacts the very process that has brought it to life. Thereby Achmatova paradigmatically captures the unfolding movement of creative solitude telling, at the same time, the *story* of creation—the story that every creation is. Not only is creation a process and not the instantaneous action of an intellectual intuition, creation is also never just a beginning but is rather the moment of advancement out of the beginning. For, creation is not the absolute beginning out of nothing—neither for Plato's *Demiurge*, nor for the G-d of *Bereshit* or the *logos* of *Genesis*, nor for the pure thinking of Hegel's *Logic*. In fact, even the absolute spontaneity of Kant's transcendental freedom happens in the phenomenal world.

The creative beginning is truly no absolute beginning but the advancement, the moving on out of primordial chaos or out of solitude and silence and night—in force of solitude and silence and night. It is the unique rearrangement of preexisting elements into an utterly new order. Only in solitude, however, can the preexisting world (the chaos of unrecognized voices, the formless void of darkness) be wiped out and reconfigured or recreated. The process of creation starts with the narrowing of the "secret circle" represented by the surrounding internal and external world; it starts with the world's fading into indeterminateness and silence. It is here that the first transfiguration takes place, that solitude becomes creative "in the abyss of whispers and ringing/Rises one triumphant sound"—a sound that now transfigures the world in its turn, allowing the poet to even hear the grass growing in the woods. Creation happens in solitude: "an absolute silence surrounds" the meaningful sound rising and makes it indeed audible in all its triumph by pitching it against that silence. From the indeterminate "abyss of whispers" to "silence" to "triumphant sound" to the "word" and the line of poetry, which is composed by words—this is the story of creation, the unfolding of its process. Once it meets the "snow-white page" creation has already happened, the poem has already told the story.

In sum, the secret of creation is not to find the first word to put on the blank page. At stake is rather the articulation of the process that first transforms background noise into silence and then turns sound into word and words into the unfolding of a story. Such is the process of creative solitude. Solitude (and silence) is itself a part of creation (not only its condition or its primordial source): solitude is one of the protagonists of the process of creation, as it must itself be created. It is ultimately up to us to let the noise of the world as well as its many voices recede to indeterminateness and fade into silence, and then to call them back, transformed, as protagonists of our story, as expressions of the creative process of thinking.

It should now be clear in what sense the insistence and persistence in dwelling in creative solitude is truly our most important achievement—above and beyond the works that we may (or may not) produce therein. And it should also be clear why David Farrell Krell's career is, in this respect, so remarkable— above and beyond the many works he has produced in his creative solitudes. In spite of all administrators, technocrats, and bureaucrats, creative solitude and its endurance remains the most important testimony of the creativity of human spirit. But maybe here my initial intuition finds a confirmation as well. Perhaps the struggle to maintain our creative solitudes and the effort to make the process advance is a necessary part of our job; they are struggles that no one can persuade us not to undertake. And perhaps they are also struggles that no one can ease for us.

It is on this basis that I propose viewing the work of fiction or literature and the arguments of the philosopher, which make for what Walther Brogan has aptly called Krell's "two heads,"[9] as stemming from the same root, namely, from creative solitude as the discursive process of finite thinking. In both cases, at stake is the gesture of telling a story—the *need* to tell a story which discursive thinking can never renounce. *Mythos* and *logos* are herein united in a common movement. They are two complementary and fundamentally analogous ways of articulating solitude and its creativeness through the discrete extension of a narrative. In this regard, the argument of the philosopher (itself the response to a philosophical question or questioning) in its logical abstraction is one of the possible *stories* of discursive thinking. Hegel's framing of art, religion, and philosophy as different yet complementary forms of Absolute Spirit, that is, as expressions of the same absolute truth by human thinking in the medium of different "elements" (intuition, representation, concept) or indeed of different *narratives*, finds here a possible confirmation. Ultimately, creative solitude is mirrored and embodied in the story it tells. It should be clear that I construe here the "story" of discursive thinking in a broad sense as reflecting our finite nature, as expressing the necessity of trial and errors in all our intellectual pursuits, and as bringing to light our need to proceed through discrete unities of sense in a process that is always, for us, necessarily open-ended and incomplete. For, again, the intellectual intuition of the whole or of truth is not a human possibility.[10] Perhaps we should be thankful for this, as we would otherwise have no story to tell—and even if we had one, it would be impossible for us to tell it. Again, it may turn out that the predicament of Plato's "light dove" is an enviable one.

"From One Solitude to Another"

I want to conclude these reflections with some brief remarks concerning the role communication plays in the process that, as I have maintained, creative solitude is for our human discursive thinking. The sterile loneliness of Maupassant's "Solitude," due to the incapacity to dwell in the intuition of truth (as the window that has opened on it immediately shuts closed) is the human equivalent of the solipsism of divine intellectual intuition, which is predicated on the fundamental incapacity of thinking to extend to something and to someone other than itself. Unlike this loneliness, creative solitude implies and expresses the essential communicability of discursive thinking. Stories are lived, performed, and told; they are heard and then also retold. No story is, in principle, incommunicable (only intellectual intuition is). To use Krell's apt formulation, the movement of creative solitudes is the movement "from one solitude to another"[11]—and this in the twofold sense of the process that connects one's solitude to another's and also of the process that continues one solitude into the next. It is precisely in the movement of transition and extension taking place in communication that solitude reveals its creativeness and thereby the distance that separates it from empty loneliness and solipsistic isolation. Krell's formulation means to bring to light the necessary connection between the solitary dimension of creative reading and writing and our activity as teachers. His point is that this crucial connection is generally missed or downplayed by the enemies of creative solitudes, and this to the detriment of both activities (administrators want to cut teacher's creative, yet for them unprofitable, reading and writing, and increase profitable teaching). Yet one cannot exist without the other—severing their fruitful communion destroys both. There is nothing to teach if nothing is creatively thought in solitude; solitude, on the other hand, should be preserved and cherished even when we are teaching. Accordingly, effective teaching should be the movement of communication that goes "from one solitude to another."

But at this point I wish to emphasize the converse relation as well—a relation that directly follows from what has been discussed so far. The movement of creative solitude requires communication (one of its forms taking place in teaching). Properly, communication is the extension or the true continuation of the process of creative solitude. As argued above, creative solitude is the process of telling a story: the weaving of a philosophical argument, conveying the narrative of a short story or a novel, or composing a poem or a piece of music. And this is the most fundamental act of communication. Communication is not an external interruption of creative solitude; it is not its end, but its necessary continuation. It is the necessary moment of internal expansion or growth in the creative process. As suggested above, our task is to keep the process going and not to shy away from the essential moment of communication that shapes our creative solitudes as communicative ones. The story truly becomes a story as it is told. Indeed, while communication is an episode of the ongoing story that creative solitude *is*, it may itself become an element of the story that creative solitude *tells*. This is what happens in Krell's recounting of his exchange with Kevin Miles during his work on the Hegel novel. The exchange becomes an episode in Krell's own creative solitude; but the communication that has taken place between them—this time, Miles's telling to Krell stories of illegitimate children important to his own life—resurfaces transfigured, in the story of *Son of Spirit*.[12]

In suspending the noise of the world and plunging it into silence, creative solitude prepares the scene for the possibility of a fresh, new look at the same world where the possibility of hearing those voices anew and more truthfully arises. As Achmatova notices in "Creation," the silence is so absolute that "one can hear the grass growing in the woods." Creative solitudes lead to a new way of perceiving the world and thereby communicating (with) it.

I have opened these considerations claiming that the most fascinating aspect of creative solitude (and, paradigmatically, of David Farrell Krell's life of creative solitudes) is its endurance, that is, the fact that it unfolds in a process that is up to us to maintain in its duration and to make it continue despite the obstacles and the distractions we encounter and the risks it implies. Ultimately, communication is that which sustains creative solitude as a process and allows it to unfold uninterrupted. Communication is what permits us to endure the solitude of creation without falling into the sterility of loneliness or into the illusion of a narcissistic solipsism. In this connection, "from one solitude to another" indicates the internal unfolding of creative solitude as a process—the movement of (and the struggle for) its continuation and renewal. At this juncture, solitude becomes plural—"creative solitudes" in the most proper sense. Herein I would also place the movement from philosophy to fiction and/or from fiction to philosophy—the alternation between two ways of telling (and communicating) the same story or the many stories that populate creative solitudes, the expansion that leads from one to the other (and back again).

> Wenn du etwas wissen willst und es durch Meditation nicht finden kannst, so rate ich dir, mein lieber, sinnreichender Freund, mit dem nächsten Bekannten, der dir aufstößt, darüber zu sprechen. Es braucht nicht eben ein scharfdenkender Kopf zu sein, auch meine ich es nicht so, als ob du ihn darum befragen solltest: nein! Vielmehr sollst du ihm selber allererst *erzählen*.[13]

The importance of communication for creative solitude, precisely in its being the unfolding of a discursive process, is clear in Heinrich von Kleist's vivid portrayal of our thinking process in the short "philosophical" piece "Ueber die allmähliche Verfertigung der Gedanken beim Reden." Significantly, herein Kleist describes the very same process that he himself undergoes during the composition of the piece as he turns to his "dear, perceptive friend" in order to let his thoughts flow and develop. The writer, in other words, does the same thing that he describes. What he presents us is the unfolding of a creative solitude in and through communication, thereby displaying the essential unity of the process of thinking and communicating.

To involve the other (a random other, any other can do), we do not need to ask her anything nor should we try to teach her anything (in fact, Kleist notices, we are rather trying to teach something *to ourselves*); we should not require of her a particular expertise in the matter at hand nor even expect pointed questions from her. We should simply turn to the other and begin with "*erzählen*"— we must simply start telling the story, narrate what occupies us, open up our solitude. This gesture is indeed a seamless continuation of our creative solitude; it is its expansion "from one to another." And we need it precisely in order to let our solitude continue, and continue creatively. For, "l'idée vient en parlant," jokes Kleist.[14] He presents us with the image of himself, the writer, concentrated at his desk, focusing on the interpretation of a law or on the solution of a mathematical problem. He is peacefully alone; he knows that the interpretation or the solution will eventually come to him. But he knows of a much livelier and pleasant way to achieve the result—a way that is truer to the nature of the thinking process itself. It is to turn to his sister, who is at work on her own behind him, and simply begin telling her his thoughts. This simple gesture triggers the real creative process: it is here that we encounter the full sense and the full potential of creative solitude as a thinking process and as the movement of communication. Kleist brings us deep into the "Werkstätte der Vernunft"[15] to let us see how ideas do not just sprout immediately and already made in our mind (again, as for intellectual intuition) but how they progressively develop, taking the time it takes for their development to occur.[16] The beginning of communication is not even articulated sound (is "unartikulierte Töne")—we are still searching for expression. The beginning is the simple gesture of "opening our mouth."

Expression begins to take shape in connection with random gestures coming from the other person. In particular, it is the movement in the other person's face and eyes that seems to bring the movement of thinking together, to allow it to coalesce in the emergence of a meaning. To be sure, the connection between our thoughts and words and the other's gestures has nothing to do with the content of the thought (with *what* we are saying) but has everything to do with the process in which thinking acquires its meaning (with *the fact that* it allows us to keep on saying it). As Kleist puts it, "ein Blick, der uns einen halbausgedrückten Gedanken schon als begriffen ankündigt, schenkt uns oft den Ausdruck für die ganze andere Hälfte desselben."[17] We offer a first, in communication, and we gain, as a "gift," the second that completes our first. This is the movement of creative solitude.

Perhaps we should learn from Kleist not only how to write—how to follow the flow of thoughts without having to force ideas (alleged "good" ideas) to come to us, preoccupied as we always are that we are "wasting" our time. We should try to follow Kleist also in the way in which we teach—and "waste" more time, indeed. What would administrators—and evaluators with their quantitative assessments—think of that? In fact, the best teachers have always done this. Be it as it may, Kleist is right: this is how the courage of all revolutionary movements—in thinking and in reality—carries these movements on.[18]

Notes

1   See Aristotle, *Nicomachean Ethics*, Book I, 1095b.

2   See David Farrell Krell, "Creative Solitudes."

3   Imagination belongs to discursive thinking; imagination is itself discursive in the sense that I am here proposing.

4   G. De Maupassant, "Solitude," in *Contes et nouvelles*, vol. 2 (Paris: Albin Michel, 1957), 923–928, 923 (my emphasis). Editor's note: "I do not know why, I breathe better here, at night, than everywhere else. It seems to me that my thought is enlarged. I have, at times, these sorts of glimmerings in my soul that make me believe, for a second, that the divine secret of things is to be discovered. Then the window closes again. It's ended." Translation courtesy of Andrew K. Whitehead.

5   I take it that even the most experimental form of 'non-narrative' is, in this sense, in its very subversion still a narrative (just as a philosophical aphorism in its refusal of argument is still, in its own way, an argument).

6   In *The Tragic Absolute* (Indiana University Press, 2005), Krell has discussed the temptation of intellectual intuition to follow the lead of discursive thinking and dissolve the punctuality of its creation in the extension of a story.

7   I. Kant, *Critique of Pure Reason*, A5.

8   A. Achmatova, "Creation," in *The Complete Anna Achmatova* (Boston: Zephyr Press, 1997), 413.

9   See W. Brogan, "The Impossible Voicing of Philosophy's Double," appearing in this volume (already published in *Philosophy Today*, SPEP Supplement [2010]: 31–37, 31).

10   This, importantly, does not mean that truth is not a human possibility.

11   Krell, "Creative Solitudes."

12   Ibid.

13   H. von Kleist, "Ueber die allmähliche Verfertigung der Gedanken beim Reden," in *Erzählungen* (Frankfurt am Main: Insel, 1986), 453–459, 453 (my emphasis). Editor's note: "On the Gradual Construction of Thoughts During Speech": "If there is something you want to know and cannot discover by meditation, then, my dear, ingenious friend, I advise you to discuss it with the first acquaintance whom you

happen to meet. He need not have a sharp intellect, nor do I mean that you should question him on the subject. No! Rather you yourself should begin by *telling* it all to him." H. von Kleist, "On the Gradual Construction of Thoughts During Speech," trans. M. Hamburger, *German Life and Letters* 5 (1951): 42–46, here: 42.

14 Kleist, "Ueber die allmähliche Verfertigung," 453.

15 Editor's note: "Workshop of Reason." H. von Kleist, "On the Gradual Construction of Thoughts During Speech", trans. M. Hamburger, *German Life and Letters* 5 (1951): 42–46, here: 42.

16 Kleist, "Ueber die allmähliche Verfertigung," 454.

17 Kleist, "Ueber die allmähliche Verfertigung," 454. Editor's note: ". . . a glance which informs us that a thought we have only half expressed has already been grasped often saves us the trouble of expressing all the remaining half." H. von Kleist, "On the Gradual Construction of Thoughts During Speech", trans. M. Hamburger, *German Life and Letters* 5 (1951): 42–46, here: 43.

18 See Kleist, "Ueber die allmähliche Verfertigung," 458f.

4

Solitude, Creativity, Delinquency

Charles E. Scott

Solitude: 1. State of being alone, remote from society; loneliness, seclusion. 2. A lonely place, as a desert. Antonyms: association, fellowship, companionship.

I am writing in considerable solitude.[1] One of the strange aspects of this solitude is that it is not, and I think could not be, in solidarity with David Farrell Krell's solitude, because that word (solidarity) implies unity and an active and present community of interests and responsibilities and constitutes a violation of solitude. Perhaps I could say without misleading that I feel myself to be in a position to understand at least something of what David Krell . . . not what he has in mind, but something of what he experiences in solitude and at least a bit about the way solitude is left to itself when one speaks of it. It is also left to itself when a person understands it. So, one of the difficult aspects of this writing is that I leave David Krell to his solitude when I address him and his thoughts on the topic, although I am also interrupting it; and yet I am writing out of friendship, respect, and deep appreciation for him and his work. There is in these feelings inevitably a call to him to bring him into companionship and away from his solitude as I address him and his work. This inevitability means to me that in this instance violation accompanies friendship, that my writing of this constitutes a misdeed as it reaches out to him while at the same time intending to affirm his creative solitude. At least I can say that he and I have delinquency in common, and I will return to some issues regarding delinquency and companionship in the course of what follows.

To bring something into being, to procreate, to produce in solitude—I find that a strange experience as well as a strange thought. The elusiveness of the implied parenthood helps to explain, I suppose, why Krell likes to refer to dark nights, opacity, and ghosts when he writes of creative solitudes. People might wonder too who they are as they bring things into being in solitude.

Self-reference and autobiography are appropriate when creators wonder what is going on when they are productive, when the creative process happens, or when, for that matter, they are ruminating and struggling with something that has not begun to emerge and become manifest. Are they as alone as their solitude feels like they are? Is the creative process always one of self-reference on the part of the producer? Krell says it is not a species of narcissism or self-absorption in spite of the loneliness and aloneness. But as he accounts it, the creative process is nonetheless solitary, a kind of isolation in which much of life is missing and one that takes a toll on those who are closest to us, whether or not they choose the pain the creator's life occasions for them. Krell is clearly aware that there is much room in this kind of situation for self-delusion, self-absorption, and a type of protected self-love that makes reliable and loving commitment to others difficult if not impossible.

An Unlikely Pairing

David reports that "it turns out that I have been making my way toward ruse-driven fiction writing for a long time." I note that before he turned to write in the genre of fiction he was a well-known, established philosopher, a successful teacher of philosophy, and a much-respected translator of philosophical articles and books. I learned so much from him as he carried out his professional activities. I attended seminars that he taught, listened to his presentations, and read his books, essays, and translations. Now, given his retrospective interpretations of himself, I see even more clearly that in some ways his professional work was a subterfuge and did not constitute accounts of plain accuracy about anything, certainly, and was not intended as enlightening or wise or direct. His work composed a type of thought and writing that were on their way to maturation into "ruse-driven fiction writing." I suppose I vaguely knew that, insofar as translations in their "trans" quality are riven with errancy. A "literal translation" is an utterly fictional image, and I'm quite sure that David Krell knew that. But all of his writing led his reader into a cosmos that is not systematically ordered, at least not in the way many philosophers think it is. In fact, if people read his philosophical work as rigorously systematic (but how could they?), they would miss the direction not only of the content but also of his style that puts the lie to most forms of philosophical, systematic rigor and develops a discipline all its own. So I begin by saying that I am not so sure where his philosophical work ends and his ruse-driven fiction begins.

I turn now to some remarks about Mark Twain.[2] Although he and David Krell are so far apart in their work and temperament that pairing them even slightly might seem deviant as well as delinquent, I would like to open a space of difference that will allow me to approach the issue of solitude from an angle that is different from Krell's as well as complementary to his approach. Ruse-driven, delinquency, and a sense of "darkness," on the other hand, are among the characteristics that Twain and David Krell share. Krell also orients his "Creative Solitudes" around his life, and he and Twain (in his *Autobiography*) are similar in their understanding of the gap between systematic, "factual" narratives and the ways lives happen. I mean, they both show that ruse and a kind of delinquency are necessary if fiction is to give us a sense for living people and events.

Concerning his autobiography, Twain said, "I don't believe these details are right, but I don't care a rap. They will do just as well as facts."[3] He added later, "The truth is, a person's memory has no more sense than his conscience and with no appreciation whatever of values and proportions."[4] He also writes in his Preface: "In this Autobiography I shall keep in mind that I am speaking from the grave. I am literally speaking from the grave, because I shall be dead when the book issues from the press. I speak from the grave rather than with my living tongue for a good reason: I can speak thence freely . . . . It has seemed to me that I could be as frank and free and unembarrassed as a love letter if I knew that what I was writing would be exposed to no eye until I was dead and unaware and indifferent" (xiv). People have considered his autobiography to be unreliable and fatally unsystematic. But *he* is telling the story of *his* life, and that is a very different project, he says in effect, from one that is built on a systematic structure of what people take as facts. Such a project would be merely well organized and . . . factual. Twain knew that neither memory nor lives happen that way. They do not make systematic sense, and events lose much of their vitality on the way to "becoming facts." They happen, rather, like a good story: some sense here, some nonsense there, and a lot of ruse and subterfuge—and sometimes with more chaos than order. If the person is alive when the autobiographical story is read, he is saying, the memory and life will be cleaned up by a good bit of editing, omission, factuality, and lying in the name of telling the truth (whether consciously or not). Further, Twain tells his story with the ruse of speaking "literally" from the grave. (I think that when people read that sentence it's better to laugh than to try to figure it out literally, and I think that is part of Twain's point.) I note that the ruse of speaking from the grave appears to give Twain a special freedom to speak as one might in a highly personal love letter, and

I suspect that kind of freedom in ruse-driven fiction writing is fairly close to what David wants too.

David says that his mother wrote him a note on his fiftieth birthday: "To my . . . son David, who renounced a promising career as a juvenile delinquent to become a sober philosopher instead—while retaining the *joie de vivre* of a ten year-old." David adds, "Well, then, from here on out, let it be the joy of life, with a dash of delinquency—and that sounds pretty much like fiction writing." I will revisit this joy of life when I turn to his strong inclination toward darkness and obscurity. I am focusing now more on his delinquency.

Twain wrote: "When I was younger I could remember anything, whether it had happened or not; but my faculties are decaying now and soon I shall be so I cannot remember anything but the things that never happened. It is sad to go to pieces like this but we all have to do it" (3). This manifest finitude in one of his most cherished faculties did not detour him from continuing to write stories and essays and dictating his autobiography. In one sense, his "going to pieces" did not change his writing in its capacity to bring people into a world where *what* is written is lost in such a way that something unwritable might become manifest. Or at least it did not change his writing the way the deaths of his daughters and wife changed it. Their loss belongs to a different order in comparison to loss of the time of his youthful memory when he "could remember anything, whether it happened or not." Experiencing the death of a loved person does not happen like ruse-driven fiction happens. Relations of love among people are in another magnitude of life in comparison to writing and its memorial dimensions. There is a lot of fiction about love and death, of course, and I believe that a good bit of dying takes place in the transfer of the experience of losing someone you love when it is expressed in writing. Twain certainly knew about the loss of life in writing from early on as he turned into fiction his experiences, beginning in his childhood, of cruelty, suffering, insensitivity, injustice, and death. I believe he both enjoyed and suffered the losses and transformations provided by the ruse of writing in those instances. As he aged, however, he became more acutely aware of the way writing removes what cannot be written, how writing holds experiences of death and loss at bay in the very way it carries out processes of dying loss in its translations, the way, as he put it shortly before he died and after his second daughter died, writing *about* the deaths of people he loved helped to keep him sane in the impact of what could not be written. By that time, his writing had more to do with surviving the days and nights of unmitigated loss than with the joy of life. I think that his love of writing and its art prevented him from ever distorting it into images of something sufficient to itself: he was always aware that fictional writing is driven by ruse and that when ruse had to do with experiences of love, death, and injustice, the facts did not matter a whole lot because the nub of the matter was far outside the domain of factuality as well as beyond the circumference of writing. That distance gave him room for a lot of fiction, humor, and delinquency as he wrote of living events in their excessiveness to the decency of literal truth and the art of writing.

Many of Twain's fictional characters and situations are based on people and events that figured prominently in his life—slaves, friends, relatives, folks, and happenings that felt familiar to readers in his culture. He both transformed them and kept many of their characteristics as he remembered them when he elaborated and often exaggerated them. And always his "interest in the arts of language was unbounded" (xviii). His ability to bring together in writing extraordinary humor in connection with the full range of human emotions and everyday experiences allowed him to write in the power of what I will elaborate as the heart/mind of his cultural world at the same time that it allowed him to present in the midst of laughter the wordless cruelty, meanness, carelessness, suffering, and absurdity around which most of us are unable to find a detour.

Twain's pessimism and "darkness" are much remarked, and I will only note that his humor accompanies a clear perception of a nonfictional world that contains no moral or metaphysical basis for anyone's situated and fragile experiences of love, hope, and meaningful engagements. As he aged, his humor provided affirmative distraction from what some people would describe as a tragic view of life. I doubt that Twain would have used the word *tragic* in that context. Instead, he noticed, on his terms, the ways things seem to fall out even when people behave themselves as best they can under the circumstances. I'm not sure that his point of view is either pessimistic or dark, but I'll take up that question later.[5]

Twain was a gregarious man who was fascinated by many aspects of technology and who fancied himself as something of an inventor. He participated in speculative business ventures, and he often wrote because he needed money. He loved to throw big parties, to host frequent dinners, to take part in festive family games and plays. He was not a loner. I speculate that he loved some of the distractions that took him away from the many hours he wrote during most days. I further speculate that he often enjoyed engaging his characters as well as himself in fiction without an overlay of much seriousness. Accompanying all of this robust activity and turn of mind, however, was profound sorrow and remorse—sorrow in experiences and memories of death, senseless suffering, and unjust treatment of people. He felt remorse over his own contributions to suffering and injustice.

I believe that his sorrow arose not only from specific instances but also from his sense that suffering, death, injustice, and the loss of all loved people would not go away or find ultimate meaning. Given Twain's nonphilosophical turn of mind, I believe I would mislead if I said he was speaking of the metaphysical nature of things. That statement would say too much and turn his experiences into a doctrine. His sensibility was too plain and nonspeculative for a shift to a metaphysical turn of mind. Further, he did not often write directly about his sorrow, although I believe it always accompanied him as he wrote. Rather, he wrote with a belief that too much sense and systematic order and too many facts clouded things unnecessarily and lost touch with the lively ordinariness of what he was writing about in his fiction. His humor especially was like a detour *with* sorrow that held it in a strange enjoyment of the possibility of life and laughter that can accompany its pain.

David Krell, on the other hand, does not seem to find his creative solitude as a possible experience in his everyday life when he is in frequent and often close interaction with other people. He does not simply withdraw to his writing desk for a few hours or days and then turn to his email, committee reports, and teaching duties. He finds our institutional lives and information technology as such to "invade our creative solitude . . . subvert our language and our thought processes . . . and . . . encourage our most rancorous side—the side that loves gossip and mean-spiritedness . . . . [I]nformation technology is invidious to creativity, civility, and community." Rather than speak of creative and connective potentiality in contemporary technology, David Krell says in concert with Henry David Thoreau that creative solitude requires "terrible aloneness" and "isolation." Gregariousness is not compatible with creative solitude. Indeed, in such solitude much of ordinary life is missing. The creative writer is alone, alone enough to allow the lonely ghosts to visit and lend us their "uncanny, unhomelike sensations." In very important ways, creative solitude allows a writer time and space to be with the dead and to write in the affects of their haunting spirits. Further, in Maurice Blanchot's words that he quotes with approval, "To write is to enter into the affirmation of solitude . . . ." Franz Kafka adds to this observation: "One cannot be sufficiently alone when writing; the night itself is still too little night."

Creative solitude, as Krell describes it, appears to call some people from their very "nature," as the poet, Hölderlin, said. Their deepest inclinations call them to "being solitary" and writing not only in their solitude but also inscribing that solitude in their writing. I cannot discern in David Krell's "Creative Solitudes" whether he wants to say that all genuinely creative writing requires the solitude he describes (whether he intends to make a universal claim about creative writing) or whether he intends to speak of his solitary experience and to contextualize it by reference to some other great writers who have "natures" similar to his. *If* we count Twain as a great writer (as I do), we can find a considerable space for allowing different "natures" to operate in writing processes. But I believe we need to address more than the inclinations of various writers when we speak of writing, creativity, and solitude, and that will be the topic of the next section.

One of the striking similarities between Twain and Krell, in spite of their seemingly irreconcilable differences, however, is the remarkable quality of life affirmation that accompanies the unfounded opacity of their experiences of life. I find gladness and happiness expressed in Twain's humor, and one of Krell's major accomplishments in his writing is the *joie de vivre* that infuses his fiction. This joy is expressed in their creativity, in their bringing their fiction to life, and in their pronounced enjoyment of the uniqueness of fictive life. Consider how lonely, isolated, and dark solitude can be, how deathly and hopeless, even when it occurs as a person is with other people without a sense of connection and life-giving interaction.[6] Both writers bring life to accompany what David Krell calls darkness. That active affirmation, as I see it, is what creative solitude is about. It constitutes a kind of delinquency with the abyss of darkness that both Twain and Krell found himself to inhabit, a temporary refusal of its vacant power, a moment of—may I use this word, David?—light when meaning is true, vitalizing, and fictional.

Creative Attunement: *Xin*

I will begin with a story.[7] I spoke last November with a young philosophy professor who was a scholar-in-residence for a year at Vanderbilt. In addition to his research, he audited several seminars, including two of mine. He came by my office to say goodbye before he returned to his homeland in China. He had come to this country with exceptional knowledge of the continental tradition in philosophy and continued his reading and research in that area with remarkable understanding and dedication.

When he came into my office he was troubled. He said that in his early years of work in continental thought he *enjoyed* his work—he emphasized "enjoyed" and used the word several times. He noted that I too had used the word several times in one of my books. "I no longer enjoy it," he said. "Maybe I have a disease in my head. Maybe I am nihilist. But I see nowhere to go now. Where do people go with their thinking after they understand many of the great continental philosophers?"

In the process of the conversation he found a metaphor for himself: a fish in a desert. "I do not know what to ask. I do not know what to think."

Our talk turned to his own background. He asked if in the West "mind" could also mean "heart." He was referring to the Chinese word, *xin*, which is variously translated in English as mind, as heart, or as heart/mind and suggests feeling and thought occurring with awareness together as though in a space without transcendental meaning. At the time, I understood him to be asking whether in the continental tradition we can experience feeling and thought together. Can we think with our hearts? Can we feel with our thoughts? He put his hand over his heart and said, "In China we speak of heart when we love and when we think."

I asked him if in his work in continental philosophy he had lost a sense of heart. He nodded, yes.

We spoke of return, in this case his return to China. He told me a Chinese story of a man who became tired of walking like everyone around him walked. He went to another country where people walked totally differently compared to those in his own country. He loved the new way of walking, and after years of practice he could walk their way. He forgot how to walk like the people in his own country. He returned home, and after several years there, with everyone walking so differently from his way, he became confused. He forgot how to walk like he did in the other country. But he couldn't walk like the people now around him. Finally, he couldn't walk at all.

I asked him if he thought he could return to the heart of his interest in philosophy. He wasn't sure. I asked him if he could walk in China as a Chinese, think as a Chinese, and teach continental thought there with *xin*. He was quiet for a moment and said, "Maybe." I think we both knew that if he succeeded, Chinese continental thinking would be something I could not do, that it would be translated into Chinese heart/mind. And we both knew that without *xin* his own thinking would die.

In this section, I would like to introduce the thought that what my Chinese friend calls *xin* and what I will name heart/mind plays a major role in communicative, creative writing and that it constitutes a non-solitary and nonindividual dimension of writing. My friend's experience was one of intense engagement in distinctly European ways of thinking and intellectual life. Whereas Heidegger, Derrida, and Foucault, for example, were vitally connected with the cultures in which they lived, vitalized by problems, violations, and creative options within those cultures, my friend, after profound intellectual engagement with their thought, was left without vitalizing—without a heart/mind—that inspires creative and meaningful engagement with experiences of life. He felt like a fish in a desert—out of his element for life. The *xin* factor, the distinctive heart/mind of a culture (as I am using the term), provides *geistige* nourishment for a people, a kind of intangible and elusive commonality that gives inspiration and a depth of relatedness that qualifies experiences of aloneness. I believe it provides a preconceptual sense of communication with a readership (unless a person writes only for himself or herself). Writing is one way of being with others. My friend needed to return to China, to cross back across a culture's border, and to discover how to transform what he had learned into his own cultural world. In that transformation, the European philosophy would no longer be definitively European. It would find its meaning in the way it came to fit within the *xin* of Chinese life.

These thoughts lead me to ask about the difference between David Krell and Mark Twain beyond the differences of the times of their writing. Twain's "nature," his disposition and character, were directly associated with the lives of ordinary people in the United States. His imagination was fired by all manner of events and associations and by his remarkable and distinctly North American sense of humor. His art is found in bringing events and humor together, often in contexts of implied social and religious critique that were informed by a passion close to outrage over injustices and human foolishness. In the process, he was definitely a North American who was a creative beneficiary (for better or worse) of the heart/mind of the United States.

David Krell's creative genius, as I understand it, arises in significant measure out of his departure from the North American heart/mind. This departure requires periods of intense isolation, a continuous leaving of the element that defined his native culture's life. It requires a profound refiguration of his *geistige* life as he joins a heritage with its own, distinctly European resources for creation. In this departure, he is especially able to find commonality with the isolation of some other writers as he works in what I will call the heart/mind of the interplay of departure (from culture in the United States) and engagement with European culture. I project that interplay as a lonely site. It requires more than the time to write. It also requires deep spiritual aloneness, a writing site that is not quite a home site—a site without a sense of a living, present community. I believe that spiritual aloneness provides something like the signature of what he writes in addition to what I think he would accept as a certain delinquency regarding what might be considered proper if an author is to conform with what most people know as "normal" authorship.

There are so many dispositions among creative people. Karl Marx reportedly could write with his children clamoring around him and on him. I know some people who prefer background noise as they write and think. Some prefer to walk as they compose. Others require absolute silence. Some break off from an activity they are engaged in and sit down to write wherever possible (a bench, a curb, a chair) when their muse appears. Whatever the disposition might be regarding solitude, they all, I believe, require a cultural region moved by its own intangible elements that define its difference and that can inspire within its context unique creativity—a distinctive heart/mind that no one controls and that can give communal inspiration even in dark and solitary nights.

I would like to close with a note of gratitude—gratitude for David's disposition, for the creations that come from his attunement and loyalty to it, and for the strength that his creative solitude requires. I believe that I have come to know him best by listening to the silence that seems always to accompany his words, whether written or spoken. I am especially grateful for this silence. It is one of the elements that makes his words light in their combinations—makes them enlightening—in the sense of *lichten* and *Lichtung*. Light, not heavy. Like when an anchor is raised—the German verb is *gelichtet*—and the ship is freed (cleared, as it were) to sail.[8] David Farrell Krell's words, especially in their rused and delinquent quality, shelter this enlightening silence. They make light. His phrase at the end of his essay, "bubbles for being," might apply.

Notes

1   This chapter assumes familiarity with David Krell's paper, "Creative Solitudes," which is included in this volume.

2   A reader might notice a certain—and here I can use the word—solidarity with David's delinquency in my use of Twain's writing in connection with his.

3   *The Autobiography of Mark Twain*, ed. Charles Neider (New York: Harper and Brothers, 1959), xiv.

4   Ibid., 50. I will insert in the text the page numbers when a reference is to his *Autobiography*.

5   You might have noticed that I am stepping aside of the polarity of light and darkness with its rich metaphysical and religious lineage. I make this move in order to intensify David Krell's own nonmetaphysical orientation as well as to give emphasis

to Twain's utterly nonphilosophical complementarity with Krell's more philosophical perception. I note also that the value David gives to "darkness" constitutes an interesting delinquency when we recall the optimism and emphasis on light in mainstream North America.

6 Given what he writes, I believe David Krell must feel something like that kind of solitude in routine committee meetings, for example.

7 The following six paragraphs appeared in my article, "Cultural Borders," published by *Research in Phenomenology*, vol. 42, no. 2 (2012): 157–205.

8 See his *Intimations of Mortality: Time, Truth, and Finitude in Heidegger's Thinking of Being* (University Park: Penn State University Press), 1986, 82.

5

Reticence, Solitude

Alphonso Lingis

Ryoan-ji Garden by Kimon Berlin.
Creative Commons

Immense cities sprawl over immense cement lakes, out of which, like petrified trees, the glass and steel stumps glitter from the fiberglass shells of innumerable automobiles. The universe is crystalized, and electronic impulses circulate through its reprogrammed circuitry. Thoughts race through them on infinite wires no longer knowing where they took origin. All is on the verge of conflagration. The reasons are hidden. They are not in the words of language, because the words are not fixed; they creep and slip and divide like gelatinous cells. In the cement, steel, and glass there are cracks, many invisible. In high noon of cities unendingly held in suspense, in the sun whose center is everywhere and circumference nowhere, shadows appear and grow. (J. M. G. Le Clézio, Haï)

"There's a hyena over there." "It looks like a puddle of water on the road, but it's a layer of light." "There's another guy acting suspiciously on the subway." Our utterances do things to things and events—indicating things and events, focusing in on them, separating them from the continuous flow of the perceptual field, questioning if they exist or how they exist, exclaiming our surprise or fear or wonder about them, doubting whether they are as they appear, grouping them with other things and events. With our words, things and events that were enmeshed and passing in the continuous flow of the environment about us come into relief; our words cast into the air take hold of them. Our words make things and events present and repeatably present. The great shared narratives of a community, its myths, are the primordial language that first articulates, extends, and reveals the world, the forces and the powers, the dimensions of space, the gods, the origin of the people, the direction of time.

But language also separates us from the environment, forms a screen before the environment, or functions as blinders and filters attached to our organs of perception. Every researcher, in biology, medical pathology, or psychiatry, knows that he or she has to put aside the ways things and events are described and analyzed to look with one's own eyes. We have felt the need to break through the screen of language to go see for ourselves the Baltimore slums, Finnish Lapland, the Sahara. Some of us go to countries and landscapes we know nothing about, to encounter them without words. How often, when we have experienced the grandest and most overwhelming things we find, we have no words—there *are* no words—to describe them.

No two humans have the same fingerprints or the same pattern in the irises of their eyes; no two feathers on a hummingbird are identical. The vibrancy of light constantly shifts, our restless eyes cannot hold still; no appearance is the same from one moment to the next. But words exist in repetition. A sound or a visual mark that was never, could never be repeated could not function as a word. Words drop the particular, the singular, to designate the general lines of series and classes of things and events. Words, like nitric acid poured on a copper plate, Yukio Mishima said, eat away at the substance of things, leaving but their beautiful skeletons. However completely a building or a person has been described to us, the moment we face that building or are face to face with that person, there is shock, astonishment, and discovery.

Words do not simply direct attention to what is present and visible; they refer to things and situations in their absence. They situate what is present in a class or a series of things and events that have passed on or are anticipated. Words are a safeguard against loss. Discourse is an operation of appropriation. Every name survives its owner: Julius Benway is dead, but his name is still there, intact, functioning as it did when he was alive. Indeed, when he was alive, his name functioned as it will when he is dead. Each statement survives its object: nothing changes in the meaning or the truth of the statement "Elsbeth went to Los Angeles and got a face-lift" after Elsbeth returned to the Hamptons or after she died.

Words that condense the complex colors of a pheasant or an evening cloud, that drag over upon situations names and classifications from other situations only the general lines of which are designated, enable us to pass quickly over things and situations, to skim over reality. "When I recognize a strange bird as a sparrow," W. Percy notes, "I tend to dispose of the bird under its appropriate formulation: it is only a sparrow" (Percy 1954, 274).

Words solidify, encrust the things upon which they are attached. Once something is named a "porcupine fish," a "mongrel dog," a "rogue lion," a "shack," a "professor," or a "wife," it, he, or she is plasticized, barnacled, by that name.

Words lose their edge, their force, their solemnity or their lilt and brightness in being repeated. Sounds uttered are words that have meaning because they are repeatable, but words empty of their meaning by being repeated. The most universally accepted principles, judgments, and values are the most empty of meaning. "Thoughts thought too much no longer think anything," Maurice Merleau-Ponty said (Merleau-Ponty 1968, 119). What is emptier than the watchwords "freedom," "democracy," "virtue"? E. M. Cioran observed:

> Words too often repeated weaken and die. [. . .] The mind should have an infinite dictionary, but its means are limited to a few expressions trivialized by use. Hence the new, requiring strange combinations, forces words into unexpected functions: *originality is reduced to the torment of the adjective and to the suggestive impropriety of metaphor.* [. . .] An *anticipated* word is a defunct one; only its artificial use imbues it with a new vigor, until it is commonly adopted, worn, corrupted. [. . .] If man invents new physics, it is not so much to arrive at a valid explanation of nature as to escape the boredom of the understood, habitual, vulgarly irreducible universe, to which he arbitrarily attributes as many dimensions as we project adjectives upon an inert thing we are tired of seeing and suffering as it was seen and suffered by the stupidity of our ancestors or of our immediate predecessors. (Cioran 2012, 89–90)

In order to sustain interest in ourselves, we had to concoct new metaphors—spirit, soul, child of God made in the image and likeness of God, consciousness, Dasein, being-in-the-world, nihilation, the brain a biological computer. These strange new words jolt the mind and make it see itself as new and astonishing. But all these metaphors undergo the fatality of all words that are used too much, become dead metaphors. Cioran foresees the time when we will have exhausted the possibilities of the dictionary, and we will no longer see ourselves as something new and astonishing in the material universe and be confronted with our life as commonplace, trivial, and boring.

People who live by words—academics, novelists, television anchormen and talk-show hosts, comedians—call what they do "work." A derisible attribution, when one thinks of telephone linemen, road construction workers, plumbers, factory workers in Haiti, and peasants in China. Yet, though talking is withdrawal from real work and writing, as we say, requires leisure, there is something in the nature of discourse that makes it akin to work.

Work begins when we detach something—a stick, a chipped stone—from the continuity of our environment and envision how it could be put in another place, foresee how its solidity could convey our force so as to detach something further. A worker detaches himself from the continuity of his environment and makes of himself a tool. She isolates her eyes, her hands and arms from the whole of her body that rests in itself and uses them as causes that produce effects, implements to reach ends. His senses cease to be disinterested; his consciousness is directed by an anticipation of the future. The passage of time is a constant reminder of irrevocable loss. The future is grasped as a compensation for decay and disintegration of things in the environment.

Her mind is made to serve; it is driven by a movement that turns it to the beyond, the absent, the future. It experiences its present and presence as wanting, failing. His mind makes itself a means for an end that incessantly moves further. The state of mind in which its present and presence are subordinated to future results is a state of servility.

To begin to speak is to launch a trajectory of time. To utter a noun is to anticipate the verb and the verbal complement that will make up a statement. A statement calls for a sequel, another sentence that qualifies it, that builds on it, draws out a consequence, evokes an objection to it, justifies it, or supplies evidence for it. As the task or goal gives its sense to a tool, so the verb and verbal complement gives its sense to the noun, and the clarification or justification gives its sense to the statement. And as the tool and the manipulation have to be continuously lined up with the task, so grammatical rules have to regulate the progression of words in the statement and logical rules regulate the progression of its clarification or justification.

Words subordinate each thing and event that presents itself to something further, to something absent, to utility, to a goal. To put words on things and events is already to make them serve.

Each of the words has its sense and its use by contrast with other words. We can be satisfied with a statement; we can be satisfied, for practical purposes, with a clarification or justification. But we remain aware that to require that one's statement be taken as true commits us to clarifications or justifications to which there is no end. Discourse is a cadence of projects, initiatives, and of the advance representations of initiatives.

There is no last word, there is no System, no Absolute Knowledge, no Unified Theory of Everything; nowadays theorists, but already Socrates, praise and prize this situation, this unquenchable restlessness of the spirit. Each of its states becomes vulnerable and dependent. But is it not an inmost experience of servility, the mind driven by a force that makes every present and every presence serve, makes them subordinate to future, absent states that when they are reached will be subordinated to further absent, future states?

Pursuing statements as they open upon more statements, questions, and objections may lead us further afield in the outlying world. But words and statements can also keep us within language. To specify the meaning of a word, we name the words with which it contrasts, and to specify the meaning of those words we would have to name the constellations of other words with which they contrast. The question "What does that mean?" leads us on and on until all meanings hover before us and vacillate.

In Witold Gombrowicz's *Cosmos*, the narrator comes back to his lodging to find a sparrow hung by the neck on a length of wire in the garden. Somebody did this. What does it mean? Is he being spied on? Followed? With what intent? Then indoors, he notices what looks like an arrow vaguely marked on the ceiling. Before long he sees signs everywhere. August Strindberg's *Inferno* invokes an individual haunted by the specter of meaning that is everywhere, equivocal and requiring interpretation. The existence of this floating, unfixable, realm of meaning obsesses him, makes unanswerable demands on him, besieges him, until he can no longer leave his room.

Language as a whole, Georges Bataille says, is ended only by the word God or by words with a sacred sense: words devoid of intelligible meaning, or whose use is prohibited. Sacred words are black holes in language.

In the Judeo-Christian West today, the word "God" is very much in use. It no longer designates the ineffable, but, in theology, a substantial reality and, in the practice of believers, an indestructible reality invoked in times of death, natural calamities, and war. The name of God has become commonplace, like any other object has come to represent a substantial reality that we can attain and use and has lost its transgressive power.

The words, then, that are sacred—separate and separating—are the words we call "profane." The word "shit" designates the expulsion of the unusable; the word "fuck" when used as a profanity designates not the reproductive and pleasurable sexual act but a nonreproductive release of energies that humiliates the one who is penetrated and violates his or her integrity. We use these words to reject explanations and justifications. These words are not only aggressions against the machinery of the working world and against the self-determination of persons but also verbal aggressions against language.

Discursive language requires the domestication of the violent elements that threaten meaning. In order to contain its transgressive potential, death must be given a meaning; it is taken to signify sleep or passage to another life. But the bald word "dead" erupts in this talk as an utterance signifying nothingness.

Poetry is allusive and elliptical; its subtle and precise phrasings put us in the presence of reality in its material singularity by making us feel not how much there is still to be said about the most familiar things, events, and mental states, but how all that has already been said and what is here being said reveals the presence of the most familiar things, events, and mental states as abysses of the unappropriated and unrepresentable. Poetry retains a sacred character that the language of religiosity has lost. There is a kinship between poetry and profanity. Poets recognize the poetic character of inner city street talk. Though the world of work and power maintains writers to produce hymns of religious and military glory and songs of everlasting love for the longings of youth, the poets write their seductive contemplations of the outcast and the abject.

In fact, does not something like an opacity, a black hole lurk in all words? At the kitchen window we see and say, "A spider is spinning its web." There is no question but that these are the right words. But at the core of those words— spinning, web—is there not an opacity, where the words are not simple windows upon the spider out there and its web, where the words do not simply diagram the inner structure of those things, but where the words themselves take form like opaque things? *L'araignée tisse son toile.* There is something inexpressive in the brief and passing words.

When an anticipated conclusion of an explanation or a narrative breaks into nonsense, when a painstaking construction or operation abruptly self-destructs, one is left with the naked things, condensed in themselves. Before the breakdown of meaning into absurdity, the collapse of efficacious work efforts, one can be left with a wretched sense of impotence. But one's forces now cut off from work, free, can sense their powers to dance intoxicated over the naked things with peals of laughter. Laughter is sovereign pleasure, pleasure of a gratuitous release of energies.

Tears and grieving disconnect the future and recognize that the force and meaning of the past has come to an end. The forces of life hold on with strength and will to the present in all its irrevocable loss, inconsolable with words and projects.

It is language itself that leads us to the depths and to the frontiers where its words no longer take hold, where our mind finds itself empty, open upon nothing words can grasp.

In moments of austere lucidity, the thought that discovers ignorance in itself assents to this ignorance, plunges into it, sacrifices itself. It lets go in an ecstatic plunge into darkness. No longer subordinated to some anticipated result, its ecstasy is the ecstasy of being an utterly self-propelled and sovereign movement.

The garden of the fifteenth-century Ryōan-ji temple—the Temple of the Dragon of Peace—in Kyoto consists of fifteen rocks of different sizes and shapes placed in a field of white sand that is raked into ripples. There are no plants, save for some moss on some of the rocks. It is viewed seated on the veranda slightly above the garden. The furrows of sand and also the rocks sunken into them appear uncannily impermanent. One views the emptiness of the garden, a space of potentiality from which a few forms—the rocks, the undulations of the field of sand—emerge and back in which they may recede. One comes to sense this emptiness about one, before one, after one. One senses one's own impermanence.

A child picks up what things are called from others. The ways things are designated, the ways they are related, the predicates, the evaluations and judgments put on things and situations are picked up from others, passed on to others. They line up our perceptions, organize our day and its tasks. We view things as others view them and we respond to things and events as others respond to them.

Communicating with words, we put ourselves in the place of others, put others in our place, take ourselves to be equivalent and interchangeable with others. Claude Lévi-Strauss called attention to the reduction of complexity, reduction of diverse organizations, reduction of energy, entropy, that occurs in communication between individuals. "Every verbal exchange, every line printed, establishes communication between people, thus creating an evenness of level, where before there was an information gap and consequently a greater degree of organization" (Lévi-Strauss 2012, 413).

Words order, organize the landscape about us, and orient, direct, order our thoughts, reveries, plans, and decisions. Order words are verdicts, death sentences. When a father orders his son "You will do this," "You will not do that," he is cutting off a trajectory of life. The son who obeys will cut others down in turn. When the new employee zealously attends to the regulations and orders, the other employees feel he is restricting their space for maneuver. The father orders his son: "Don't touch that." "You keep out of there." Every order-word limits the space in which we live. Death is not only a limit, an end, in time; it is also a limit in space. The cue that orders the talk of the group, pack, gang, milieu, "society," rational community, scientific discipline, or technological team and orders one's entry into a practicable space threatens exclusion and effacement from it. The one who is ordered to speak in his own name is being isolated, cut apart, cut down.

Demanding words, oppressive words. Abrasive words, stinging words, biting words, cutting words. Words constrict us, lacerate us, humiliate us, sicken us, mortify us.

People who talk all the time strike us as shallow. Jean-Jacques Rousseau spoke with exasperation of thought and feeling slipping away while making conversation at a social gathering: "Its progress, more rapid than my ideas, forcing me almost always to speak before thinking, has often suggested to me stupidities and ineptitudes that my reason disapproved and my heart disavowed at the moment they escaped from my mouth, but which, preceding my own judgement, could not be reformed by its censure" (Rousseau 1959, 1033). Launched into conversation, the words, sequences, anecdotes, repartees, and the civilized, witty but polite rhetoric that governs them scuttle on and pull us from insight we may have and from the uneasiness, attractions, desires, lusts, anxiety, mounting pleasure of our bodies. Conversation assimilates and generalizes, accumulates commonplaces, comforts and anesthetizes.

Because the words do not attach to the singular apparition or event, but rather designate what is common to a succession of past and future apparitions or events, words detach from things and events. They can then be arranged willfully to misrepresent, to lie. We daily resort to the polite conventions, stock phrases, evasions that cover over what we in fact see and touch. "Men have language," Voltaire said, "in order to conceal their thoughts."

In a conversation, we speak about certain things in order to not speak about certain other things and even to establish that they do not exist. A professor in her office talks about the course material in order not to touch upon the surge of lust she feels toward the student or that the student feels toward her. At a family picnic, a young man keeps the conversation going about his aunt's preparations for her daughter's wedding, knowing that she is on the verge of asking him why he doesn't have a job or why he doesn't have a girlfriend. A guy keeps asking his brother-in-law more about his managerial advertising executive job, about his big new suburban house, his Porsche, his deep-sea fishing vacation, his taste in fine wines, in order to make clear to himself and to the brother-in-law that "I am not one of you." Aristocrats speak a refined language in order to make clear to the hoi polloi that they are not one of them, and drifters speak in obscenities to make clear they are outside the straight world, the mass of squares.

Jean Genet, an unwanted birth, a foundling, was adopted by a couple to work on their farm, and from the beginning he heard that he was unwanted, rejected, a thief, and a deviant. He is incarcerated in prison already in adolescence. He begins to write, originally masturbation fantasies, while there. Some of these writings leave the prison and fall into the hands of Jean Cocteau, who is struck by the intensity of the language and assembles a committee of writers, including Jean-Paul Sartre and André Malraux, to petition the government for Genet's release. But out of prison, Genet writes to mark how he loathes right-thinking society, including artists and intellectuals, to isolate himself from them. "I love murder," he writes, "for I love murderers."

The Marquis de Sade carried out exhaustively the use of language to isolate himself from humanity. In his *The Hundred Days of Sodom*, his libertines violate all the laws and conventions with which humans come together for protection, for support, for common undertakings. The supreme libertine act is sodomy, not understood, as we understand it today, as anal eroticism pursued for pleasure, but instead understood biblically, as the ejection of sperm into excrement. A refusal to serve the generation of life, an attack on the species, on humanity. In Sade's writings, Pierre Klossowski explains, all libertine acts are conceived as acts of sodomy, acts by which the libertine separates himself from the human species (Klossowski 1991, 24–28).

Where did I put that bracelet? So there was frost. I better go scrape the car window. I better not take the freeway. All day, in our minds, we are constantly saying things, planning things to do, commenting on the weather, on the traffic, commenting on the success or frustration in what we are doing, going back over what we did and what happened. When we are absorbed in conversation with someone, there continues an inner commentary on what they are saying, a rehearsing what we might say about it. When we are watching two dogs fight, or watching the waves pounding against the rocks, that commentary goes on, inarticulate, clumsy, inane. Mostly, we carry on all this talk silently. Some of it is addressed to someone: we rehearse what we will say to our boss, what we will say to our lover who is upset with us. We rancorously rehearse what we should have said, what we would have liked to say to someone who slighted us. But most of the inner monologue will never be said to anyone. Most of the inner monologue is trite, hackneyed, repetitious to the point that it becomes meaningless.

About us are an array of flowers, a towering tree, a cascading brook, waves of the ocean advancing and receding, the fathomless blue of the sky—all that are on the verge of advancing upon us, invading, saturating the space of our awareness. Silent things. That can silence the inner monologue.

"As for me, I think we should . . ." "I object to what you say . . ." "Shopping bores me." It is what we call self-consciousness. Ludwig Wittgenstein had said there is no private language; we formulate our inner life in the common language. Friedrich Nietzsche argues that this language of our inner life was developed only under the pressure of the need for communication (Nietzsche 1974, 297–300). Our organism consumes energy, requires sustenance—food and drink—is exposed to cold and heat, needs protection. As infants, we were not able to supply our needs ourselves; we needed adults, and we needed to communicate our needs to them. Thus, self-consciousness developed in the form of a language of our needs and wants. In the measure that we formulate ourselves as a bundle of needs and wants, we make ourselves dependent on things and on others, servile.

This language, Nietzsche writes, formulates the most superficial and worst part of ourselves (Nietzsche 1974, 299). A living organism is not simply a material composite in which lacks form that are experienced as needs. A living organism generates energies, energies in excess of what it requires to search for and obtain what it needs. Needs and wants are not the core of life; they are superficial and intermittent. The core of life is the production of excess energies; surging within, they are felt in exhilaration. Actions that discharge these excess energies, without needing, without requiring anything in return, actions that are driven by inner exultation are, Nietzsche writes, "incomparably personal, unique and infinitely individual" (Nietzsche 1974, 299). They are actions driven by the compulsion and exhilaration that discharge energies generated within oneself, energies discharged on one's environment that arrays its surfaces singularly around oneself.

In 1978 in Philadelphia in the United States, a passerby happened upon a pile of cardboard boxes and bags put out for trash collection in a side street. He noticed that they contained hundreds of bundles wrapped with wire containing all sorts of things—bolts, magazine cutouts, electrical parts, batteries, and coins. There were also a number of abstract drawings. He took them home and kept them in his attic. In 1982, they were seen by and acquired by the owner of a gallery devoted to outsider art. There were more than 1,200 of these bundles, now called sculptures, most of them four to six inches long. The gallery owner and, later, journalists and amateur detectives made exhaustive inquiries but found nobody who knew anything about these objects or their maker. Because the people in the neighborhood are mostly black, it is supposed that the maker was African American; because many of the wires are heavy gauge and were apparently bent without tools, it is supposed that the maker was a man; and because all the inquiries did not locate the maker, it is supposed that he is dead. He has come to be called Philadelphia Wireman.

These bundles are bound with rubber bands, tape, and twine, but especially they are bound with wire. Often several kinds and gauges of wire are used, excesses of wire wound in dense coils. The variety of shapes and designs is astonishing. The maker never seemed to have started a series of similar bundles.

These pieces of plastic, glass, reflectors, foil, packaging, toys, watches, eyeglasses, earrings, tools, and costume jewelry, these pieces of wire are there now without the uses for which they had been made. They had been dropped, discarded, dismissed as trash, as litter. But here they are now, bound up, cocooned in these wire exoskeletons, existing on their own, containing energy, power that is still there when the functions and uses that had been put on them are gone.

Unlike collages and installations made by acknowledged artists, they do not celebrate or reflect critically or ironically on pop culture. Their force is immediate and earnest. They materialize transformation, "like cocooned insects undergoing metamorphosis, like a cast binding a broken bone, like mummification to ensure safe passage from this world to the next" (Kettner 2011). Some of the tightly bound bundles express bondage and oppression. Some of them are cocoons concealing small objects like precious treasures. Some of them are bound like a

Image of Philadelphia Wireman's works by Velvet.
Creative Commons

spider's dying prey. Some emanate warmth and vibrancy. These sculptures show us the powers that subsist in things we dismiss and discard.

The compulsive force in this artistry—1,200 sculptures! The artistry that is everywhere in nature, in fields and forests, deserts and coral reefs, is somehow precipitated, concentrated in Philadelphia Wireman. Every day he walked the streets, where a bolt, a cheap earring, a piece of glass attracted his look, called out to him. Back in his room, he saw that some of these things fitted together; he intently twisted wires about them. We study the sculptures and cannot discover what drives, cravings, conflicts were in him. Nowhere was he projecting his subjectivity into them. He did not make these sculptures to express, exteriorize his inner self, such that others could recognize him and he recognize himself. He did not show these sculptures to anyone. He— or she?—in fact, it is only a guess that the artist was a man. In the oceans, mollusks make the intricate designs and colors of shells they do not see, no one sees.

References

Cioran, E. M. 2012. *A Short History of Decay*. Translated by Richard Howard. New York: Arcade.

Kettner, Em. 2011. "Things That Do: African Power Objects, Emery Blagdon, Philadelphia Wireman." Title. http://www.title-magazine.com/2011/11/things-that-do-african-power-objects-emery-blagdon-philadelphia-wireman/.

Klossowski, Pierre. 1991. *Sade my Neighbor*. Translated by Alphonso Lingis. Evanston, IL: Northwestern University Press.

Lévi-Strauss, Claude. 2012. *Tristes Tropiques*. Translated by John Weightman and Doreen Weightman. New York: Penguin.

Merleau-Ponty, Maurice. 1968. *The Visible and the Invisible*. Translated by Alphonso Lingis. Evanston, IL: Northwestern University Press.

Nietzsche, Friedrich. 1974. *The Gay Science*. Translated by Walter Kaufmann. New York: Vintage.

Percy, Walker. 1954. *The Message in the Bottle*. New York: Farrar, Straus & Giroux.

Rousseau, Jean-Jacques. 1933 (1959). *Oeuvres Complètes*. Paris: Pléiade.

6

"An Incarnation Openly Bearing Its Emptiness": Life, Animal, Fiction, and Solitude in the Work of David Farrell Krell

Peg Birmingham

David Farrell Krell is a thinker of mortality. He is also a writer of fiction. From his earliest essays, his work has been guided by the fundamental insight that thinking mortality is not a separate or unrelated activity from writing fiction. The one, mortality, demands the other, fiction. Most generally, for him, this is because mortality, our radical finitude—death—confronts us with a crisis of discourse in which we are robbed of speech. Thus, radical finitude is a radical solitude which must not be mistaken for solipsism. How then to find a language of radical finitude in an experience in which words fail? Krell's answer is that thinking mortality requires a transformed relation to language; it requires, in other words, fiction. In what follows, I want to trace this relation between mortality and fiction in David Krell's thought, specifically by following the thread in his work that intertwines life and animal with writing fiction.

Taking his departure from what for Heidegger remains in scare quotes, Krell thinks mortality or radical finitude as *life*. In *Daimon Life*, he writes:

> In Heidegger's *Being and Time* "life" proves to be both essential to existential analysis and utterly elusive for it, quite beyond its grasp. Life falls in the gap that yawns between beings that are of the measure of Dasein and beings that are altogether unlike Dasein. Life neither precedes nor succeeds existential analysis, but remains outside it, being both necessary to it and inaccessible for it. In short, life supplements Dasein, and like all supplements it is the death of Dasein. Fundamental ontology discovers a kind of being-there that is born and that dies, an existence it "fixes" terminologically as Dasein; what it is unable to determine is whether such a being is ever properly alive, or what such "life" might mean. (34)

Life is included in Dasein's existence in scare quotes, separated off, included only as a radical estrangement different from either ontic everydayness or ontological anxiety. Still further, if ontological anxiety reveals the authentic possibilities of Dasein's existence, then life is the negative outline of these possibilities, an empty possibility, "empty" in the sense of being inherently unqualified and enigmatic.

In an early essay in *Intimations of Mortality* entitled "Strokes of Love and Death," Krell reminds us that this estranged and enigmatic possibility is outside anything like the will or agency. Life, mortality, is pathological; it is something that happens to us, strikes us, and deals us a double blow of death and love. Heidegger, he points out, relates *Schlag* (the blow of mortality) with *Geschlecht*, embodiment, sexuality, generation. In the blows of death and love (which for David Krell are the two fundamental mortal events), we are struck, blindsided, knocked off our feet. The Germans have an expression—*Lebens-schlag*: to be cracked upside the head by life. Caught unawares, *Lebens-schlag* is also a wake-up call. Cracked open by life through this blow to the head, David Krell suggests that the mortal is an incarnate (*Geschlecht*) openness bearing an empty, enigmatic possibility.

Krell's reading of Trakl in this same essay illuminates this estranged and enigmatic possibility removed from rationality and will: "Georg Trakl seeks and finds an image to counter it [that is, what Heidegger calls 'the decomposing form of man']: *ein blaues Wild*, an animal untamed but fragile, deep azure in hue, that haunts the forest rim at dark. It is associated with the poet's sister . . . and with the poet himself, shivering on the threshold of his dead father's house or treading the dark paths of passion . . ." (IM 167). Going further, he points out that Heidegger names *ein blaues Wild* the mortal "who wanders with the stranger down to their native soil, the earth" (IM 167). Mortality is animal life. The mortal is the animal that haunts the shadows of the earth.

In the essay, "I, an Animal of the Forest," in *Lunar Voices*, an essay on Blanchot and Kafka, David Krell returns to mortality and animal life. He states, "The animal in the forest is not an *image*, but a *life*, a life of exile from the world and exclusion from the customary sources of hope" (119). And in *The Purest of Bastards*, in an analysis of Husserl's passive synthesis and the question of an "affective awakening" of what is no longer memory as such, of what in the retentional process has disappeared into what Husserl calls an encrypted vault, a reservoir in the heart of being no longer within the reach of constituting consciousness, Krell again returns to the animal: "Only through this undiscussed slippage or passage between inside and outside, only through such cryptic haunting—as though phenomenological consciousness were like an animal huddled in the moss near the trapdoor of its burrow, believing itself to be inside and outside at once—can there be waking and awakening" (132). Contrary to the cheerful Husserlians who, as he puts it, ". . . roll up their sleeves and prepare to tackle any and every human experience, no matter how recalcitrant, no matter how chilling, with gusto and elan" (131), Krell reads Husserl as posing the question of the *Lebens-schlag*, the wake-up call, of this incorporated and encrypted figure haunting the living present, putting into radical question the very possibility of self-givenness, eidetic essence, and evidence.

David Krell's question is how to think mortality, the estranged animal, without once again reducing it to the all too familiar *animal rationale*: "One thing is certain: as long as 'man' remains the shuttlecock of metaphysics, batted back and forth between *animalitas* and *ratio*, such thinking cannot succeed" (IM 174). How to think mortality freed from representational thought? Rejecting a move to hermeneutics insofar as he claims that it still retains a "violent force" exerted upon the overpowering appearance of mortal being, he suggests that we must move from language as assertion to language as gesture (*Geheiss*). In this experience of mortality in which all words fail, only the poetic gesture remains: "Only in the bidding gesture does the mortal let language speak, and the gesture that wraps itself in folds of silence so as not to frighten the world away, the most faithful gesture, is poetizing thought" (IM 161). In *The Purest of Bastards*, in an analysis of the voice and the glottis, Krell elaborates on the relation of gesture to language, asking, "Can the speaking voice—leaving the phenomenological voice to enjoy its chronic laryngitis—ever refrain from plunging into the space of the world? Is not the space of motility, the motility of . . . glottis, tongue, teeth, lips, and lungs, inevitably a space in the world, a space of embodied situation rather than location?" (94). Krell insists on the rootedness of speech and writing in the spatiality of the gesturing body, claiming that talking and writing must be understood in terms of kinesthetic structures (95).

Mortality, animal life (*Geschlecht*), he suggests, is inseparable from *Geheiss*, gesture. Again, it is a question of an embodied language rooted in gesture. Here we need to recall that the question of language and gesture is both a philosophical and a political question. We need to recall that Rousseau in *The Origin of Languages* begins with the recognition that language is rooted first in the throat, the glottis, and through this to the passions; however, he immediately ties the glottis to a national throat, a national language of a people.[1] Krell, on the other hand, thinks gesture, language, the glottis in relation to emptiness, the estranged animal, the "negative outline," wandering on the edge of the earth in its shadows. Traveling with the stranger, this enigmatic possibility is not rooted in any native soil or national body. Nevertheless, Rousseau recounts (and this is where he and Krell would agree) in the *Second Discourse* that gesture is older and more originary than conceptual expression. It is the stratum or medium of language that bears language and is not exhausted by it. Krell goes further, suggesting in his work that gesture reveals the emptiness of language which cannot be filled in. In other words, it is the dimension of language that reveals the impossibility of speaking; it is the speechless dwelling in language. Gesture, then, is the incarnate bearing of mortal emptiness. It seems to me that Agamben's work on gesture is very close to Krell's view of language as gesture when he (Agamben) writes: ". . . what is at issue is not a nameable substance, but, rather, a figure of annihilated human existence . . . and, at the same time, its self-transcendence not toward a beyond but in 'the intimacy of living here and now,' in a profane mystery whose sole object is existence itself."[2] Nothing is more intimate, nothing more identifies the person, than her walk, the turn of his head, the movement of her hand. Certainly, one is recognized first by gestures and only later by the face. Could we even go so far as to say that there is no face without its gestures? And yet, nothing is more mysterious. Indeed, it is through gesture, Agamben argues, "life returns to its secret." And like Krell, he argues that this mystery of the everyday and the worldly is "the poet's possession."[3]

Eckhart's and Heidegger's *Gelassenheit* is David Krell's early term for the poetic gesture that reveals mortality. In his essay, "Strokes of Love and Death," he writes, "At the outset it may be enough to dwell on the fact that for all our readiness to confront Eros and Thanatos we have nothing to say to them—whereas they have a long tale to tell us. Let our responses to them therefore be coined in *Gelassenheit*, a kind of thinking that combines traces of twofolds so as to form a third, 'foreign' strain, itself beyond the dialectics of activity-passivity, willing-nonwilling, advancing-waiting" (IM 175). The poetic gesture, *Gelassenheit*, allows for mortality, animal life, to tell its tale; it allows language to be infected, contaminated by this "foreign strain" of mortality. In this early essay, one sees already that Krell's constant concern with contamination, contagion, infection is rooted in his attempt to think the "foreign strain" of mortal animal life.

In *Contagion*, following Novalis, he calls the poetic gesture of *Gelassenheit* a "poetics of the baneful," a poetics that celebrates "the attractive force of the dire" and that tends to "identify the forces of good health with illness" (50). Novalis, he claims, gives us a "thaumaturgic idealism" which is "as much pathology as an epistemology, as much an experience of something that is happening to him as a project." Krell uses Hölderlin's term *aorgic* to describe this poetics of the baneful, defining it as ". . . that which resists the formative, organizing power of reason and even imagination, whether false or true" (LV 149). Fairy tales, he suggests, provide the best source for this poetics of the malignant as they are often, if not always, about the transformation of the beautiful and the monstrous, frogs and princesses, the impossible and possible occurrences: ". . . as soon as the princess overcomes her disgust in the face of the frog, as soon as she does the impossible and confesses her love of the beast, bestowing on it her first philosophical kiss, the frog is transformed into a prince" (C 50). And this occurrence, he claims, depends upon the beautiful coming to love the ugly, because otherwise the magic will not work (C 50). And yet it seems to me that as David Krell continues his thinking of mortality and his writing of fiction, he abandons the fairy tale. There are no happy endings—the kiss is never transformative no matter how much the beast is loved. Hansel and Gretel go into the woods and never come out. Indeed, it seems (and I will come back to this at the end) that his fictions increasingly have at their center an absolute loss or lack, the negative outline of the animal haunting the edge of the forest. Krell's continuous reflection on mourning, the impossible transformation of loss at the heart of radical finitude is certainly part of what leads him to abandon the fairy tale, if indeed he ever embraced it. His fictions are situated in what he describes as "baleful incorporation rather than successful introjection of the person (or object) mourned . . ." (PB 130). He cites Husserl's phrase "the vacant horizon of what has foundered" (PB 132) to describe this radical loss that cannot be recovered or incorporated.

Krell follows Blanchot by calling this vacancy the "neutral," the invasion of the other into all discourse. This other, he argues, is not the other personalized by psychoanalysis or capitalized by ethics, but rather something that is "even more recalcitrant to discourse" (LV 136). The neutral is the distance opened up in language itself; it expresses the limit-situation of language. Reading Blanchot's "The Outside, the Night," and hesitating at certain key moments with Blanchot's reading of Kafka's *Der Bau* ("The Burrow"), Krell suggests that this limit or distance in language is the animal life that haunts the edge of the forest, the negative outline of mortal life at the limit of language, ". . . whose hissing or rustling sound is scarcely distinguishable from the subterranean silence. What the burrower hears is the sound of its imminent immanent absence . . ." (LV 147). Writing today, he argues, has moved infinitely closer to this limit, to this disquieting absence which announces itself from the depths of language. Like Kafka's beast, "a creature of the cellar" (LV 149), language now listens from the bottom of its burrow to this disturbing rustle that marks its source. Yet, as I just suggested, Krell hesitates in embracing completely Blanchot's neutral/narrative voice: "Had I more space, time, and courage, I would pay more and better heed to pungent sulphur, gruel, vomit, mud, and moss. Elements of, on, or beneath the writer's earth, elements that cling to words as lint or talc or moon stain, incarnate elements that can never be neutralized" (LV 145). And the question for him is whether discourse can invoke the elemental or the granting of time and being. In other words, can brute being be said without reference to beings?

For David Krell, the torment of language is that it cannot name this lack. He writes: "The impossibility of finishing with death and dying, of ending the day, of finalizing the meanings of things, the impossibility of being anything but survivors in a sanctuary that can never be refused but is never guaranteed, a refuge as secure as a penitentiary . . ." (LV 130). How then to attract language into a possibility of saying that would be telling—without saying being and the elemental and yet without denying them? In other words, he asks, how do we trace in their own right the motifs of death as the possible impossibility and impossible possibility of human existence, of exteriority, of the other, the neuter/neutral? (LV 124).

Here again, it is a question of *Gelassenheit*, the poetic gesture. I submit that as Krell continues to write, the only writing possible for him is the writing of fiction. He describes the work of fiction as telling the mortal tale wherein "all given meaning is in *retrait,* both redrawn and withdrawn" (LV 133). Fiction is both destitution and disappropriation. There is no command center, no *chez soi,* no one is telling the tale. Fiction, he argues, is the architecture of contingency and residue (LV 135). To think mortality, life, requires the lucidity and denseness of fiction—its essential passivity, its exposure, its vulnerability to many readings, many times; its plurality of singular voices that have passed through an essential mortal solitude that can never return them to the general.

David Krell's fictions present a dizzying and dazzling array of singular voices, all of which have passed through this solitude. Think for a moment of *Son of Spirit*: Louis, his father, Goethe, Christiana Burckhardt, Minna Herzlieb, to name only a few. A medley of voices that echo around the "son of spirit" from his birth to his death in Indonesia only eighty-five days before the death of his father in Berlin. This is a fiction in which ultimately spirit devours itself. In *The Recalcitrant Art*, there is not only a plurality of voices but also a plurality of temporalities—the fiction moves from the present to the past and back again. The voices of Hölderlin and Susette echo with those of the banker husband Jacob, their son Henry, the translators Doug Kenney and Sabine Menner-Bettscheid— all caught up in the strife of love and death. We can say of these singularities what David Krell describes of Kafka's work: "In the present instance, in the letter to Milena from the forest animal, singularities that bespeak the forest: anxiety and torment, muddy hollow and pestilence, and the eventual return to darkness" (LV 124).

In conclusion, I want to return to a question that David Krell asks Blanchot, because it seems to me that it is key to thinking life, animal, and fiction in Krell's own work. At the outset, I suggested that from the earliest essays to the later fictions, David Krell's thought is struck by the twin blows of love and death. The question he asks Blanchot is the following: "Why should love affairs constitute the obsessive last word, albeit an ironized, abashed, and constantly superseded last word, for one who sole obsession is writing?" David Krell answers his own question: "Perhaps because they serve (in Kafka's case, but in his alone?) as the supreme instances of the conflict or strife that prevails between *the law* and *solitude*, or between *the shared word* and *silence*. Perhaps because such love relationships offer the writer at least some hope that errancy in the desert, exile, and the surrender of every possible abode need not last forever" (LV 120).

But it seems to me that David Krell's fictions perhaps give us a different answer and this is something we must think through as we grapple with his work. In other words, I want to suggest that his fictions offer no such hope that the surrender of the abode need not last forever. Instead, his fictions suggest that the surrender of every possible abode does last forever, although there are moments of grace—short reprieves from the silence and solitude. Louis goes home and is given his father's name; Susette and Hölderlin spend a few summers together. But all of it is short-lived—Louis is again turned out, his name revoked; Susette is dead within two years and Hölderlin remains alone in the tower. Krell's novel, *Nietzsche*, of course, is all silence and solitude. His fictions suggest that mortality is contaminated by the "foreign strain," the enigmatic, negative outline that haunts the edge of the forest. We are contaminated by the world and by the word, struck by love and death, cracked upside the head, cracked open by life. It is no wonder that giving birth, natality, is a constant theme in his work.

And yet David Krell's fictions suggest that nonetheless this incarnate animal existence can be borne through the poetic gesture that allows mortality to tell its tale. Here I am reminded of Faulkner—a writer I believe Krell admires above all others, although Faulkner's name is mostly absent from his work. Recall that *The Sound and the Fury* opens with Benjy's refrain, "Caddy smelled like trees," and ends with Dilsey's enduring efforts to assuage Benjy's mourning: "But he bellowed slowly, abjectly, without tears; the grave hopeless sound of all voiceless misery under the sun." Like Faulkner's, David Farrell Krell's fictions originate in the elemental and say nothing other than what Faulkner's appendix to *The Sound and the Fury* says about Dilsey and her race: "They endured."

Notes

1   A version of this essay appeared in *Philosophy Today*, vol. 25, no. 1 (Fall 2010).
    I owe this insight of the relation between language, the passions, and the throat to
    Will Meyrowitz who pointed out in a graduate class on Rousseau the reference to the
    glottis in the opening paragraphs of Rousseau's *Origins of Language*.
2   Agamben, *Potentialities*, ed. and trans. Daniel Heller-Roazen (Stanford, CA: Stanford
    University Press, 1999), 84.
3   Ibid.

References to works by David Farrell Krell

C   *Contagion: Sexuality, Disease, and Death in German Idealism and Romanticism*,
    Bloomington: Indiana University Press, 1998.
D   *Daimon Life: Heidegger and Life-Philosophy*, Bloomington: Indiana University
    Press, 1992.
IM   *Intimations of Mortality: Time, Truth, and Finitude in Heidegger's Thinking of
    Being*, University Park: Pennsylvania State Press, 1986.
LV   *Lunar Voices: Of Tragedy, Poetry, Fiction, and Thought*, Chicago: University of
    Chicago Press, 1995.
N   *Nietzsche, A Novel*, Albany: State University of New York Press, 1996.
PB   *The Purest of Bastard: Works of Mourning, Art, and Affirmation in the Thought of
    Jacques Derrida*, University Park: Pennsylvania State University Press, 2000.
RA   *The Recalcitrant Art: Diotima's Letters to Holderlin and Related Missives*, University
    Park: Pennsylvania State University Press, 2000.

7

An Enigmatic Solitude

William McNeill

For David in the silent mountain valleys

In his last lecture course *What Is Called Thinking?*, delivered in 1951–52, Heidegger, speaking of the path of thinking, of thought's emergence and of its precursory character, remarks that this precursory character of thinking for its part resides "in an enigmatic solitude, taking this word in a high, unsentimental sense."[1] The word "solitude," in German, *Einsamkeit*, is notably absent from Heidegger's lectures in the earlier Freiburg and Marburg periods—absent too from the major published work of that period, *Being and Time* (1927).[2] It begins to make an appearance, albeit tentatively, around 1929, most prominently in the title of the Freiburg lecture course from the winter semester of 1929–30, published under the title *The Fundamental Concepts of Metaphysics*, bearing the subtitle *World—Finitude—Solitude*;[3] and from that point on it remains a recurrent theme in Heidegger's thought, even though he invariably broaches it with some hesitation and by way of warding off a certain misinterpretation. It will indeed always be a matter of reserving a certain height, a dignity and even unreachability for this phenomenon named as solitude, and of distinguishing it from phenomena such as loneliness, isolation, and being alone, and from the commonplace interpretations of such phenomena. Solitude names a kind of inner sanctum or sanctuary, yet one that is never simply given in advance, but that must rather be brought about in and through a certain engagement and accomplishment of thinking.

In my present remarks, I shall simply try to trace something of the semantic resonance and hermeneutic significance of this word in Heidegger's thinking, and to indicate the phenomenon to which it refers. I shall propose three theses: First, that such solitude is inextricably linked to what, in Heidegger's earlier work, was called the finitude of original, ekstatic temporality, and that this connection points to a profound continuity of the later thought with the earlier, important differences notwithstanding. Second, that Heidegger's appropriation of the term *solitude* occurs under the influence of Nietzsche and of a renewed reading of Nietzsche that begins at least as early as 1929.[4] And third, that this theme of solitude in Heidegger, not least by way of this Nietzschean influence, dwells in inevitable proximity to questions concerning the human–animal relationship, concerning *phusis* and life, in short, concerning what Heidegger at one point refers to as "abyssal kinship."[5] For solitude, we shall see, is paradoxically nothing other than a word for kinship and belonging, for abyssal kinship or for the abyss of kinship itself.

Solitude and Ekstasis

With regard to the first point, as I noted above, the apparent first usage of the term "solitude"—at least in a terminologically circumscribed sense—is a tentative one. For according to both Walter Bröcker and Heinrich Wiegand Petzet (both of whom attended this course), the original subtitle of the 1929–30 course listed, in Heidegger's handwriting, on the notice board that announced the schedule of courses at Freiburg University was not "World—Finitude—Solitude" but "World—Finitude—Individuation." The manuscript of the course, however, substitutes the word "solitude" in the subtitle.[6] "Solitude" thus appears to be a translation of sorts of the word "individuation," *Vereinzelung*, a word that is used extensively in *Being and Time*.[7] And this is indeed confirmed by the initial discussion of the phenomenon of solitude in the 1929–30 course itself. While *world* is identified with "being [*Sein*] as a whole," and *finitude* with our relation to this whole, with a fundamental way of being that must be safeguarded and preserved through our becoming finite, this appropriation of our finitude entails individuation, an individuation that transports us into solitude. Heidegger writes:

> Finitude is not some property that is merely attached to us, but is *our fundamental way of being*. If we wish to become what we are, we cannot abandon this finitude or deceive ourselves about it, but must safeguard it. Such preservation is the innermost process of our being finite, i.e., it is our innermost becoming finite [*Verendlichung*]. Finitude only *is* in truly becoming finite. In becoming finite, however, there ultimately occurs an *individuation* [*Vereinzelung*] of man with respect to his Dasein. Individuation—this does not mean that man clings to his frail little ego that puffs itself up against something or other which it takes to be the world. This individuation is rather that *solitariness* [or becoming

solitary: *Vereinsamung*—the word suggests the arising or undergoing of solitude]
in which each human being first of all enters into a nearness to what is essential
in all things, a nearness to world. What is this *solitude [Einsamkeit]*, where each
human being will be as though unique?[8]

Becoming finite, or undergoing finitude, *Verendlichung*, entails individuation,
Vereinzelung, which, properly conceived, is nothing other than a becoming
solitary, *Vereinsamung*: an entry into solitude or the undergoing of solitude,
in which each will be as though unique or singular, *einzig*. Heidegger here
coins the terms *Verendlichung* (a word used already in the inaugural Freiburg
lecture, "What Is Metaphysics?"[9]) and *Vereinsamung* (a word that appears in
a letter to Karl Jaspers dated December 3, 1928) to underscore the temporal
becoming, yet also a kind of undergoing, entailed in this appropriation
of our ownmost being: it is indeed a matter of "becoming what we are."[10]
The term *Vereinzelung*, by contrast, as just noted, appears frequently in
Heidegger's earlier work and, together with the associated verb *vereinzeln*,
plays a pivotal role in *Being and Time*. There, we recall, individuation occurs
as a key moment of transition, of the transition from the inauthenticity of
Dasein's falling everydayness to its authentic appropriation of its ownmost
potentiality for being. This critical moment of transition happens via the
fundamental attunement of Angst which, in first bringing Dasein before
the phenomenon of world as world and before the fundamental possibilities
of authenticity and inauthenticity, is said to *individuate* Dasein: Angst,
writes Heidegger, "individuates Dasein down to its ownmost being-in-
the-world"; it discloses Dasein as being possible, as a being possible "that
it can be solely of its own accord, as individuated in its individuation."[11]
Angst is an exceptional attunement precisely "because it individuates," in
an individuation that retrieves Dasein from its falling and makes manifest
the fundamental possibilities of its being, authenticity and inauthenticity.[12]
Yet the very characterization of this event—an event that is nothing other
than the happening of Dasein's "mineness"—as individuation was (and
continues to be) all too readily misunderstood as a kind of factical isolation
of Dasein, or as an egoism or subjectivity, and this was a misunderstanding
that Heidegger continually had to defend against. The situation was certainly
not helped by his unfortunate appeal to this individuation as entailing an
"existential 'solipsism' " in *Being and Time*, where, well aware of the misleading
connotations of the word "solipsism," Heidegger already tried to ward off
such impending misunderstandings. Angst, the text states,

individuates and thereby discloses Dasein as "solus ipse." This existential "solipsism," however, is so far from transposing an isolated subject-thing into the harmless vacuum of a worldless occurrence that it brings Dasein in an extreme sense precisely before its world as world, and thus brings itself before itself as being-in-the-world.[13]

Similarly, a course delivered just before the 1929–30 course, the *Introduction to Philosophy* from winter semester 1928–29, continues to use the word *Vereinzelung* while defending it against being misunderstood as isolation: *Vereinzelung* "does not mean isolation [*Isolierung*], but in each case brings Dasein, rather, in the whole of its relations into the midst of beings."[14] What is at stake, he explains, is not isolation, but individuation (*Individuation*), a temporal individuation: "individuation from out of the being itself: temporality"[15]—an individuation that would first clarify the proper meaning of the traditional thesis concerning time as the principle of individuation, a topic that Heidegger had addressed as early as the 1924 "Concept of Time" lecture.[16] Might one not indeed speculate, therefore, that the shift to the language of solitude and away from that of individuation—a term that certainly recedes, perhaps even disappears, in Heidegger's work from the 1929–30 course on—occurs precisely in an attempt to avoid the misleading connotations of egoism, solipsism, and isolation that the term individuation all too readily implies?[17]

Now the appropriation of Dasein's ownmost potentiality for being, a possibility brought before it in Angst, is Dasein's taking up, understandingly, this liminal individuation as its own in authenticity. And this occurs in and as the movement of anticipation, of anticipatory being-toward its ownmost end, being toward death. Anticipation, *Vorlaufen*, which is literally a running ahead or *precursion*, is the temporalizing of the authentic futurality of Dasein, its coming back toward itself in and from out of its ownmost possibility, the happening of its ownmost individuation. And this individuation is nothing other than the happening of the *finitude* of originary, ekstatic temporality, which temporalizes primarily out of the future. "The ekstatic character of the originary future," Heidegger writes, "lies precisely in the fact that it closes our potentiality for being, that is, is itself closed, and as such enables the resolutely open, existentiell understanding of nullity"[18]—that is, enables an authentic self-understanding, Dasein's becoming authentic. Dasein's appropriation of its individuation—of an individuation, therefore, that is not entirely, never yet its own, but rather brought before it in the *Unheimlichkeit* of Angst—thus occurs in the thoughtful understanding of its ownmost potentiality for being, in Dasein's running ahead or precursiveness, as a preserving and safeguarding of its finitude, an appropriation of finitude, a becoming finite. Its undergoing finitude is its "passing under the eyes of death"[19]—of death which "individuates Dasein."[20] And would this not be precisely what, in 1929–30, Heidegger calls the human being's solitariness, his or her entry into solitude? Running ahead, *Vorlaufen*, as authentic being toward death, Heidegger emphasized in *Being and Time*, is indeed nothing other than the thoughtful, explicit retrieval and appropriation of the very movedness of Dasein's being: "Being toward death is running ahead into a potentiality for being of that being whose way of being is running ahead itself."[21] And is it not in terms of this very precursiveness that Heidegger continues to understand the movement of authentic thinking or authentic thoughtfulness some twenty-five years later, in *What Is Called Thinking?* Thinking, he there insists, is "the most precursory of all precursory activities of man"[22]—not because it is something provisional that would be superseded by action, but because it occurs as a running ahead, always in advance, into that which withdraws, that which has, from time immemorial, withdrawn: into the not yet of what is most thought-provoking, namely, that we are still not, not yet, thinking. If the precursive character of thought's being underway lies in an enigmatic solitude, it is because it is drawn into this happening of finitude—now thought as the withdrawal of being—that cannot be superseded (that is unsurpassable, *unüberholbar*), an event of withdrawal to which thought is always exposed in advance.

The Shadow of Nietzsche

At this point, I wish to turn to my second claim: that Heidegger's appropriation of the word *solitude* in the 1929–30 course occurs under the marked influence of Nietzsche. The text of the 1929–30 course everywhere bears indications that Heidegger was, at this juncture, engaged in a renewed reading of Nietzsche, even though there is no sustained interpretation of Nietzsche presented in the course. We do indeed find several pages in §18 identifying Nietzsche as the underlying source of prevailing diagnoses of culture that operate in terms of the opposition between life and spirit (the interpretations of Spengler, Klages, Scheler, and Ziegler), and indicating that Nietzsche is the place where "the confrontation proper" must occur—a confrontation or *Auseinandersetzung*, which, as we know, would not be explicitly articulated until the Nietzsche lectures of the mid- to late 1930s. The opposition between life and spirit is said to arise from Nietzsche's distinction between the Dionysian and the Apollonian, although Heidegger provides no real interpretation of this here but merely cites a number of passages from *The Will to Power* that discuss the significance of these terms. More significant than these references, however, and more striking, is the fact that, at the end of an extensive, philosophical investigation into what world is— an investigation that proceeds, we recall, via an interpretation of the attunement of boredom and its various forms; and then through a comparative examination that contrasts the world-poverty of the animal with the world-forming essence of man—after, that is, more than 500 pages (in the published volume) of incisive philosophical and conceptual analysis, Heidegger concludes the lecture course by reciting part of "The Intoxicated Song" from *Thus Spake Zarathustra*, telling us that it is here, in this *poetic* word, that "we experience what the world is." A strange ending to a work of unprecedented philosophical rigor!

Yet it is not just in these explicit references to Nietzsche that the presence and influence of Nietzsche is palpable in the 1929–30 course. Although not explicitly named there, Nietzsche's presence is manifest not least precisely in the section that introduces the theme of solitude (§2 in the published text). Who can fail to hear the echo of Nietzsche in the insistence that we human beings are a "transition" (*Übergang*), underway toward the whole, toward world, yet torn back by a "gravity" (*Schwere*) that draws us downward; in the exhortation to "become what we are"; in the reference to the "hammer" of conceptual comprehension;[23] or in the question "What is man? A transition, a direction, a storm sweeping over our planet, a recurrence [*Wiederkehr*] or a vexation for the gods?"[24] Significantly, however, all of these allusions, together with the Nietzschean theme of solitude, are inscribed within the over-arching perspective of a word from Novalis, namely, the claim that philosophy "is really homesickness, an urge to be at home everywhere."[25] The 1929–30 course not only ends with the word of a poet (or of a philosopher-poet), but finds its proper beginning in the word of a poet—and this despite Heidegger's introductory insistence that philosophy should be determined only on its own terms, solely from out of itself, and not by way of detours or circuitous paths (*Umwege*), such as art or religion! The Freiburg lecture course of 1929–30, its intensive engagement with biological science and with the apophantic *logos* of philosophical conceptuality (the *logos* of assertion) notwithstanding, is thus already underway toward inhabiting the proximity between poetizing and a thinking more originary than philosophy, a proximity that will attune the later lectures on *What Is Called Thinking?* from beginning to end.

How does Heidegger, in this introductory section of the 1929–30 course, develop this word of Novalis that philosophy is really homesickness, *Heimweh*? Does homesickness, he asks, even exist today? Is it not a romantic notion, a kind of nostalgia that has long since been eradicated by contemporary city man, the "ape of civilization"? What is implicit in Novalis's elucidation that philosophy, as homesickness, is "an urge to be at home everywhere"? Manifestly, philosophy can be such an urge only if we who philosophize are not at home everywhere. What, asks Heidegger, does it mean "to be at home everywhere"? He writes:

> To be at home everywhere—what does that mean? Not merely here or there, nor even simply in every place, in all places taken together one after the other. Rather, to be at home everywhere means to be at once and at all times within the whole. We name this *"within the whole"* and its character of wholeness the *world*. We are, and to the extent that we are, we are always waiting for something. We are always called upon by something as a whole. This as a whole is the world.[26]

Philosophy, as an urge (*Trieb*) to be at home everywhere, would thus first find its fulfillment, its answer and its end, in our coming to be at home everywhere, in our coming to dwell within the world, a learning to inhabit the world as our proper dwelling place. Such dwelling would mark the end, perhaps, of philosophy— which, we may recall, begins in a certain withdrawal from the immediacy of worldly dwelling in order to contemplate the world by way of *theōria*—and the beginning of a thoughtful, yet poetic dwelling. Yet this proper dwelling place, our home or *Heimat*, is, Heidegger goes on to insist, nothing other than solitude. It is in individuation, correctly conceived as becoming solitary or entering into solitude, *Vereinsamung*, he states, that "each human being first of all enters into a nearness to what is essential in all things, a nearness to world. What is this *solitude*, in which each human being will be as though unique?"[27]

Two points merit special attention here. First, this identification of solitude as our proper home or dwelling place is, of course, an eminently Nietzschean theme, or more properly, that of Zarathustra—despite the fact that Heidegger does not explicitly relate this theme to Nietzsche or to Zarathustra here, in this context. It is in Part Three of *Thus Spoke Zarathustra*, at the opening of the section entitled "The Homecoming," that Zarathustra proclaims:

> *O Einsamkeit! Du meine Heimat Einsamkeit! Zu lange lebte ich wild in wilder Fremde, als daß ich nicht mit Tränen zu dir heimkehrte!*

> O Solitude! Solitude, you my home! Too long I lived in the wild, in wild and foreign parts, not to return home in tears to you!

Second, however, if solitude is indeed our proper home and dwelling place, it is a place we can never entirely inhabit, just as we can never entirely inhabit the world. Solitude may bring us into a nearness to world, but this proximity, this nearness to what is essential in all things, remains exposed to the unsettling happening of finitude, of what Heidegger has identified as a fundamental unrest:

> This is where we are driven in our homesickness: to being [*Sein*] as a whole. Our very being is this restlessness. We have somehow always already departed toward this whole, or better, we are always already on the way to it. But we are driven on, that is, we are somehow simultaneously torn back by something, resting in a gravity that draws us downward. We are underway to this "as a whole." We ourselves are this underway, this transition, this "neither the one nor the other." [. . .] What is this unrest of the "not"? We name it *finitude*.[28]

Our not being at home is not something to be overcome: it is, rather, precisely what must be brought to the fore, acknowledged as the fundamental *Unheimlichkeit* of our being—as occurs in *Being and Time* through the attunement of Angst, which, in individuating Dasein, first brings it before the world as world. If solitude is our home, is it not, paradoxically, a home that is no home at all, a being at home or coming to be at home in not being at home, a dwelling within and from out of a fundamental uncanniness—an *Unheimlichkeit* that, as Heidegger insists already in *Being and Time*, is more fundamental than any and all being at home?[29]

Solitude and *Phusis*

Although Heidegger does not explicitly connect the theme of solitude to the Nietzschean discourse in the 1929–30 course, as just noted, he does devote considerable attention to *Einsamkeit* in the second of his major lecture courses on Nietzsche, the course on "The Eternal Recurrence of the Same" from 1937. The first communication of this "thought of thoughts," the thought of eternal recurrence, occurs in aphorism 341 of *The Gay Science*, entitled *The Greatest Burden*, which opens by addressing the reader in his or her "most solitary solitude"—yet also in relation to the spider, the moonlight, and the trees:

> What would happen if one day or night a demon were to steal upon you in your most solitary solitude and say to you, "You will have to live this life—as you are living it now and have lived it in the past—once again and countless times more; and there will be nothing new to it, but every pain and every pleasure, every thought and sigh, and everything unutterably petty or grand in your life will have to come back to you, all in the same sequence and order—even this spider, and that moonlight between the trees, even this moment and I myself. The eternal hourglass of existence turning over and over—and you with it, speck of dust!"

In his reading of this aphorism, Heidegger initially asks what kind of knowing is meant to be invoked as the "science" of *The Gay Science*: it is, he claims, "science" in the sense of a "stance and will toward essential knowing,"[30] which he will go on to characterize as tragic knowing—that knowing that is first portrayed poetically in the figure of Zarathustra, whose downgoing is announced in the opening words of the next and final aphorism of Book Four: *Incipit tragoedia*. It is in terms of such knowing that we must then reflect upon what it means that a thought, the thought of eternal recurrence, can become a "burden": a determinative force and center of gravity that weighs upon all of our actions. Yet no less decisive are the circumstances under which this thought arises, namely, in one's "most solitary solitude." Such solitude is not found in one's everyday, self-oblivious running around and busyness, comments Heidegger, nor does it mean the human being's simply withdrawing and becoming occupied with his ego. It is found, rather, "where the human being is altogether himself, standing in the most essential relations of his historical Dasein in the midst of beings as a whole."[31] And this sense of solitude must once again be differentiated from individuation, or more precisely, from individuation misunderstood as isolation:

> This "most solitary solitude" lies prior to and beyond every distinguishing of the I from the You, and of the I and You from the "We," of the individual from the community. In this most solitary solitude there is no trace of individuation [*Vereinzelung*] as isolation [*Absonderung*]. It is rather that kind of individuation [*Vereinzelung*] that we must grasp as *becoming authentic*, in which the human self authentically comes to itself [*sich zu eigen wird*]. The self, authenticity, is not the "ego"; it is *that* Da-sein in which the relation of the I to the You [singular], and of the I to the We, and of the We to the You [plural] is grounded.[32]

Solitude is once again affirmed as indeed a certain kind of individuation, and explicitly related to authenticity, to the authentic appropriation of oneself. Significantly, not only does Heidegger here, in 1937, once again resurrect the language of authenticity from *Being and Time*, but coins a word for becoming authentic that explicitly resonates with the language of the 1929–30 course, namely, *Vereigentlichung*: a word that continues the chain of verbal substantives with the prefix *Ver-*, suggesting a becoming or coming to be that we explicitly undergo, that happens to us: *Vereinzelung* is *Verendlichung*, *Vereinsamung*, and now, *Vereigentlichung*—a word that, to the best of my knowledge, here makes its sole and unique appearance in Heidegger's work.[33]

In poetizing the figure of Zarathustra, notes Heidegger, Nietzsche projects the space of this most solitary solitude.[34] Yet, such solitude is not only to be understood in terms of individuation correctly understood and, ultimately, in terms of the Moment (*Augenblick*) of thinking the thought of eternal return. The space and realm of solitude is also first delineated in relation to Zarathustra's animals, the eagle and the serpent, representing pride and wisdom respectively. These animals are Zarathustra's own animals, emphasizes Heidegger, "they belong to him in his solitude, and when his solitude speaks, it is his animals who are speaking."[35] Yet Zarathustra's animals, Heidegger insists, are not pets— not *Haustiere*, not animals of house and home; they are remote, rather, from all that is habitual and accustomed, from the realm in which we normally dwell—indeed, they alienate us from this very realm. And in so doing, they "first determine our most solitary solitude," which is something other than habitual opinion conceives it to be. Whereas habitual opinion regards solitude as freeing and releasing us from everything, so that we are no longer disturbed, quite the contrary is the case, Heidegger emphasizes. For "in our most solitary solitude precisely that which is most grave and perilous is let loose upon us ourselves and upon our task, and this is something that cannot be deflected onto other things or other people; it must pass through us, not as something to be eliminated, but as something to be known in its belonging, known in authentic knowing and supreme discernment."[36] It is this "magnificent concept" of solitude, Heidegger remarks, that must be thought here, and thought in relation to Zarathustra's two animals.

I cannot here recount the entire richness of Heidegger's 1937 interpretation of Zarathustra's animals and of the solitude that arises in their proximity and in dialogue with them, an interpretation that contains Heidegger's most extensive and explicit remarks on the theme of solitude. But what is particularly intriguing is that it is precisely in the company of these animals that the solitude of the thinker—here of the thinker of eternal return, of the finitude and individuation of the Moment as the Moment in which world is disclosed—is said to arise. "*A love of animals*," writes Nietzsche in a note from the *Nachlaß*, which Heidegger here cites, "—in all eras people have recognized those who are solitary [*die Einsiedler*] from this."[37] It is as though it is only in and through the presence of these non-domestic animals, alien to house and home, and of their strange speaking (of what and how they speak, for their speaking, we recall, is a critical dialogue in the section of Zarathustra called "The Convalescent")—or, let us say more broadly, the presence of *phusis*—that the solitude of the human being in the midst of beings as a whole can properly emerge and resonate in the full spectrum of its abyssal character. Certainly, one could relate this issue to the traditional determination of man as *animal rationale*, the "rational animal," and to Nietzsche's characterization of man as "the as yet undetermined animal," as the rope stretched over an abyss between animal and Overman, that figure of man whose essence will first be cast in and through the thinking of eternal return. Yet, if the suspicion is correct that it is from Nietzsche that Heidegger adopts the term *Einsamkeit* in 1929, then this also casts a somewhat different light on the whole of the 1929–30 course and its trajectory. For in that course, having introduced the theme of solitude in his initial remarks via the tentative translation we have mentioned, Heidegger then leaves it suspended, so to speak, over the entire lecture course, never again to return to it, beyond the briefest mention. He leaves it suspended, we may recall, in order to devote himself, first, to an interpretation of the attunement and its temporal oscillations—an interpretation in which the Moment of world-disclosure is pivotal—and second, to an extensive comparative interpretation of the animal and of animality in relation to the Dasein of man. The characterization of the animal as "poor in world" by contrast with the world-forming Dasein of the human being does not simply drive a wedge between man on the one side and the animal on the other, but opens up a rift, so to speak, in which each is held toward the other, held in proximity to the other, precisely over and across the abyss of world.[38] Must one not suspect that the sustained engagement with the animality of the animal that Heidegger pursues in the 1929–30 course is just as much an unspoken confrontation, at a distance, so to speak, with Nietzsche's thinking of animality, and of life in general as drive and instinct (*Trieb, Instinkt*), as it is the elaboration of a problematic announced in *Being and Time*, that of a "privative interpretation" of "life"—yet a confrontation in which the theme of solitude is, for the time being at least, quietly removed from the purview of animality?

Heidegger's Solitudes

A few remarks by way of conclusion:

The enigma of solitude in its high or elevated sense lies not only in the paradox that, in the very event of temporal individuation, it brings us into a proximity to being as a whole, to the presence of all those beings that manifest themselves on a given occasion. Solitude is not just the temporal moment of the happening of finitude that enables us, in our most extreme individuation, to participate in the presence of other beings, to share in that very presence—in short, to participate in a world. When Heidegger, after naming the enigmatic solitude which the precursory character of thinking inhabits, immediately adds: "No thinker has ever entered into the solitude of another. And yet every thinking speaks only from out of its solitude in a concealed manner into the thinking that follows or precedes it," this suggests that solitude is also an overarching attunement, an attunement into which, in a concealed manner, a thinker's thought is gathered in advance, a singular attunement that attunes his or her thought from beginning to end.

To the attunement of solitude—of Heidegger's solitude—there belongs, I would suggest, a certain experience of *phusis*, of the being or *Walten*—the prevailing, as he called it in the 1929–30 course—of nature that prevails through yet exceeds the human, and of the animal. And it is perhaps in his more personal and autobiographical reflections, rather than his public lectures, that one can intimate most directly Heidegger's solitudes and their vicissitudes. Allow me, in closing, to cite just two such reflections.[39] In December 1931, just eighteen months or so after the conclusion of the 1929–30 course, he writes to Karl Jaspers:

> Tomorrow, we [i.e., the family] move to the cabin [the *Hütte* in Todnauberg] for the entire holiday. Then there will be snow storms once again, and the howling of foxes in the snowy woods, and the vault of the heavens at night, and solitary excursions into the silent mountain valleys.[40]

In his 1933 reflection *Why Do We Remain in the Province?*, following his characterization of "the high time of philosophy" as occurring in the midst of a snow storm that rages around the cabin, Heidegger again appeals to the attunement of such philosophical work as that of solitude:

> City dwellers often wonder about the extended, monotonous being alone among the peasants amid the mountains. Yet it is not being alone, but presumably solitude [*Einsamkeit*]. In the big cities the human being can indeed readily be *so alone* as *scarcely anywhere else*. But he can never be solitary there. For solitude has the properly primordial power that it does not *isolate* us [*das sie uns nicht vereinzelt*], but casts our entire Dasein away into a far-reaching nearness to the essence of all things.[41]

Is it not in a certain dwelling with "nature," or more precisely, with *phusis*, exposed to the howling of foxes amid the silent mountain valleys, in the space opened up by the vault of the heavens—is it not amid all of this that uncanniness, *to deinon*, *das Unheimliche* arises, and that one may first experience what Heidegger seeks to describe as solitude, which is, above all, an experience of uncanny belonging?[42]

Notes

1 *Was Heißt Denken?* (Tübingen: Niemeyer, 1984), 164. Henceforth WHD. Translated as *What Is Called Thinking?* by J. Glenn Gray (New York: HarperCollins, 1976), 169 (translation slightly modified). Henceforth WCT.

2 Significantly, there is not a single occurrence of either the noun *Einsamkeit* or the adjective *einsam* in *Being and Time*.

3 *Die Grundbegriffe der Metaphysik: Welt—Endlichkeit—Einsamkeit.* Gesamtausgabe Bd. 29/30 (Frankfurt: Klostermann, 1983). Henceforth GA 29/30. Translated as *The Fundamental Concepts of Metaphysics: World, Finitude, Solitude* by William McNeill and Nicholas Walker (Bloomington: Indiana University Press, 1995). Henceforth FCM.

4 I say renewed because Heidegger certainly read Nietzsche much earlier, and Nietzsche has a considerable presence in *Being and Time*. On this point, see my essay "On the Nietzschean Legacy in Heidegger's Phenomenology," in *Nietzsche and Phenomenology*, ed. Andrea Rehberg (Newcastle upon Tyne: Cambridge Scholars Publishing, 2011), 103–20.

5 I am thinking here, of course, of the "Letter on 'Humanism,'" where Heidegger writes of "our abyssal bodily kinship with the animal." See *Wegmarken.*

Gesamtausgabe Bd. 9 (Frankfurt: Klostermann, 1976), 326. Translated as *Pathmarks*, ed. William McNeill (New York: Cambridge University Press, 1998), 248 (translation modified). Henceforth GA 9 / PM.

6 See the Editor's Epilogue to GA 29/30 for details.

7 Perhaps significantly, the term *Vereinzelung* and the associated verb *vereinzeln* appear to be largely absent in Heidegger's earlier work, suggesting that the introduction of this terminology in *Being and Time* was itself tentative.

8 GA 29/30, 8 / FCM, 6.

9 See GA 9, 118 / PM, 93 (here translated as "the process of finitude").

10 GA 29/30, 8 / FCM, 6.

11 *Sein und Zeit* (Niemeyer: Halle a. d. S., 1927), 187–88. Henceforth SZ. Translated as *Being and Time* by Joan Stambaugh (Albany: State University of New York Press, 2010), 182 (translation slightly modified). Henceforth BT.

12 SZ, 191 / BT, 184 (translation modified).

13 SZ, 188 / BT, 182 (translation modified). The reference to *solus ipse* suggests that Heidegger understood this individuation of Dasein as a corrective to Husserl's rejection of the *solus ipse* view of the individual in §18f.) of *Ideas II*.

14 *Einleitung in die Philosophie*. Gesamtausgabe Bd. 27 (Frankfurt: Klostermann, 2001), 334.

15 Ibid.

16 *Der Begriff der Zeit* (Tübingen: Niemeyer, 1989), 26–27. Translated as *The Concept of Time* by William McNeill. Bilingual edition (Oxford: Blackwell, 1992), 21.

17 I owe this suggestion to my colleague Michael Naas, in the context of a seminar on the 1929–30 course held at DePaul University in the fall of 2011. My thanks not only to Michael, but also to my colleague Elizabeth Rottenberg and to the graduate students who participated in that seminar.

18 SZ, 330 / BT, 315 (translation modified).

19 SZ, 382; cf. 384 / BT, 364 (translation modified); cf. 365–66.

20 SZ, 264 / BT, 253 (translation modified).

21 SZ, 262 / BT, 251 (translation modified).

22 WHD, 161: "*Das Denken ist das Vorläufigste alles vorläufigen Tuns des Menschen …*" / WCT, 160. In the same vein, Heidegger elsewhere characterizes "authentic thinking" as a "thinking ahead" (*vorausdenken*). See the 1937 lecture course on Nietzsche, "The Eternal Recurrence of the Same," in *Nietzsche*, Bd. I (Pfullingen: Neske, 1961), 398. Henceforth NI. Translated by David Farrell Krell as *Nietzsche*, Volumes One and Two (New York: HarperCollins, 1991), Volume Two, 135 (translation slightly modified). Henceforth N2.

23 GA 29/30, 8–9 / FCM, 6–7.

24 Ibid., 10 / 7.

25 Ibid., 7 / 5. Nietzsche too, of course, characterizes philosophy as homesickness: *German* philosophy, as a homesickness or nostalgia for the Greek

world. See the fragment reproduced as §419 of *The Will to Power* (original in: Nietzsche, *Werke. Kritische Gesamtausgabe*, edited by Giorgio Colli and Mazzino Montinari (Berlin: De Gruyter, 1967ff.), 7. Abt., 3 Bd., 412.) In the 1929–30 course, Heidegger is concerned with the issue of "metaphysical" homesickness, and not yet with the question of the historical determination of homesickness and homecoming in relation to the Germans and the Greeks that would become his focus with the turn to Hölderlin's poetizing from 1934 to 1935 onward.

26 Ibid., 7–8 / 5.

27 Ibid., 8 / 6.

28 Ibid., 8 / 5–6.

29 SZ, 189 / BT, 183.

30 NI, 271 / N2, 20 (translation modified).

31 NI, 275 / N2, 24 (translation slightly modified).

32 Ibid., 275–76 / 24–25 (translation modified).

33 Since this essay was written, a second instance of *Vereigentlichung* has come to my attention, apparently dating from 1936. See *Zu Eigenen Veröffentlichungen*. Gesamtausgabe Bd. 82 (Frankfurt: Klostermann, 2018), 46.

34 NI, 286 / N2, 34 (translation modified).

35 Ibid., 298 / 45 (translation modified).

36 Ibid., 300–301 / 47 (translation modified).

37 Ibid., 298 / 45 (translation modified).

38 For references to the "abyss" (*Abgrund*) in the 1929–30 course, see GA29/30, 384, 411 / FCM, 264, 283. In the first, Heidegger suggests that if the animal is unable to apprehend "something *as* something, something *as* being," then "the animal is separated from man by an abyss." In the second reference, however, the abyss is no longer simply between the human and the animal, but is an "abyss of Dasein in the midst of Dasein"—an abyss, that is, that opens up in and as the phenomenon of world itself. I have elsewhere suggested that Heidegger's equating of the apprehending of "something as something" with "something as being (something)" is too hasty. See *The Time of Life: Heidegger and Ēthos* (Albany: State University of New York Press, 2006), chapter 1, 45–46; for comments on the abyss, see 49–51.

39 To be sure, there are numerous other mentions of solitude by Heidegger to which one might refer here, and not all convey the same attunement. A few years after the reflections cited here, following the disastrous failure of the Rectorship, one cannot help but hear a very different pathos in his use of the word *Einsamkeit*, one not so readily removed from the commonplace connotation of loneliness. Writing to Jaspers in 1935 to acknowledge receipt of some lectures that Jaspers had sent him, Heidegger states: "I thank you from the heart for this greeting, which made me *very* happy; for my solitude is almost total [*denn die Einsamkeit ist nahezu vollkommen*]." Letter to Karl Jaspers of July 1, 1935, in *Martin Heidegger*

/ *Karl Jaspers: Briefwechsel 1920–1963*, ed. Walter Biemel and Hans Saner (Frankfurt: Klostermann, 1990), 157.

40   Letter to Karl Jaspers of December 20, 1931, in *Martin Heidegger / Karl Jaspers: Briefwechsel 1920–1963*, ed. Walter Biemel and Hans Saner (Frankfurt: Klostermann, 1990), 145.

41   *Denkerfahrungen* (Frankfurt: Klostermann, 1983), 11. Here, Heidegger apparently concedes the inevitable connotation of isolation that attends the verb *vereinzeln* and explicitly distances it, together with loneliness, or being alone (*Alleinsein*), from the experience of *Einsamkeit*.

42   A first version of this essay was presented at the 30th annual meeting of the North Texas Heidegger Symposium, held at El Centro College, Dallas, Texas, in April 2012. I thank the participants at the symposium for their helpful feedback and suggestions.

8

Solitude and Other Crowds

Jason M. Wirth

Who can protect teachers against the institutionalized war on creative solitudes?
No one.

—David Farrell Krell

Preface

It is strange that many philosophers so quickly circumscribe the kinds of questions that they regard as genuine philosophical questions. While we are busy arguing about what we can know, what we should do, what we should appreciate, and who we are, we spend strikingly little time inquiring into what it is that we do when we do philosophy and even less time investigating the conditions under which philosophy is at all be possible. Is it sufficient for the philosophical life merely to assume uncritically and automatically the prevailing norms according to which philosophical research is produced, verified, and evaluated? If that is the case, then the conduct of philosophy only requires a high level of competence in the contemporary institutions of philosophy.

The inadequacy of this answer has again and again been demonstrated by the works, both philosophical and resistant to "professional" philosophy, of David Farrell Krell and by the "creative solitudes" out of which they were possible. The tenor of his works are well known to all who read from his impressive bibliography, but in this essay I would like not to speak from a mere rehearsal of these published fruits, but rather from out of their self-acknowledged source. "Yet our great teachers were not full of chat; they were not 'personalities,' and certainly not song-and-dance performers or talk-show hosts. Rather, they spoke well about what they had read and contemplated well; they brought something of their solitary reading and thinking and writing with them when they entered a classroom." I could add here: this same solitude is demanded when we write about Krell, about his own ventures into solitude, and about the solitude that one enters in order to appreciate (or rebel against) such solitude, a solitude that we share, paradoxically, each in our own way. I share Krell's suspicion "of the very singularity of the *solus ipse* and of the emphatic egocentricity that seems to derive from the metaphysics and morals of both late antiquity and European modernity since Descartes." The singularity of which I will speak has nothing to do with an isolated self-same individual.

How then does one speak of creative solitudes without merely recapitulating the works that made their way to the light of day from the solitude of another? How does one speak to the singularity of another without that singularity becoming the trap of solipsistic individualism? Such traps are what Charles Olson, speaking of Ahab's rage against the unconquerable solitude of the sea and its symbol, the white Leviathan, called "hate—huge and fixed upon the imperceptible . . . solipsism that brings down a world."[1] One can only speak to the singularity of another from one's own shared singularity, from, in Nancy's felicitous articulation, our sharing in the *being singular plural* out of which creativity finds, always on its own terms, it way to expression. The task of this essay is therefore to speak *from* my solitude *to* David F. Krell's solitude *on* the problem of solitude as such. It is a task, I would like to suggest, that is critical to the question of philosophy's own enabling (and disabling) conditions, a question that opens up the space for the possibility of being more philosophical about the life of philosophy.

I

In remarking on how "creative solitudes" is a "wonderful title," Krell muses that "both Ralph Waldo Emerson and Henry David Thoreau, and perhaps even William James, would have written stirring essays on it." Even a cursory familiarity with the dawn of the North American philosophical tradition, generations before the rise of a philosophical culture that engages in increasingly bellicose arguments about decreasingly important issues, indicates that the strangeness of the philosophical life in its strange new home required not merciless debating but rather a willingness to surrender the gregarious life of institutional and societal reassurances for a life that involved a profound commitment to periods of genuine solitude without the guarantee that the fruits of such a solitary life would be rewarding. The philosophical life, unprotected by institutional policies and protocols, uncertain of having an audience, even a hostile one, would have to wager itself on solitude. Such a life is vulnerable before an uncertain future, and the works that emerge out of it are, in Schelling's exquisite phrase, *unvordenklich*, unprethinkable. Who knows what one is getting into when one affirms solitude?

Looming solitude, with all of its uncertainties, can produce anxiety and, as we assess its risks, chief among them is the threat of loneliness. "And solitude? No one has ever been able to distinguish it properly from aloneness or loneliness, even though we know that these states or conditions are far from identical." This is the problem that shall here guide our initial reflection.

The proximity of solitude to loneliness is part of solitude's risk. When we see people living and working alone, we often habitually conclude, perhaps as a prophylactic against our own looming solitude, that they must be terribly, unbearably lonely. Indeed, Krell senses "that aloneness and loneliness are essential components of creative solitudes. They may be self-inflicted wounds, but they are not accidents." As solitude looms, it threatens "a terrible aloneness" and such terror is also implicated in the premonition that solitude is haunted, that "every creative solitude entertains ghosts." I remember a dream in which I realized I was dying yet I was wholly unable to move or to speak. I could not even scream out to my wife, who I could see was sleeping right next to me. As death came over me, I sensed it as relentlessly hermetic, as Ahab's final despair, "Oh, lonely death on lonely life" (chapter 135, The Chase—Third Day). Of course, this was just a nightmare, but I could detect in it my anxiety about my own finitude, an anxiety that also flares when solitude looms. We write as we die: in some very real way alone. Creativity demands that we, in some very real way and for some significant time, actually be alone. As Kafka wrote to Felice Bauer: one "cannot be sufficiently alone when writing; . . . never enough silence around oneself when writing; the night itself is still too little night." Solitude is not the same thing as always being alone and being alone does not necessarily entail feeling lonely, but there is also no assurance from the outset that such borders will not blur.

When Henry David Thoreau spent his two years, two months, and two days in solitude in a cabin on Walden Pond,[2] abandoning "the mass of men" who "labor under a mistake" (W 4) and "lead lives of quiet desperation" (W 7), people wondered if he had been lonely—"Some asked what I got to eat, if I did not feel lonesome . . . (W 1); "men frequently say to me, 'I should think you would feel lonesome down there, and want to be nearer to folks, rainy and snowy days and nights especially'" (W 143). To walk freely away from what Krell calls "the celebrated global village" as well as the "information highway down which we are tearing, roaring along so confidently in the direction of ignorance, ugliness, and bad style": surely that is to inflict a grievous wound upon oneself, to condemn oneself to isolation, to self-destructively cast aside the comforts and glories of human accomplishment. Moreover, it seems even madder to do so with no recourse to metaphysical comforts or a promise of a transcendent payoff. Solitude is not the ascetic ideal of the hermit who rejects the vainglory of this world in favor of a better world beyond. Solitude is not trying to escape the earth, but rather seeks to be true to it and to win insight into the mistakes to which we otherwise anxiously root ourselves.

The silent sway of *das Man* may foster group think about what really matters and consequently dismiss philosophy as *eine brotlose Kunst*, but one of the enduring philosophical motifs of the last century is Dasein before its death—a guarantee that promises the loss of all the ways in which one relates to oneself and one's world, but which opens up the enigma of the future, an enigma that is one's ownmost, what is in each case mine (*Jemeinigkeit*), the *solitude* that death (and the open horizon of the future) allows to emerge. Although, as Jean-Luc Nancy (in *Being Singular Plural* and other works) and others have shown, Heidegger may not have sufficiently developed the thought of our *Mitsein* and our being together; it does not follow, even for Heidegger, that solitude is tantamount to forlorn individuality and ontological orphaning. We are not simply abandoned to ourselves with all of the loneliness that this entails.

Such solitude, however, will probably always remain a hard sell. Is not the result of our resistance to *Öffentlichkeit* loneliness, as my first year students tell me year after year in order to explain why they find themselves constitutively closed to philosophical discourse? That Socrates was denigrated as ἄτοπος, out of place, and thereby strange and unclassifiable, does little to endear him to students who know all too well the traumatic fickleness of the "mass of men" even though they can also already appreciate the exorbitant price that they reluctantly pay for inclusion: to become what Thoreau called the "slave-driver of yourself" (W 6). Why would one elect to cultivate what prima facie appears to be the role of the pariah? Is not therefore the "private business" (W 19) of Thoreau's Walden experiment the painful isolation of a world without the "mass of men"? To twist free of this conclusion is to again take up the question of the relationship of solitude to loneliness.

Thoreau's *Walden* remains popular and inspiring to this day, but in the institutionalized self-assurance that takes philosophy and its tasks to be self-evident and needing no philosophical examination (what we might here call the "mass of philosophers"), *one still has to argue that Thoreau is a philosopher,* that he does not deserve to be banished to the supposedly thoughtless and a-philosophical hinterlands of what is ruinously (in the eyes of professional philosophers) denigrated as literature. (From this same point of view, literature always suffers in the philosopher's eyes because its modes of thought are not recognizably philosophical. Its chief crime is that it is not philosophy and therefore not serious thought.) The editors of the fine new collection of essays, *Thoreau's Importance for Philosophy*, lament that "many members of the academic philosophical community in the United Sates would be reluctant to classify Thoreau as a philosopher at all." Indeed, "Thoreau's work is seldom taught or studied in most American philosophy departments."[3]

To be fair, Thoreau's excoriation of professional philosophy and its practices likely does little to endear him to the "mass of philosophers." "There are nowadays professors of philosophy, but not philosophers" (W 14). The "mass of philosophers" talks the talk, so to speak, but they do not walk the walk. They write papers about the body, but dine on processed foods and deliver their work in the basements of conference hotels that seemed designed for *das Man*. They speak endlessly of ethics, but they are despotic teachers and punitively petty colleagues. In other words, philosophy is something that is satisfied with producing accounts. It is not, as Pierre Hadot said of Greek philosophy, a "way of life" and "spiritual exercises,"[4] a personal embodiment of the questions that animate one's thinking. For Thoreau, philosophy was not the production of arguments but rather experiments with the conduct of living.

> To be a philosopher is not merely to have subtle thoughts, nor even to found a school, but so to love wisdom as to live according to its dictates, a life of simplicity, independence, magnanimity, and trust. It is to solve some of the problems of life, not only theoretically, but practically. (W 14)

Students, for their part, "should not *play* life, or *study* it merely . . . but earnestly *live* it from beginning to end. How could youths better learn to live than by at once trying the experiment of living" (W 53–54)? Solitude belongs not only to the necessary conditions for the possibility of writing, but it is also that by which we break away from the established account of who we are and how we are to live, and once again take up the question—the experiment—of the practice of living. Thoreau spoke of himself as "my own experiment" (W 42) and in the case of the experiment of Walden: "I went to the woods because I wished to live deliberately, to front only the essential facts of life, and see if I could not learn what it had to teach, and not, when I came to die, discover that I had not lived" (W 97).

Although our being unto death reveals our solitude just as much as the isolation required for creative work does, this solitude comes in the form of a question and a problem. Regardless of our current obsessions and ambitions for life, death confirms none of them. As Tomas realized in Milan Kundera's *The Unbearable Lightness of Being*, "We live everything as it comes, without warning, like an actor going on cold. And what can life be worth if the first rehearsal for life is life itself?"[5] Tomas had his own experiments, and his beleaguered wife Tereza had her own. For Thoreau, the challenge was to experiment with the solitude at the heart of human living in such a way that one awoke to and was more mindful of the experience of solitude as such. What does solitude, even the solitude of living philosophically, reveal, despite the tacit conspiracy of the "mass of men" and the "mass of philosophers" who resist it? In his solitude, Thoreau did not come to see new things or produce new philosophical conclusions. Rather, he came to see in a radically new manner, what Nishitani Keiji, following the Zen tradition, called "the infinite freshness, pervaded with an infinite fragrance"[6] of awakening. His senses no longer took the world for granted, but became mindful of it in its granting. This is what the Zen tradition calls beginner's mind (初心, *shoshin*)—"in the beginner's mind there are many possibilities, but in the expert's mind there are few."[7]

> To him whose elastic and vigorous thought keeps pace with the sun, the day is a perpetual morning . . . Morning is when I am awake and there is a dawn in me . . . To be awake is to be alive . . . We must learn to reawaken and keep ourselves awake, not by mechanical aids, but by an infinite expectation of the dawn, which does not forsake us in our soundest sleep. (W 96)

Fleeing what they fear is a looming loneliness, the "mass of men," with considerable irony, lose themselves in the loneliness of crowds, mass movements, fads, and best practices (the current denomination of herd mentality). In the explosion of mass living, is not the image of loneliness more readily large groups than a person lost in the solitary art of reading or painting? It is the mass of men who flee loneliness by abdicating solitude for the protection of the herd and the school. Thoreau, to the contrary, left the loneliness of the "mass of men" for a different kind of community, the awakening to what Mahāyāna cultivates as the originary community (or *sangha*) of *pratītyasamutpāda* or dependent co-origination. Hence Thoreau concluded that "I love to be alone. I never found the companion that was so companionable as solitude" (W 146). "I am no more lonely than the loon in the pond that laughs so loud, or than Walden Pond itself"

(W 148). Here is the primordial community—"beneficent society in Nature"—
to which Thoreau awoke:

> I have never felt lonesome, or in the least oppressed by a sense of solitude, but
> once, and that was a few weeks after I came to the woods, when, for an hour,
> I doubted if the near neighborhood of man was not essential to a serene and
> healthy life. To be alone was something unpleasant. But I was at the same time
> conscious of a slight insanity in my mood, and seemed to foresee my recovery. In
> the midst of a gentle rain while these thoughts prevailed, I was suddenly sensible
> of such sweet and beneficent society in Nature, in the very pattering of the drops,
> and in every sound and sight around my house, an infinite and unaccountable
> friendliness all at once like an atmosphere sustaining me, as made the fancied
> advantages of human neighborhood insignificant, and I have never thought of
> them since. Every little pine needle expanded and swelled with sympathy and
> befriended me. I was so distinctly made aware of the presence of something
> kindred to me, even in scenes which we are accustomed to call wild and dreary,
> and also that the nearest of blood to me and humanest was not a person nor a
> villager, that I thought no place could ever be strange to me again. (W 142)

No place could ever be strange not because everything suddenly becomes
familiar but rather because one awakens to being at home with the strange, to
the dignified bizarreness of being. That the world was ever familiar is now the
strangest thought of all. Those who are at home in the familiar, who think that
the home is the familiar as such, not only are not awakened by what Heidegger
thematized as *Unheimlichkeit* (the uncanniness of no longer being familiarly at
home), but it is they who most repress the homelessness looming within the
home. As Krell speaks of this uncanny haunting:

> We are always writing with them and for them, even when we are writing against
> them. No matter how joyous and exhilarating our solitudes may be, they are
> always haunted. We may feel at home in them, yet our being-at-home is riddled
> with uncanny, unhomelike sensations.[8]

Solitude emerges in a reversal of how we ordinarily think about the personal
forlornness that we experience as loneliness. In departing from the "mass of men,"
Thoreau wondered if this departure was a sundering of ties, an elective crisis
within our sense of belonging. Thoreau experienced the opposite: the delusional
belonging of the masses, their surrender of the freedom that comprises solitude,
is an experience not of literally being alone, but of being isolated in their manner
of belonging together (as slave drivers of themselves as they labor uniformly for

their wants as if they were their needs). It is the mass of men who are lonely—loneliness is our isolation in *Öffentlichkeit*, not the community that we share, each in our singular way, with all people, all animals, and all beings. In solitude we discover another manner of belonging, a manner that we have abandoned in confusing this way of being together with mass living and group think. One can sense in Thoreau's recovery of the solitude of belonging with all beings a presentiment of what Jean-Luc Nancy would much later, thinking critically within Heidegger's wake, articulate as a being singular plural that touches the being singular plural of nature itself:

> But this circulation goes in all directions at once, in all the directions of all the space-times opened by presence to presence: all things, all beings, all entities, everything past and future, alive, dead, inanimate, stones, plants, nails, gods— and "humans," that is, those who expose sharing and circulation as such by saying "we," by saying we to themselves in all possible senses of that expression, and by saying we for the totality of all being.[9]

The point of solitude is not that each of us should live in a cabin in the *Schwartzwald*. These are particular experiments within the dignified problem of solitude. "I left the woods for as good a reason as I went there. Perhaps it seemed to me that I had several more lives to live, and could not spare any more time for that one. It is remarkable how easily and insensibly we fall into a particular route, and make a beaten track for ourselves" (W 351). Thoreau would soon have other experiments, including the civil disobedience that resulted in a night in the far lonelier confines of jail.

In the *Origins of Totalitarianism*,[10] with its incisive analyses of the hermetic closure of the great ideological systems of mass living, Hannah Arendt elucidated the unprecedented scale of the loneliness of our age when she demonstrated that the "common ground for terror, the essence of the totalitarian government" (OT 612) is the "experience of being abandoned by everything and everybody" (OT 613). Starving, I ask you for food and you look at me as if you did not speak my language. "Loneliness is not solitude. Solitude requires being alone whereas loneliness shows itself most sharply in the company of others" (OT 613). Solitude is the scene of thinking as "a dialogue between me and myself," a "two-in-one" that "does not lose contact with the world of my fellow men because they are represented in the self with whom I lead the dialogue of thought" (OT 613). Thoreau, in writing *Walden*, is having a spirited exchange with the "mass of men" and even the "mass of philosophers." Krell's "own call to creative solitudes wants to be a call to this society of selves each of us is." In loneliness, however, "I am actually one, deserted by all others" (OT 613). I am abandoned to a forlorn individuality.

Perhaps we see in the reveries of Thoreau's solitude the "braggadocio" about which Krell (and Emerson) worry. Fair enough. Thoreau may not fully own up to his bouts of loneliness and sufficiently acknowledge the pain of how we isolate each other even as we absorb each other into our groups (the cruelty by which the vulnerability of creativity is institutionally administrated and normalized). We may even at times in our history produce systems of loneliness that are so ruthlessly efficient that all hope for solitude is lost. What solitude is there really in concentration camps and refugee camps and the urban squalor of slums to which we condemn billions of our sisters and brothers? Thoreau is nonetheless among the clearest about the decisive bifurcation that holds loneliness and solitude apart, despite their prima facie confusion: shared singularity versus forlorn and abandoned individuality. The loneliness that Thoreau only claims to have tasted in a "slight insanity in my mood," may be more pervasive than he admits, but there is an ontological divide between solitude and loneliness. How often have we tasted the loneliness of seeking philosophical solitude in professional life! Krell: "Who can protect teachers against the institutionalized war on creative solitudes? No one. Nor should we expect understanding on this point from persons who no longer teach much." How rare are the successful experiments like Walden! How far away is the *experimental* classroom from administrative imperatives! John McCumber recounts arriving at the New School for Social Research in 1980 and learning that the American Philosophical Association had considered the New School's most justly celebrated philosopher, Hannah Arendt, "unproductive . . . because her works were not cited in important journals such as the *Journal of Philosophy* and *Philosophical Review*."[11]

II

And so now the question becomes clearer: If there is nothing intrinsic to solitude (the being singular plural that is our community with all things) that includes the idea of loneliness (which is a forlorn individuality, the trap of being only one), why does loneliness so often accompany solitude? It is the strength of Thoreau's experiment to distinguish solitude clearly from loneliness, so why are the solitary so often subjected to loneliness? Why is the refusal to acknowledge this at the heart of Krell's charge of Thoreau's "braggadocio" as well as his insistence that solitude is "sometimes also heroically" solitude? If solitude, as

I think Krell rightly sees, has nothing whatsoever to do with the nascent egoism of "existential solipsism"—it is precisely not utter individuality, the *solus ipse*— *why is it subject to such desolation?*

Although it would be futile to hope to answer my own question adequately within the limited confines of this essay, if at all, I would nonetheless like to suggest that a part of the problem is that *we do not know how to be together in our solitude.* We lack skillful practices and wise insights about the *life* in philosophical life. This is painfully true for we philosophers, trained to subjugate all of humanity, even the earth itself, with our knock-down arguments and aspirations to the universal. At the heart of the challenge is a formidable *aporia*: when we are in a sense the least alone (in our solitude), we are in another sense the most alone (exposed to the singularity at the heart of solitude, albeit a singularity that we share with others and as others). What we most lack is not more publications, but better, wiser, more skillful, even more forgiving, practices of friendship, with each other, with other forms of life, with the earth itself.

Looking back upon his many achievements, both philosophical and literary, a bureaucrat would likely say that "Krell has always gone his own way," but this seems to me to misplace the emphasis on a willful individuality (on the individuating force of the will as such). This mistakes the problem of solitude for the egocentric imperative of eccentricity (the less others are like me, the smaller the set of my colleagues, the more I get to be myself all by myself). I leave the mass of men because I believe that I am one of the few elect, that I was born special, that I should have the limelight all to myself, that I should be the only star in the sky. Zarathustra, having "tirelessly enjoyed his spirit and his solitude [*Einsamkeit*] for ten years" in the mountains, as suddenly and creatively as Thoreau leaving Walden Pond, "had a change of heart." At dawn he addressed the sun, remarking that it could not have had its happiness if it had not also had "those for whom it shined."[12] Like the sun setting, Zarathustra then went down the mountain to share the fruits of his solitude and on the way came upon a hermit who had abandoned humanity for God. Zarathustra's solitude, however, was not the life of *der Einsiedler* or hermit and it is not founded on a rejection of humanity in favor of transcendence. As Georges Bataille, writing of Nietzsche's solitude, asked, "Is there a silence more stifling, more sound-proof, further beneath the earth?"[13]

Krell has not gone his own way. He is not a hermit, simply taking reactionary refuge in the *Schwartzwald* from the toxic banality of our institutions. Without the hermit's recourse to transcendent escape routes and the illusion of individuality and independence, but with the long-lost deities of Samothrace, he *is* the insistence and miraculous fecundity of the way of his solitude, with its experiments, questions, problems, passions, discoveries, mistakes, and demons.

It is from the cultivation of this place that Krell is wary of what I might here call "the mass of technology" and the technological reproduction of mass living and mass society and its flight into loneliness as if it were escaping it. Information technology "invades our creative solitudes in a particularly pernicious way." Writing of the recent invention of the telegraph, Thoreau claimed that these "pretty toys" are "but improved means to an unimproved end . . . . We are in great haste to construct a magnetic telegraph from Maine to Texas; but Maine and Texas, it may be, have nothing important to communicate" (W 55). In an age of smartphones, an array of apps verging on the mathematical sublime, blue tooth, social media, including Twitter and its tweets and the relentless limelight that is Facebook and its ceaseless pages, each in their death struggle for recognition, even email is becoming antiquated almost as quickly as it burst on the scene. Does not Thoreau's worry about the telegraph and Morse code, which promised written communication (γράφειν) at a distance (τῆλε), or even Krell's worry about email, now seem hopelessly quaint and obsolete? Alas, as the toys grow prettier, they do not become less so toys. "As if the main object were to talk fast and not to talk sensibly" (W 55). To talk sensibly requires a commitment to solitude. "Some of our colleagues have given up entirely on creative solitudes; their supreme need is to interrupt those who have not yet succumbed. Misery loves . . . e-mails about committee meetings."

That technology is in effect increasingly enclosing us within a hermetic seal of *Gerede* and *Geschwätz*[14] from which escape and retreat are increasingly taxing and unlikely is not a cause for celebration. "To a philosopher all news, as it is called, is gossip, and they who edit and read it are old women over their tea. Yet not a few are greedy after this gossip" (W 100–101). And not a few are in thrall to what Heidegger called *Neugier*, the greed, so to speak, for the new and for news, the endless demand for novelty that only leads to the demand for more novelty.[15] Loneliness and its ontological alienation from the earth drives us in our panic to a manic verbosity, but the way out of verbosity is not more verbosity about verbosity, but rather, as Heidegger counseled: "Necessary in the contemporary world-crisis [*Weltnot*]: less philosophy, but greater mindfulness [*Achtsamkeit*] in thinking; less literature, but more cultivation [*Pflege*] of the letter."[16]

Real communication, however, is not desperate and it is not reactionary. We *communicate solitude to solitude*—solitude is the possibility of communication. Krell states: "True, those words of support must be spoken. Yet they must be spoken discreetly, and that means *communicated from one solitude to another,* otherwise they are simply empty 'validations' cast to the winds."

In the "mass of words" of contemporary electronic communication, solitude is ruinously inefficient and produces little that we recognize or already know how to consume. Where are the outcomes by which to evaluate the fruits of solitude when solitude, as the possibility of creativity, makes itself vulnerable to the open horizons of the future? Indeed, "one cannot dedicate oneself to reading and writing without also committing oneself to what will be an extravagant waste of time, or, at the very least, a maddening inefficiency. Perhaps that explains why we are losing the capacity and the courage to read and write. And even if we are not wasting time when we engage with words, time is wasting us."

Georges Bataille, the great defender of waste and inefficiency, whose *La part maudite*[17] is a "book that no one awaits, that answers no formulated question" (PM 11/51), but which affirmed that the earth's "energy economy," contrary to its topsy-turvy misunderstanding, is analogous to a wildly inefficient sense of time and space: "*the sexual act is in time what the tiger is in space*" (PM 12/51), that is, wildly inefficient, wasteful, and excessive. "Luxury [*le luxe*]," not efficiency or necessity, comprises humankind's "fundamental problem" (PM 12/52). "Woe to those who, to the very end, insist on regulating the movement that exceeds them with the narrow mind [*l'esprit borné*] of the mechanic who changes a tire" (PM 26/64). Alas, in the current crisis of the university in which everything is being rendered more efficient as if universities were factories of learning or corporate enterprises designed to extract maximum yields, we are changing student minds like a mechanic changes tires. Krell laments, I think rightly so, that "no cunning and calculating efficiency expert will ever lend a sympathetic ear to a teacher, not even if it is the case that without creative solitudes the life of a school, college, or university is doomed." Bataille's formulation about sex and tigers— space and time for the strategic waste that is thinking, teaching, and writing— immediately demonstrates both the poignant fragility of the institutionalization of thoughtfulness and its fatal contradiction.

This, then, is another paradox of creative solitudes: in order to be *creative* of the works and arts that are teaching and writing, we need to be less *productive* in the sense of efficiently producing the commodities that are part and parcel of our factories of learning and teaching. We can only laugh with recognition and a sense of the absurd when we read the words of the young Schelling, still confident in his hopes for the university, when he lamented that "certainly there is in the realm of science more than enough sexless bees, who, because they will fail to produce anything from themselves, externally replicate moulds of their own lack of spirit [*Geistlosigkeit*] in the form of inorganic subsections" (I/5 217). We continue to produce dead parts of a whole whose life is lost on us, endlessly prolonging tasks whose value is found simply in the fact that we continue to do what we have always done. Was it ever possible for institutions of knowledge production and transmission to be more than nominally able to protect and foster this critical distinction between *creativity* and *productivity*?

Perhaps not all of us can leave so successfully the convalescence that remains a defensible promise of the philosophical life, for it is "a kind of hospital stay, as Hölderlin says of philosophical work in general." Nonetheless, we owe much to Krell's capacity to communicate in deed and word and from solitude much wisdom about the promise of φιλία amid the din of the professionalization and commoditization of φιλοσοφία.

Notes

1 Charles Olson, *Call Me Ishmael* (Baltimore: The Johns Hopkins University Press, 1997 [1947]), 73. I apologize in advance for my footnotes. "As for scholarship, it inspires footnotes, and that's another way to spoil a pleasant walk."

2 Henry David Thoreau, *Walden*, ed. Jeffrey S. Cramer (New Haven: Yale University Press, 2006 [1854]). Henceforth W.

3 James D. Reid, Rick Anthony Furtak, and Jonathan Ellsworth, "Locating Thoreau, Reorienting Philosophy," *Thoreau's Importance for Philosophy*, ed. Rick Anthony Furtak, Jonathan Ellsworth, and James D. Reid (New York: Fordham University Press, 2012), 1.

4 Pierre Hadot, *Philosophy as a Way of Life*, ed. Arnold Davidson and trans. Michael Chase (Oxford: Blackwell, 1995).

5 Milan Kundera, *The Unbearable Lightness of Being*, trans. Michael Henry Heim (New York: Harper & Row, 1984), 8.

6 Nishitani, "The I-Thou Relation in Zen Buddhism," *The Buddha Eye*, 2nd edn., ed. Frederick Franck (Bloomington: World Wisdom, 2004), 51.

7 Shunryu Suzuki, *Zen Mind, Beginner's Mind* (New York and Tokyo: Weatherhill, 1971), 17.

8 All David Farrell Krell quotes are from his "Creative Solitudes" in this volume.

9 Jean-Luc Nancy, *Being Singular Plural*, trans. Robert D. Richardson and Anne E. O'Byrne (Stanford, CA: Stanford University Press, 2000), 3.

10 Hannah Arendt, *The Origins of Totalitarianism* (New York: Schocken Books, 2004 [1951]). Henceforth OT.

11 John McCumber, *Time in a Ditch: American Philosophy and the McCarthy Era* (Evanston, IL: Northwestern University Press, 2001), 51.

12 Friedrich Nietzsche, *Also sprach Zarathustra, Kritische Gesamtausgabe* 6.1, ed. Colli and Moninari (Berlin: Walter de Gruyter, 1968), 5.

13 Georges Bataille, *Inner Experience*, trans. Leslie Anne Boldt (Albany: State University of New York Press, 1988 [1943]), 156.

14 *Sein und Zeit*, §35.

15 *Sein und Zeit*, §36.

16 Martin Heidegger, Brief über den "Humanismus", *Wegmarken*, Gesamtausgabe vol. 9 (Frankfurt am Main: Vittorio Klostermann, 1976 [1949]), 364.

17 Georges Bataille, *The Accursed Share*, vol. 1, trans. Robert Hurley (New York: Zone Books, 1988 [1949]). *La part maudite* (Paris: Les Éditions de minuit, 1976). Henceforth PM, with the English citation followed by the French citation.

Part Three

Imagining Krell's Solitudes

9

Sounion

John Sallis

For David Krell—

Recalling how we once read together the Fragments of the early Greek philosophers, especially Heraclitus, at a time when a more attentive way of reading Plato also began to open up, as we marveled at how wonderfully the *Timaeus* departs from what at the time was considered Platonism.

Recalling, too, that this was only the beginning of a discourse that, from our own solitude, we nonetheless shared, a discourse that never strayed far from the Greek beginning.

* * *

Its place is other, utterly so. Its remoteness is so unyielding that any attempt to measure its distance from anything familiar could only have the effect of setting it still more insistently apart. Yet precisely as a place of such alterity, this site is most impressive to behold in its sheer presence. Perfectly framed by sea and sky, as if raised by the earth itself up out of the intensely blue surface of the Aegean, the site belongs uniquely to these elements. Even in antiquity, indeed even before the magnificent temple was erected there, travelers of many sorts were attracted. Today, in still greater numbers, tourists come with cameras in hand to have a look at this remarkable site and to capture its image. Yet the distraction is no more than momentary. As soon as one is again alone in what remains of the sacred precinct, from the moment when solitude returns and there is left only these stones shining there amidst the elements, the utter strangeness of the site is again announced in the silence that surrounds.

What remains at this site comes from another world, from what we call—already beginning to mediate, to break down the difference—Greek antiquity. Yet, precisely in its otherness, this world is the origin of origins, the absolutely archaic. It first released all that was to come: the course of what came to constitute the West, and now the global figure into which those lines have extended. It is an origin that, from the beginning, continued to animate what it had released, coming, to this extent, always from the future. Thus, its remoteness is irreducible to mere pastness; and even now, in the wake of closure, it summons from beyond. It is an origin thus withdrawn into both past and future, hence doubly remote from the present, so that the remains of it that are now still to be seen—as in the stones preserved at this site—cannot but appear utterly strange. The place is, at once, displaced, almost as into a void, and yet it is set firmly on the earth, shining before our eyes in the brilliant Greek sunlight. Its conjunction of consummate presence and staunch remoteness, of stark manifestness and utter strangeness, is cast in the light itself, in the almost blinding intensity of its illumination.

A portion of the wall that once surrounded the sacred precinct is still to be seen. Little remains, however, of the marble-covered propylaea through which one would have entered the enclosure. The location is marked by an inscription—recent no doubt—on a slab of marble; but the remains are meager, merely three sections of a column and a few other slabs. An inscription also marks the location of the large stoa that extended laterally from the propylaea; but here, too, very little remains, only the stylobates or bases of five columns. Even as one is present at the very spot where the propylaea and the stoa once stood, the visible traces that remain can sustain only a vague image of how these would have looked: that the propylaea, as the opening to the temple, would have been especially magnificent and that the marble surfaces of both structures would have shined luminously.

At such a site where one is faced with ruins, what is called forth is never just pure phantasy, not even just phantasy sustained by memory of images previously seen or of familiar descriptions. Rather, if one is intent on envisaging, to the extent possible, what once stood at this site, then the imagining called for will be such as to circulate between the visibly present ruins and an image of the ancient structure, hovering between these, letting each inform the other.

But it is in face of the ruins of the temple itself that imagination is sustained and hence soars. These ruins are extensive enough and sufficiently well preserved that from them alone many features of the temple are evident. The columns display its Doric order, and their configuration indicates that the temple was peripteral. The majority of the columns along the longer sides of the temple are still standing: nine on the more seaward, southern side, five (along with a couple of sections of another) on the other side. The marble, which came from nearby quarries, is more purely white than that of many other such edifices (such as the Pentelic marble used for the Parthenon); but the material is also softer, and it was presumably in order to strengthen the columns that the architect reduced the fluting from the usual twenty to sixteen. The distinctive radiance with which the stone gives back the light it receives is not unrelated to these features.

On top of the columns, running horizontally, are the epistyles, rectangular blocks on which the superstructure would have rested. On the two shorter sides much less remains. On the eastern side, which would have formed the entrance to the temple, there is one column, the base of another, and two stacks of rectangular blocks, many of them almost cubical. The stacks, which are the same height as the columns, are connected to columns by epistyles. Protrusions from them toward the interior of the temple indicate that these stacks of square blocks form the extremity from which the solid inner walls would have extended; these are the only traces of the inner walls that remain. On the western side of the temple, nothing remains standing.

The blocks that form the base of the edifice are mostly intact: the stylobates of course on which the columns rest but also most of those that would have formed the floor of the chambers. The entire temple is elevated above the surrounding grounds, most conspicuously so on the lower side of the sloping ground, where the base is several meters high and requires for each vertical section eight to ten rectangular blocks.

The promontory on which the temple stands lies at the extremity of the cape of Sounion, which forms the southernmost tip of Attica. The strategic importance that the location had for Athens let to its being fortified in 413 BCE, shortly after the magnificent temple had been erected (c. 440 BCE) to replace a porous rock temple that after only a few decades had been completely destroyed by the Persians. This very remarkable site is mentioned already in the *Odyssey*. In a passage in the Third Book, Odysseus relates that as he and Menelaus were sailing back from Troy they "came to holy Sounion, the cape of Athens." There, Menelaus's steersman Phrontis was slain by unseen arrows of Apollo. To pay full honor to this most excellent of all men in piloting a ship through strong storm winds, Menelaus interrupted their journey at Sounion and there buried his comrade. Two centuries before the great marble temple came to be erected on the promontory at Sounion, several marble *kouroi* were placed there, presumably as votive offerings whose presence might ensure that sailors passing by would escape what had befallen Phrontis. One such *Kouros of Sounion*, quite well preserved, can be seen in the National Archaeological Museum in Athens.

The temple is placed so as to overlook the sea. From the north side, one looks across an inlet; to the south and the west, one looks out across open sea stretching to the horizon. From the perimeter of the temple, a few paces in any of these directions bring one to the precipitous edge of the site. One's vision plummets almost straight down to the rocks and the sea far below. Near the rugged shore, there are areas where the water is almost emerald green; but as one looks farther out, it is consistently such a deep blue that, at the horizon, the sky appears, by contrast, unusually pale, almost washed-out, by contrast, in turn, with the intense blueness of the sky overhead.

Yet while the presence of the sea is what most decisively determines the character of the site, the history borne by it enlivens that presence. The Homeric passage alone suffices to show that the Greeks experienced that presence, not as totally unreserved exposure to panoptic vision, but rather as harboring also a depth from out of which something barely describable can unaccountably appear and then just as unaccountably—that is, mythically— vanish. The very idiom on which one most readily draws could not be more indicative: presence was experienced as if, like the sea, it withdrew into its depth and as if there were secret inlets, harbors, where things could be hidden away.

What could be more appropriate than the encompassing presence of the sea? For what stands there is a temple of Poseidon, and Poseidon is god of the sea. But what does it mean for a temple, an edifice constructed by humans, to belong to the god? And what does it mean to say that Poseidon is god of the sea? What kind of comportment to the temple and to the sea would be appropriate for the figure that the Greeks called Poseidon? How is it that what once stood at Sounion overlooking the sea and stands there still in ruins can be called a temple of the god of the sea?

At the site there is not only the intense presence of the sea but also an elevation above it. While overlooking the sea, the temple stands at a height befitting a god. It is as if raised from out of the wine-dark sea into the brilliant sunlight above. There, far above the sea, its columns of purely white marble, outlined against the intense blue of the diurnal sky, shine with incomparable radiance. The temple lays out a place where the elements come to be ranged alongside—and as they run together with—one another. It is a site of concurrence of the elements, of earth and sky, sea, and light. It brings into proximity what seem to be simply opposites: the massive solidity of stone and earth and the insubstantial spread of atmosphere and sky; the invisibility of light itself and the radiance of the marble illuminated by the light. As the very medium of irreducible elemental differences, it is itself utterly remote from ordinary things; it is something quite other, incomparably strange.

As the place where these elements come together in their very differences, the temple is not simply a temple of Poseidon but spreads around itself a precinct to which other gods, too, may draw near. For many centuries it was believed, on the basis of an erroneous report by Pausanias in the second century CE, that the temple at Sounion was dedicated to Athena. In fact, in antiquity there was a temple of Athena at Sounion; it stood some five hundred meters from the temple of Poseidon, on a lower hill, and is believed to have been the older of the two edifices. Today, it is preserved only as a few blocks of marble outlining the rectangular shape of the temple. Yet not only Athena, patron goddess of the great maritime city, but also others of the immortals too were vitally linked to the sea and even, in some cases, as the Homeric passage shows regarding Apollo, to the sea gathered around the promontory at Sounion. Considering also, however, the complex identity of Apollo and especially his connection with light and the sun, this passage serves, in addition, to indicate that the site of the temple is distinctively related not only to the sea but to the elements at large.

Yet the great temple, erected on the highest plot of ground in the entire region, has a unique relation to Poseidon; and as a temple of Poseidon its character is preeminently determined by the sea, precisely as it is set high above on the rocky promontory. It is known that a sculpted figure of Poseidon once stood in the *sekos*, the middle chamber of the temple, though today no trace of it remains. For the ancients, such sculpted figures were not mere representations of the gods, not mere copies or images showing how the gods looked, displaying their appearance, compensating thereby for the incapacity of humans for actually beholding the all-too-elusive gods. Rather, the sculpted figure served for enacting the placement of the god in the temple, his being offered the temple as a place where he was invited to enter and where, now and then, in his own elusive manner, he might reside. Just as the magnificent elevated site paid honor to the god, so the precipitous drop to the rocks and sea below displayed at this very site the destructiveness that Poseidon with his trident could unleash. Through the installing of the sculpted figure in the temple erected to house it, the god was invited to be present in the temple, was offered this presence in the hope, no doubt, that his graciousness rather than his destructiveness would prevail. In this sense, the sculpted figure was nothing other than the god himself, his very way of being present in the temple.

But what, then, about the sea? How is it that the god who could come to be present in the temple remained, even when present there, the god of the sea? What does Poseidon—as the ancients experienced his presence—have to do with the sea?

It does not suffice to say that Poseidon inhabits the sea and reigns there like a king. For in this case, there would be no need for mortals to build a habitation for the god; the temple and its sacred precinct would be entirely superfluous. Also, whereas for a king it is essential that he be beheld in all his glorious presence, Poseidon is, like all gods, perpetually elusive, hardly to be seen at all and often, if seen, seen only in some disguise or other. Nonetheless, mortals must somehow have caught sight of him even if only in a fleeting moment; otherwise they would erect no temple into which to invite the god and in which to celebrate his presence. Where, then, will the god have been caught sight of? Where will shortsighted mortals have caught a glimpse of Poseidon? Where will their fleeting glance have chanced upon the transient presence of the god? There is no other place than the sea. Poseidon is god of the sea, not because he would reign there as the godly analogue of a king, but rather because the sea is the place of his evanescent presence, the place where, on rare occasions, he lets humans catch sight of him. The sea is his element: not only *an* element, something elemental in distinction from mere things, but *his* element, the element in which he remains even as he comes to be present in the temple. Poseidon belongs to the depth of the sea, not just depth as opposed to surface, but depth in the sense of hidden retreat, of withdrawal into the utterly indefinite. There in his element the god remains unexposed to mortal eyes, withholds all offers of presence. And yet, from out of his element, from out of the depth of the sea, the god can unaccountably and fugitively appear. It is in such fleeting appearance that the Greeks experienced the most purely mythical.

Because the sea is his element, his appearance—fleeting though it be—can give one a glimpse of the true character of the sea. In the god, in the deeds that the poets revere as his, there is concentrated the graciousness and the destructiveness that belong to the thalassic element, that are bound together in its elemental character. While welcoming the god into the temple and celebrating his presence there may calm the disquieting element, these enactments never simply supersede the glimpse into the depth; neither do they silence the poets' songs of the god's deeds, but, on the contrary, they evoke, amplify, them.

Though the temple is set overlooking the sea, its height above the sea is such that the god can enter it only by coming forth from the depth, yet without ever abandoning his element. Coming to presence in the darkened interior of the brilliantly illuminated temple, the god, glimpsed fleetingly, grants to mortals a momentary vision of other elements in their manifold concurrences with the sea.

Such glimpses, such visions, were granted—so they attest—to the Greeks.

And yet, now, one will say, the Greek gods—perhaps all gods—are dead. To whatever visions may have been granted to the ancients, we today, so it seems, can only remain blind.

And yet—

There, at that site, wonder may be evoked, wonder whether, in the presence of what remains of the temple, one can experience only the absence of the god, only the ruin of everything once sacred. Or whether, in envisioning the great temple that once stood overlooking the sea at Sounion, in engaging oneself imaginatively so as to let the temple take form from the traces that remain there, one can again experience the absolutely archaic. As the temple again takes shape—if now imaginatively—rising from the ruins at the very site where it once stood overlooking the sea and welcoming the brilliant Greek sunlight, can one sense the fleeting appearance of an origin of origins silently summoning from beyond what seems only closure?

10

Withdrawal Symptoms: David Farrell Krell and the Solitude of a Body Born of Chaos

Michael Naas

I am alone. Says he or says she. I am alone. —Jacques Derrida[1]

We had planned the course together for months and there was no way I was about to go it alone. It was an opportunity we had long anticipated, both because of the topic of the course and because of its venue—the International College of Philosophy in Paris. It was there that David Farrell Krell and I became reacquainted after a first meeting at the Collegium Phaenomenologicum some two years before, and there that David and I in March 1987 attended an event that would become a point of reference for us both, an international conference on Heidegger where Jacques Derrida would present the entirety of his magnificent *Of Spirit*. The International College of Philosophy was thus an institution that had become dear to us both, the perfect place to offer, in April and May of 1999, a team-taught course on Plato's *Statesman* and the works of Hölderlin, a follow-up to our earlier team-taught seminars at DePaul University on *Phaedrus* and *Timaeus*. But when David fell ill in early spring 1999 and was unable to travel to Paris (fortunately it turned out not to be serious), the course had to be cancelled. I briefly considered trying to do it without him, but with Hölderlin on the menu I soon realized the folly of trying to go it alone.

Here is how the course was advertised—the language mostly David Krell's, and the rough translation from French to English mine:

Chaos, Kronos, Zeus: From Plato's Politikos to the Age of Hölderlin

The central myth of Plato's Politikos is that of the Ages of Kronos and Zeus, both of them emerging out of the chaos that gives birth to the human body. We will examine [in this course] the points of intersection between temporality, historicity, and the political, against the backdrop of both divinity—in its

Olympian and Titanic forms—and incarnated mortality. We will evaluate the significance of this myth from the Politikos in relation to a whole host of other Platonic myths (in Phaedo, Phaedrus, Republic, and Symposium, for example, though also in the developments concerning the demiourgos and ananke in Timaeus). We will then look at how the literary and philosophical career of Friedrich Hölderlin can be interpreted as a detailed engagement with this myth of the Politikos. From Hyperion (1792–1796) to The Death of Empedocles (1797–1800), and even right up to the later poems and Tragedies of Sophocles (1803–1804), Hölderlin remained fascinated by the myth of chaos, Kronos, and Zeus. Along with the narrative of the ancestry of Eros in the Symposium, the myth of the Politikos serves as a constant point of reference for Hölderlin's poetic and critical works. Our project will thus consist in going back and forth between the age of Greek tragedy and philosophy and the more Hesperian age of modernity as a way of posing questions concerning our own histories, our time, and our bodies born of chaos.

So that was the trajectory; we would alternate primary responsibility for lecturing from one session to the next; there would be two sessions a week for five weeks— an entire seminar on Plato's myths, particularly the myth of the two ages in the *Statesman*, and the reading and development of it in Hölderlin. But since the seminar never took place, it itself now belongs to a mythical or imaginary past, and all I can do today is speculate about what might have been. I know pretty well what I would have done, but as for David Krell, all I can do is speculate on the basis of what he has written before and after that ill-fated venture. All I can do today, living in our Age of Zeus, as it were, is to try to imagine what might have been in that Age of Kronos.

In what follows, I would like to indulge in such speculation not in order to recover some lost past but so as to explain the unique intellectual itinerary of David Farrell Krell. My hypothesis will be that a reading of Krell on Plato, and particularly the *Statesman*, along with Hölderlin and a few other privileged Germans on Plato, will tell us just about everything about Krell's unique set of interests, his views about philosophy, and the very methodology he believes most urgent for philosophy or thinking today. I would thus like to show that this seminar that never took place will have nonetheless left traces throughout Krell's entire oeuvre, teaching us a great deal about how to rethink a certain family scene in order to return to a body born of chaos, and about what happens to that body when the Father of the family withdraws or retires from the scene.

If our team-taught course at the International College of Philosophy would have been, in many ways, unique, unpredictable and unrepeatable, it is nonetheless not impossible to imagine how Krell would have at least begun a reading of Plato, whether in the company of Hölderlin or on Plato's "own terms." For if Krell's engagement with and investment in Plato has been marked, mediated, and inflected by his reading and engagement with, say, Heidegger, Nietzsche, Schelling, and Hölderlin, Krell has also been—and from very early on—a reader of Plato in his own right. A work such as *Of Memory, Reminiscence, and Writing: On the Verge* (1990) is enough to demonstrate that David Krell never needed the encouragement of others to go back to Plato.[2] This monumental book on the question of memory treats figures ranging from Derrida, Merleau-Ponty, Heidegger, Freud, and Nietzsche to Hegel, Descartes, Augustine, Aristotle, and, especially, Plato. Indeed the book returns again and again to Plato's tropes of writing and inscription in relationship to memory in *Theaetetus*, *Sophist*, and *Timaeus*, though also in *Republic*, *Phaedrus*, *Cratylus*, *Parmenides*, *Philebus*, *Symposium*, *Meno*, *Phaedo*, *Laws*, and, briefly, in *Statesman* (*MRW* 33, 190).[3]

But almost two decades before this great book on memory, David Krell had already made his mark as an original and inspired reader of Plato. Two of Krell's first four published essays in the early 1970s are on Plato, and these were soon followed by his important essay "Female Parts in *Timaeus*," where Krell not only took on the question of sexual difference in Plato but already anticipated by about a dozen years Derrida's focus on that part of the *Timaeus*—and whether it is a "female part" or not is precisely the question—that goes by the name of *khōra*.[4] Considering everything Krell would go on to write about Derrida, about *khōra* and Derrida's influential essay on *khōra*, the opening lines of this 1975 essay appear more than prescient:

> If the importance of the receptacle in Plato's *Timaeus* is granted there is no need to belabor the point that female parts play a role in that dialogue. How central a role is debatable—like virtually every other topic concerning *Timaeus*. ("FP" 400)[5]

From this point on, almost all of Krell's works make use of Plato's dialogues and assume in his reader an intimate knowledge of them. What was just said about *Of Memory, Reminiscence, and Writing* could thus also be said about a work such as *Lunar Voices: Of Tragedy, Poetry, Fiction, and Thought* (1995),[6] where Krell has important, original readings of *Philebus* (*LV* 136), *Symposium* (*LV* xiii, 88), and, especially, *Timaeus*, with its references to Egypt (*LV* 46), "bastard reasoning" (*LV* 134 n.14), and, again, *khōra* (*LV* 137).

David Krell has thus never needed Hölderlin or Schelling, Nietzsche or Heidegger, to return to Plato, though it is in fact often under the tutelage of these favorite Germans that Krell returns to his favorite Greeks. To get back to Plato, to motivate or accelerate the return to ancient Greece, Krell often begins with a reading of Plato in nineteenth- or twentieth-century German philosophy—for example, working backward in time, in Heidegger. In *Intimations of Mortality: Time, Truth, and Finitude in Heidegger's Thinking of Being* (1986), Krell demonstrates the crucial role played by Plato in Heidegger's thinking.[7] For Heidegger, Plato marks the beginning of a certain epoch of metaphysics and, thus, the beginning of a certain understanding of being (*IM* 33–35).[8] As such, Krell shows Heidegger returning to Plato for his thinking of the being of nonbeing in the *Sophist* (*IM* 69, 76, 100), of the instant, *to exaiphnēs*, the *Augenblick* in *Parmenides* (*IM* 49–50), and of beauty in *Phaedrus* (*IM* 59).[9]

From rather early on, then, Krell's engagement with Plato will have been in part in response to Heidegger's own engagement with Plato, even if Krell ends up treating subjects that might have made Heidegger blush—female parts, sexual difference, in short, the entire question of what Krell might have called, following Derrida's reading of Heidegger this time, *Geschlecht*.[10] Heidegger will have thus been—or will have become in the course of the 1980s and 1990s—a constant companion in Krell's reading of Plato. Heidegger, but then also, still moving backward, Nietzsche, in works such as *The Good European*,[11] or else *Postponements: Women, Sensuality, and Death in Nietzsche* (1986), the title of which alone is enough to indicate what in Plato will be of interest to Krell: death, sensuality, and, once again, woman and female parts.[12] It is thus the role of Diotima in the *Symposium* that draws Krell's attention in this work (*P* 38–39) and, again, the question of *khōra* and "feminine distance"—just one more theme that will put Krell into conversation with Derrida.[13]

But if Heidegger and Nietzsche would have no doubt been in the background of Krell's reading of Plato during our course in Paris in 1999, Hölderlin would have been front and center. Clues to what Krell would have done with Hölderlin are scattered throughout his corpus, but several are concentrated in *The Tragic Absolute: German Idealism and the Languishing God* (2005).[14] As we can glean from this work, Krell would have no doubt speculated on Hölderlin's planned but never completed commentaries on *Symposium* and *Phaedrus* (*TA* 20, 43, 212, 218), on the relationship, for example, between Beauty and Eros in these dialogues (*TA* 35), and he would have spoken of the "wizened sage" who, in Hölderlin's *Hyperion*, "communicates the doctrine of Plato's Socrates in *Symposium*" (*TA* 57).

As for Krell's interest in the *Statesman*, his almost obsessive return to it over the last two decades, this too will have come in large part, it seems, from

Hölderlin. In *The Recalcitrant Art: Diotima's Letters to Hölderlin and Related Missives*, Krell (a.k.a. Kenny) tells us that "[Hölderlin's] favorite Platonic myth is of the two ages of the world, the reign of Zeus and the reign of Kronos, spinning out and then back again on a string suspended from some Titanic finger poised in Chaos" (*RA* 242). Even when Krell reads Hölderlin on Antigone, Plato and his *Statesman* are never very far away. Hence Krell interprets Hölderlin as having, in effect, subjected Antigone to the fate of humans during the mythical age of Kronos, insofar as "Antigone grows younger and more blindingly beautiful as the play proceeds. It is as though she were a creature of that Golden Age presided over by Zeus and Kronos, the age recounted in the myth of Plato's *Statesman* (*TA* 388).[15]

In all these works we see that what draws Krell most to Plato is not the account of right opinion in the *Meno* but the question of sexual difference, the presence of Plato's women, Diotima in *Symposium*, Aspasia in *Menexenus*, and the role played by female parts and *khōra* in the *Timaeus*.[16] But then Krell's repeated return to *Statesman* appears all the more strange, for, unlike *Symposium* or *Menexenus*, there are no female characters in this dialogue and, unlike *Timaeus*, there is no real emphasis on the feminine or on female parts. If anything, the *Statesman* myth is a story of fathers and sons, with no real reference to mothers or daughters or women in general. To explain Krell's interest or investment in this myth, we will thus need to look at the role played by these fathers in the dialogue and at their relationship to a universe that is, as Krell put it a moment ago, "poised in Chaos," a moment that, as he will demonstrate, defies the authority and legitimacy of all these fathers.

Though Krell was a reader of Plato in his own right, he often returned to Plato, as we have seen, under the tutelage of Heidegger, Nietzsche, and Hölderlin, these German "fathers" who will have all pointed back in some way to what comes before the father—whether to female parts, *khōra* or *chaos*. But it is really Schelling, it seems, who leads Krell toward this latter. In several of Krell's descriptions of the myth of the two ages in the *Statesman*, even those ostensibly related to Hölderlin, the reference to *chaos* suggests that it is Schelling who is always lurking in the background. While his name is not even mentioned in our abstract for that cancelled course of 1999, *The Tragic Absolute* suggests that it is even more Schelling's than Hölderlin's reading of Plato, and particularly of the *Statesman*, that has animated Krell over the past two decades. In addition to a commentary on the *Timaeus*, which Krell knows well (see *TA* 74, 81, 91 n.16, 116), the author of *The Ages of the World* wrote explicitly about the *Statesman* and its myth of the two ages. Krell comments on this reading in *The Tragic Absolute* in terms that echo our abstract from 1999: "Even the primal time of Chaos—out of which, according to the myth of Plato's *Statesman*, both the Titanic-Olympian age (dominated by Kronos and Zeus) and the anthropological age (in which no god or titan guides humankind) arise—is haunted by a still more primordial past" (*TA* 131). Hence "the problem of 'The Past,'" in Schelling, "thought as the remote, elevated past, is the problem of the preworldly time of Chaos" (*TA* 206; see 124). Krell's reading of *chaos* as what—as the course abstract put it—"gave birth to the human body" seems to have come, therefore, not from Heidegger, Nietzsche, or Hölderlin, but, precisely, from Schelling, for *chaos*, which is mentioned just once in Plato—in the *Symposium* rather than the *Timaeus* or the *Statesman*—is central only to Schelling's reading of this latter dialogue.[17] It is from Schelling, it seems, that Krell gets the interpretation of the Age of Kronos not as a time when human bodies were more divine than they are now, a time when they did not die, only grow younger and then perish, but as a time of Chaos when they were dissolute and not yet ordered or organized.[18]

The Tragic Absolute demonstrates once again Krell's unique orientation with regard to Plato. What interests Krell most is, again, not so much the elenchus, not the pursuit of the Forms, not the differences between knowledge, right opinion, and ignorance, not politics, not so much Plato's critique of the arts, but madness, sexuality, female parts—the female neck and throat, for example— and the memory of an immemorial time. And as *The Tragic Absolute* makes abundantly clear, these interests are also Schelling's. Krell writes, for example, as he follows Schelling's readings of *Symposium*, *Timaeus*, and *Statesman*:

> Figures of the feminine come to play an extraordinary role in the three drafts of the *Die Weltalter* and in *Über die Gottheiten von Samothrake*. It would take pages and pages of analysis to do these figures justice. Allow me here simply to catalogue a few of them. Woman, in Schelling's texts, is both Isis . . . and Penia, the "Poverty" of Plato's *Symposium*. She is mother and nurse. (*TA* 176)[19]

The feminine, the female body, the body in general—these interests of Krell's were also and from the beginning Schelling's. As Krell will go on to argue, Schelling's lectures on aesthetics "offer a complete portrait of the body, with Plato's *Timaeus* serving as the model" (*TA* 163). It is also Schelling who ventures to think the notion of *chaos*, which he had attributed to the *Statesman*, in relation to the *khōra* of the *Timaeus*, which Krell will have been himself following since at least 1975, that is, well before his explicit engagement with Schelling. Hence Schelling speculates, in Krell's summary, that "Hesiodic *chaos* is precisely what Plato's *Timaeus* means by *khōra*, traditionally understood as space and elementality in one, the mother and matrix . . . of all sensible things" (*TA* 401). This was, it has to be said, an interpretation for which Krell would have been amply prepared and to which he would have been wholly receptive, since in "Female Parts in *Timaeus*" he himself already spoke of a "cosmos born of chaos" ("FP" 415), even though the word *chaos* does not appear in the *Timaeus* any more than it does in the *Statesman*. Even more than Hölderlin, Nietzsche, and Heidegger, Schelling would have led Krell back to himself, as it were, as a reader of Plato.

Krell would have also found in Schelling a kindred spirit in his focus on sexual difference and on a certain way of resisting the Platonic interpretation of it. As Krell puts it in *The Tragic Absolute*, Schelling "break[s] with the long-standing tradition inaugurated by Plato's *Timaeus* when he suggests that the female sex comes first" (*TA* 133).[20] Such a break or reversal is one that Krell himself carries out when he reads just about any figure—not just Plato. When Krell thus turns to the *Iliad*, to cite just a single example, he will be less interested in Achilles, Hector, or Agamemnon than Briseïs (see *RA* 202–5, 209)—the first in a long line of women in Krell's work, from Sophie and Susette to Molly and Caddy, and the list goes on.[21] Like Schelling, Krell is thus always attentive to the role and place of women in literature and philosophy, in writing in general, right down to his rightful insistence on retaining the maternal *Farrell* at the center of his own name, and right down, as we have seen, to his reading of Plato, of Plato as a father.

What this reading of Krell on Plato is beginning to reveal is something much more than a mere history or genealogy of Krell's references and interests. It is beginning to reveal something essential about Krell's understanding and interpretation of the entire history of philosophy, a history that, to put it in a word, has always neglected the mother and female parts in the name of the father. It is thus all the more significant that the one myth Krell will have concentrated on, often with the help of Hölderlin and, especially, Schelling, will have been a story of fathers. Plato's myth of the two ages in the *Statesman* is first and foremost a family romance of fathers, of Father Zeus and his father, Father Kronos. Krell thus follows this myth, in the company of Schelling, in order to subvert it, always on the lookout for traces within the discourse of Father Plato of the female who will have come before the male and of the body in chaos before the ordering of the father. In a letter of Sophie LaRoche in *The Recalcitrant Art*, Plato is explicitly called "Father Plato" a father who will award Aspasia the laurels of rhetoric for her discourse about Athens and about women who imitate the earth: "Wieland told me that even Father Plato made her the spokeswoman for an entire dialogue of his—he said the name, but I didn't recognize it—in which Plato explains that women imitate the Earth, that we are the verdant source and the nurture of all that is" (*RA* 135; see *A* 35).[22]

This emphasis on the father—and what resists the father or threatens to upset his reign—is present as far back as "Female Parts in *Timaeus*," where Krell remarks that Timaeus—though not necessarily Plato—comes to hold a "patrogenic view" that makes him "despise and fear the female parts" ("FP" 414). Krell returns to this theme in conjunction once again with *khōra* in *Daimon Life* (*DL* 125), and then again in *Archeticture: Ecstasies of Space, Time, and the Human Body* (1997), where it becomes a guiding motif. In this book, written and published about a decade after Derrida's "*Khōra*," Krell tries to think the relationship between the Demiurge of the *Timaeus*, the Demiurge as father, artificer, and architect of the cosmos, and *khōra* as what would come before this father.[23] Krell there refers yet again to Father Plato, to the metaphysical underpinnings of the father's reign and a structure of duplicity that could take it all down: "For the original is merely the image of a duplicitous structure, the metaphysical structure of image-versus-original, and there are many who say that Father Plato himself gave us all the comic sensibility we need in order to be shaken out of the dream of originals once and for all" (*A* 172; see also *PB* 210). What becomes central, then, in Krell's reading of Plato, is the focus on a certain family scene and on the question of sexual difference as what disrupts that scene, a focus that had begun, as we saw, some two decades earlier in "Female Parts in *Timaeus*."

What Krell aims to attack or dismantle through this emphasis on female parts and figures of the feminine is thus nothing less than the legitimacy of Father Plato, even when the weapons used to carry out the attack are borrowed from the Father himself. When we read in *The Good European* that Nietzsche in *Beyond Good and Evil* "took on the entire tradition of Western metaphysics and morals since Plato" (*GE* 140), we are no doubt licensed to conclude that Krell's ambitions with regard to Plato—to Father Plato—are no less great.[24] What Krell would have thus learned from Nietzsche, though also from Hölderlin and Schelling, is the necessity not of returning to tragedy but of relearning how to philosophize again, like the ancients, in a "tragic" mode (*IM* 176). Krell's work on Schelling, Hölderlin, Nietzsche, and even Heidegger is in large part an attempt to philosophize in this tragic mode.

What is at issue in Krell's reading of Plato is thus nothing less than the past and future of metaphysics—or ontotheology—itself. In a footnote in *The Tragic Absolute* Krell gives us one of his clearest accounts of what is at stake for him in rethinking the legacy of Plato and the reason for questioning the structure of legitimation that Plato will have instituted:

What concerns me in the *closure of ontotheology* that is commencing in Schelling, Hölderlin, Novalis, and others at the end of the eighteenth century is not so much the "reinvention" of tragedy, or the shift from tragedy to "the tragic," but the need to interpret anew virtually everything we have assumed to be "Platonic" or "Aristotelian" in and about the tradition—and this by reading the texts of Plato and Aristotle in a manner that can only trouble interpreters who accept without disquiet their own Platonistic or Scholastic formation. Likewise, we should anticipate that the *end(s) of metaphysics as possibility* will enable us to experience the tragedies of Aeschylus, Sophocles, and Euripides in utterly new ways. The tragic absolute may not reinvent Plato, Aristotle, and the tragedians, but it will open the texts of antiquity to unanticipated and compelling readings—after which we will be less certain than ever about the very distinction between antiquity and modernity, the Greek and the Hesperian, the "ancient narratives" and our contemporary predicaments. (*TA* 184n4)

This is an extraordinary programmatic statement—uttered almost as an aside, in a footnote. It suggests that opening Plato and Aristotle to unanticipated readings will tell us something about our time and ourselves, about our own bodies, I would hazard to suggest, born of chaos. That would have been, as we see from the final lines of our abstract from 1999, the primary aim of our course. Krell knows well that Plato "construct[ed] his entire polity—not merely in one of its particulars but from top to bottom—in opposition to tragedy" (*TA* 280), to say nothing of the mourning and tears associated with women and tragedy. And yet there are many elements within Plato's dialogues—and Krell's ability to ferret them out is second to none—that at once underscore this subjugation of the tragic and the feminine and allow the feminine to subvert—and perhaps even tragically—the paternal order from within. In other words, there is something within the work of Father Plato that undermines the legitimating signature of the father. As Krell argues in *The Purest of Bastards*, "not even Plato's (literary and doxographic) signature is fully accomplished and fully *underwritten*, as it were, although a long and august philosophical tradition feels confident that it can recognize the marks of his signature, the distinguishing marks of his work" (*PB* 12; see 20). It is up to us then, it seems, not to accomplish this signature but to discover—to invent—new readings that will risk "illegitimacy, forgery, bastardy, and patricide" (*PB* 12). That is why Krell will call Derrida—playing in part on the *bastard* reasoning required in *Timaeus* for speaking of *khōra*—"the purest of bastards."[25]

Krell is thus always rethinking legacy and legitimation through his rereading of Plato. He is always reading in Plato a family scene, remaining always attentive to the role of women in the story, the role of the body, the body in general, to be sure, and especially female parts. This emphasis is motivated by Krell's desire to think outside or beyond the legitimate and legitimizing couple of the father and son, his desire to think the chaos that precedes this ordering couple. Krell thus rejects the family scene of a certain Plato—of Father Plato—where legitimacy and legacy are established between father and son to the exclusion of the mother and daughter and of the feminine in general. He embraces the Plato who speaks—even if in spite of himself—of the role and place of female parts, female figures, female generation, and of a reign before the reign of the Olympians and even of the Titans. That is why Krell—following Schelling—wishes to read Chaos into the myth of Father and Son, Kronos and Zeus, in *Statesman*, Chaos as what would have preceded this entire patriarchal order.

This is also perhaps why Krell's own method is always to move forward in order to move back, back to Heidegger, to Nietzsche, to Hölderlin and to Schelling in order to think our present or else the future of philosophy. And it is why he not only speaks in so many places of this myth of the *Statesman* where time goes forward in the one age and backward in the other but himself uses the strange temporality of this myth to structure one of his own narratives, the magnificent *Nietzsche: A Novel*.[26] If, as Krell suggests in the preface, madness is "a kind of eternal recurrence of the same, albeit with reversals of direction," then the best way to depict Nietzsche's madness is perhaps to let the narrative itself undergo such a reversal. Krell thus begins the novel in 1889, with Nietzsche's breakdown in Turin, and then moves simultaneously forward in time, up to Nietzsche's death in 1900, and backward to review Nietzsche's works and friendships, his childhood and, eventually, his birth in 1844. As we read in the preface, it "is a story about Nietzsche's ten years of madness, years that allow us to catch crazy glimpses of the forty-five productive years that preceded them" (*NN* ix). Moving both forward and backward, Krell's *Nietzsche* is itself mad, for what it attempts to elicit through these "crazy glimpses" is not just Nietzsche's ten mad years and the forty-five productive years before them but, in essence, an archaic time of the body in chaos. Krell's narrative thus owes even more to Plato than it does to Faulkner, even if the time of the archaic body is precisely a time of sound and fury at the limits of signification. It is here then, significantly, in the preface to *Nietzsche: A Novel*, that Krell gives us his most complete retelling of the myth that would have been central to our 1999 course at the International College of Philosophy in Paris:

In a dialogue called *Statesman*, Plato has the Stranger tell of the two great eras that make up human history. We now live under the reign of Zeus, a reign that spins out like a top on a string, except that the top is really a yo-yo: when the world spins out to the end of its tether it does not fly off into space but whirls back again to its point of origin, and the second era, the era of regress, is called the reign of Kronos. On the backspin to the origins—to the archaic time of Chaos and the body that precedes both the divine and the titanic reigns—everything seems to be topsy-turvy. People are born as cadavers out of the earth, they grow younger instead of older, their hoary heads take on color, their skin gets softer every day, and like truly rational creatures they learn to talk with the animals. The two reigns or eras enact a kind of eternal recurrence of the same, albeit with reversals of direction. Perhaps that is what madness is like: the backspin gives us all of life once again, all the way back beyond our beginnings in infancy, everything the same, only upside-down and inside out, as fusions and confusions of a primeval body. (*NN* ix)

Once again, Krell's emphasis is on the body in Chaos. The Age of *Kronos*, for *Krell*, is a time of *Khaos*—and not, as others would interpret it, a utopian golden age where no one dies, where there is no war, no need for labor and toil, where man and animals are taken care of by the gods. Rather than identifying the Age of Zeus with the Olympians and the Age of Kronos with the Titans, with nothing coming *before* these two ages, Krell speaks instead of an "archaic time of Chaos and the body that precedes both the divine and the titanic reigns." In this archaic time, everything would be, says Krell, "topsy turvey"—as if the universe and the body were subject to an uncontrollable alteration and alternation, as if this archaic time underwent not a movement forward and then backward, backward and then forward, but an uncontrollable and unpredictable alternation between the two. In the beginning, there would have been an archaic time without beginning or end, without direction or orientation, a time before Father Time, before time altogether. The reigns of Kronos and of Zeus will have thus eventually come to give order to this archaic time, all the while leaving traces of that archaic past, those moments of transition, precisely, when, according to Plato's myth, "the universe was turned back" and there was a terrible collision, as "beginning and end [*archēs te kai teleutēs*] rushed in opposite directions" (*Statesman* 273a).[27]

The *Statesman* myth would help explain why, in Krell's own works, every reading is a return and a reversal, a lurch backward that attempts not just to question received ideas or assumptions but to evoke or reinvest the body born of chaos. Had our course at the International College of Philosophy gone off as planned, we would have no doubt ourselves gone back and forth between Plato and Hölderlin, Plato and Schelling, with Derrida—the Derrida of "*Khōra*" and of *Of Spirit*—always hovering somewhere in between. We would have gone back and forth between these figures, though also, from one session to the next, back and forth between ourselves.[28] Were anyone tempted, however, to see a narrative unfolding in this alternation, Krell would have been the first to interrupt it. There would have been instead the betrayal of filiation, bastard discourse, absent thirds, and interrupted legacies. It would have thus been impossible to assign roles, in the end, since he would have been much more than Kronos and I much less than Zeus. And I suspect that at times chaos would have reigned as well.

What makes possible this return to the body in Chaos is, as I have argued, a constant questioning of the authority and legitimacy of the father and the son, though also, it should be said, the father's withdrawal or retirement—a retirement that, on this reading, would have happened *from the beginning* in order to give human mortality its space and its time. It is a point Krell does not underscore in his recounting of Plato's myth, though it is crucial and it supports his entire reading. It is the moment when, at the end of the Age of Kronos— the mythical age before our own—the Demiurge takes his hand off the universe he has been steering, off the tiller, says Plato, in order to let the universe spin of its own accord in the opposite direction. This marks the beginning of the Age of Zeus—the beginning of our time, the beginning of an age where humans are born of one another rather than out of the ground, the onset of our age of death, sensuality, and intimations of mortality. It is at this moment that the Demiurge—who seems to be identified with Kronos, though the identification is not explicit—withdraws or retires to a place of outlook, not so much in order to watch the human drama of mortality unfold below him but in order, simply, to give human time its chance, or more simply still, in order to give humans *room*—Krell's brilliantly simple translation of *khōra* some four decades ago in "Female Parts in *Timaeus*." As Plato tells it, when the time for this transition had come "the helmsman [*kybernētēs*] of the universe dropped the tiller and withdrew to his place of outlook, and fate and innate desire made the earth turn backwards" (272e).

The Demiurge retreats, retires, and all the other gods do the same, leaving humans to their own devices—to procreate on their own, to practice the arts in order to stave off death from the elements and the animals, which are no longer as mild or as tame as they once were. It is up to humans now to govern themselves, no longer under the protection of the gods, and to give some meaning and order to their time, to invent filiations and legacies, even if the

Demiurge knows that this order—this order of life and death—is only for a time. In the absence of Kronos, humans are left to their own creative solitudes and their own intimations of mortality.

A certain retreat or retirement will have thus made space—made room—for the entire realm of the simulacrum, for fathers and sons, though also mothers and daughters, who must now live—though this will have in essence happened from the beginning—in the father's absence, and only for a time. This withdrawal is accompanied not by some contemplative satisfaction after the creation of a world but by the resigned knowledge that there will be order for a time and then chaos again. That would be the lesson of Plato's myth. As Krell interprets it in the light of Schelling, what we lose along with the father's authority and paternal presence is nothing less than the order and integrity of the living body. The body born of chaos is thus always, in the wake of the father's retreat, plunged back into chaos, as beginning and end rush in opposite directions—a state as frightening as it is exhilarating. It's enough to give you the shakes, which is always the first sign of serious withdrawal.

Notes

1   Jacques Derrida, *The Beast and the Sovereign, Volume II*, trans. Geoffrey Bennington (Chicago: University of Chicago Press, 2011), 1.

2   *Of Memory, Reminiscence, and Writing: On the Verge* (Bloomington: Indiana University Press, 1990); hereafter abbreviated as *MRW*.

3   Right in the middle of *Of Memory, Reminiscence, and Writing* there is a section entitled "Plato's Dream," essentially a reading of Derrida's reading in *Of Grammatology* and "Plato's Pharmacy" of Plato's critique of writing in the *Phaedrus* (*MRW* 187–204).

4   Socrates's "Body," *The Southern Journal of Philosophy*, vol. X, no. 4 (Winter 1972): 443–451, and "On Reading Plato (After Nietzsche)," *Topic: A Journal of the Liberal Arts*, vol. 28 (Autumn 1974): 33–49. "Female Parts in *Timaeus*," *Arion: A Journal of Humanities and the Classics*, n. s., no. 2 (1975): 400–21; hereafter abbreviated "FP." "*Khōra*," trans. Ian McLeod, in *On the Name* (Stanford, CA: Stanford University Press,1993), 87–127; *Khōra* (Paris: Éditions Galilée, 1993); first version published in *Poikilia: Études offertes à Jean-Pierre Vernant* (Paris: Éditions de l'EHESS, 1987), 265–96.

5   In the footnotes to "Female Parts in *Timaeus*," Heidegger's reading of Plato's *khōra* in *Introduction to Metaphysics* is already cited (421 n.14).

6   *Lunar Voices: Of Tragedy, Poetry, Fiction, and Thought* (Chicago: University of Chicago Press, 1995); hereafter abbreviated as *LV*.

7   *Intimations of Mortality: Time, Truth, and Finitude in Heidegger's Thinking of Being* (University Park: The Pennsylvania State University Press, 1986); hereafter abbreviated as *IM*.

8   See *IM* 5, 27, 33–35, 115, 139, 144, 151, 166.

9   Krell also looks at Heidegger's interpretation of the famous myth of the cave of *Republic* (*IM* 89). Krell will later write in *The Purest of Bastards: Works of Mourning, Art, and Affirmation in the Thought of Jacques Derrida* (University Park: The Pennsylvania State University Press, 2000), hereafter abbreviated as *PB*, the "allegory of the *Republic* . . . serves as an 'icon' of all blindness and insight in Western art and letters up to and including the back room of 'Plato's Pharmacy'" (*PB* 76).

Six years later, we see the same emphasis on Heidegger's reading of Plato in *Daimon Life: Heidegger and Life-Philosophy* (Bloomington: Indiana University Press, 1992); hereafter abbreviated as *DL*. Krell refers to Heidegger's interpretation, at the end of his 1942–43 Parmenides lecture course, of the myth of Er of the *Republic* (*DL* 301) and to the way Heidegger ends his first lecture course on Nietzsche with a reading of *Phaedrus* (*DL* 230, 235). There are also references throughout *Daimon Life* to Plato, to *Cratylus* (20), *Sophist* (49), *Parmenides* (101), the *Seventh Letter* (101), and, of course, the Aristophanes myth of *Symposium* (187). See also *Lunar Voices* 57–58 and 107 where Heidegger's reading of Plato is again at issue.

10   Krell evokes Derrida's *Geschlecht I* in the penultimate footnote of *Intimations of Mortality*: "The most remarkable reflection on these matters I take to be Jacques Derrida, '*Geschlecht*: différence sexuelle, différence ontologique' . . ." (*IM* 190 n.17).

11   *The Good European: Nietzsche's Work Sites in Word and Image*, David Farrell Krell and Donald L. Bates (Chicago: University of Chicago Press, 1997); hereafter abbreviated as *GE*. In this work, Krell clearly takes delight in following Nietzsche's teaching and writing career, and especially where Plato is concerned. He thus evokes Nietzsche's teaching of Plato in the Gymnasium in Basel, citing a letter from 1869 where Nietzsche writes: "So far, it is a pleasure. Because we are reading [Plato's] *Phaedo*, I have the opportunity to infect my pupils with philosophy" (*GE* 108; see also 66, 69, 81, 98, 121 for references to Plato).

12   *Postponements: Women, Sensuality, and Death in Nietzsche* (Bloomington: Indiana University Press, 1986); hereafter abbreviated as *P*.

13   Krell thus already seems to be responding to Derrida's *Spurs: Nietzsche's Styles / Éperons: Les Styles de Nietzsche*, bilingual edition, trans. Barbara Harlow (Chicago: University of Chicago Press, 1979). Krell writes in *Postponements*: "The question of feminine distance, of the dream and risk of death, encompasses the entire problem of space and time, the problem of *proximation* as posed in the history of metaphysics, from the 'crater' or mixing bowl of Plato's *Timaeus* (the

'matrix' and 'nurse' of all genesis and the source of all madness and disease) to the phenomenology and poetics of Heidegger (the 'undistancing' of finite Dasein and the 'withdrawal' of Being as propriation)" (*P* 10; see also 41 and 73). Krell asks in this same work "whether and how Nietzsche successfully mates *aisthētikē* with *epistēmē*, that is, whether and how Nietzsche overcomes the strict segregation of these two in the universe of Plato's *Timaeus* and in the realm of subsequent metaphysics" (*P* 34).

14 *The Tragic Absolute: German Idealism and the Languishing God* (Bloomington: Indiana University Press, 2005); hereafter abbreviated as *TA*. Krell reads Hölderlin's *Death of Empedocles* with Plato's *Timaeus* and *Critias* in mind, speculating that Hölderlin would have had them in mind (see, e.g., *TA* 242 and 245). He also makes several references to the divine madness of *Phaedrus* (*TA* 132, 206, 360).

15 As Krell puts his thesis in the preface to *The Tragic Absolute*, "One may read *Antigone* as though Antigone herself were subject to the reign of Zeus and Kronos as portrayed in Plato's *Statesman*. For Antigone seems to grow ever younger and more tender as the rush of scenes takes her relentlessly to her womb-tomb. Like mother, like daughter" (*TA* 11).

16 *The Recalcitrant Art: Diotima's Letters to Hölderlin and Related Missives* (Albany: State University of New York Press, 2000); hereafter abbreviated as *RA*. Another letter of Sophie LaRoche makes reference to Aspasia from Plato's *Menexenus* (*RA* 135), and there are multiple references to Diotima from the *Symposium* (especially in the "Translators' Afterword: Children of Penury," 200–55).

17 "Schelling compares the mix of colors in fleshtones to the mix that occurred during the reign of *Chaos*, described in Plato's *Statesman* and Hesiod's *Theogony* as the eon in which the flesh of the human body itself originated" (*TA* 162). Krell recalls that the only reference to *chaos* in Plato is in the *Symposium*, as Phaedrus cites Hesiod on Love's venerable birth: "Hesiod says that Chaos came first into being— 'and thereafter rose / Broad-breasted Earth, sure seat of all for aye, / And Love'" (*Symposium* 178b).

18 Even when Krell is considering the way in which the *Statesman* myth "accompanies Hölderlin throughout the gestation-period of *Hyperion*," he seems to have Schelling's reading of the myth in mind: "The categorial *reversal* of time, along with the reversal of the eternal tendency in the direction of an earthbound, temporal tendency, may best be understood through a reading of the myth of Plato's *Statesman*, that is, the myth of the Golden Age, when human beings were still under the guidance of Kronos and Zeus" (*TA* 313).

19 Reading the myth told by Aristophanes in the *Symposium*, Schelling, not unlike Krell, comes to see that "in order to understand the nature of the forlorn we must

presuppose a prior union with what is now lost," "a sundering or separation [that] somehow precedes what is said to be initially unified" (*TA* 142; see also *PB* 212 for a reading of the Aristophanes myth).

20 The author of *Daimon Life* will have also found in Schelling a thinker of the *daimon*, of Dionysus as "a *daimōn* in Plato's sense," "a middle essence or middling creature, *ein Mittelwesen*, midway between sky and earth, immortals and mortals, and halfway between male and female" (*TA* 400 and 228).

21 This is yet another place of intersection between Krell's interests and my own. The chapter of *Daimon Life*, "Where Deathless Horses Weep," remains one of the most moving and insightful pieces ever written on the *Iliad*. It begins with the scene of Achilles' immortal horses weeping for Patroclus and then goes on to refer to a line from the *Iliad* on human tenderness that will be crucial for Krell in so much of his later work: "Human beings are like olive trees. Not the ancient trunks but the tender shoots thrusting from them" (*DL* 101). Death, mortality, mourning, tenderness— all these themes will have come in part from Homer, though also from Hölderlin (*Zärtlichkeit*, tenderness, will have been a favorite word of Hölderlin) and from Plato (once again in the *Symposium*, though this time it's more Pausanias' speech—and the distinction between heavenly and earthly love—than Aristophanes'). Krell thus writes in *The Purest of Bastards*: "In the second of his 'Contributions to the Psychology of Love Life,' Freud cites a widespread difficulty in the development of libido in Western culture, the difficulty of experiencing a love that is both *tender*, as tender as motherly care, and *sensual*, as disturbing and powerful as predatory Eros. He cites the ancients' division of love into heavenly and earthly aspects, the division that philosophers associate with the speech of Pausanias in Plato's *Symposium*. 'Where they love, they do not desire, and where they desire, they do not love' " (*PB* 63–64). See also Krell's "Tenderness: Aristotle, Hölderlin, Freud, Lacan, Irigaray," *Mosaic*, vol. 39, no. 1 (March 2006): 25–43, especially 39.

22 After noting that "Plato's *Menexenus* says (at 238a) that the Earth does not imitate women; rather, women, when they conceive, give birth, and nurture, imitate the Earth," he adds, "Perhaps both men and women—and even all third things—have to imitate women in this respect, who themselves imitate the Earth, not only in their bearing (in every sense) but also in their intelligence" (*A* 35).

23 *Archeticture: Ecstasies of Space, Time, and the Human Body* (Albany: State University of New York Press, 1997); see 5–6, 8, 9–37, 43, 135–40, 148, 162, 189–90 n.6, 198 n.2; hereafter abbreviated as *A*. See also 19 for a reference to *Sophist*, 113 for the *Phaedrus*, and 102–3 for a reading of Plato's myth of Er in the *Republic*.

24 Krell cites a letter of Nietzsche's from 1885 in which Nietzsche characterizes St. Augustine's *Confessions*: "Philosophical value = zero. *Platonism for the masses . . .*" (*PB* 180).

25 Krell writes of this theme of legitimacy in Derrida: "Derrida's genealogy of writing
in 'Plato's Pharmacy' is by now classic. If the *logos-père* is that-which-is, then
the *logos-fils*, mimicking that-which-is, writes itself in two forms or moments of
familial repetition. The traditional domesticity of being and *logos* depends on our
being able to distinguish between two repetitions of writing: the one sort of writing
is putatively originary, memorious, *endothen, für sich, ganz-bei-sich, chez soi*; the
other sort is derived and deprived, hypomnesic, *exothen*, extrinsic, estranged,
and errant" (*PB* 206). Near the end of *The Purest of Bastards*, Krell recounts this
anecdote: "I once asked Giorgio Agamben at the Collegium Phaenomenologicum
in Perugia (the year was 1987) whether the bastard reasoning of Plato's *Timaeus*,
which he was addressing in his seminar, might be more accessible to a 'real bastard'
than to a poet or thinker of *Gelassenheit*. Derrida turned to me and interjected: 'But
that is the problem, isn't it? What is a *real* or *true* bastard?

Herewith my response, somewhat delayed, but well considered" (*PB* 205).

26 *Nietzsche: A Novel* (Albany: State University of New York Press, 1996); hereafter
abbreviated as *NN*.

27 Plato, *Statesman*, trans. W. R. M. Lamb (Cambridge, MA: Harvard University
Press, 1975).

28 After the mid-1980s, Derrida would have also always been there, right along
with Schelling, Hölderlin, Nietzsche, and Heidegger. To cite just a single sign, the
dedication of Krell's 1992 *Daimon Life*: "*for jd for life*".

Hölderlin's Solitude

Françoise Dastur

Is solitude an unavoidable fate or the result of a choice? Does it define in an essential manner the individual human being or is it an experience that characterizes *par excellence* the modern way of existing? We know that at the beginning of modern times, Descartes placed the individual in the center of the philosophical way of thinking, opening thus the door to the extreme solipsism that can be found in Berkeley's philosophy. But the same affirmation of individualism can also be found later in Kierkegaard, who is considered as the father of existentialism. The solitude of existing has been further sustained by Levinas who, in one of his first books, explained that "the acuity of solitude" consists in "the indissoluble unity between the existent and its existing"[1] since "one can exchange everything between beings except existing."[2] This led him, as he said, "to repudiate the Heideggerian conception that views solitude in the midst of a prior relationship with the other," a conception which may be "anthropologically incontestable," but nevertheless "ontologically obscure."[3] For Levinas, the ontological obscurity of the Heideggerian conception of *Mitsein* as the fundamental structure of *Dasein* comes from the fact that the relation with the other is understood as a coexistence and not as this face-to-face relationship, which is, for him, the basis of all possible encounters with the other. But the face-to-face relationship presupposes that the "subject" who encounters the other is already constituted as "one," so that there is, for Levinas, "the existent's mastery over existing" which does not allow to understand solitude as a negative state, but rater "as a virility, a pride and sovereignty."[4]

Conversely, for Heidegger, the human being cannot be defined as ever having a mastery over its existing, since existing means for him primarily to be thrown into the world and thus be "with the other" in the sense that, as anthropological research actually shows, at the primary level of the everydayness, "others are not definite others" so that "one belongs to the others oneself."[5] For Heidegger, the "they" is the basis of the being "with" the other, of collectivity, and defines the level on which the existant is not yet a singular being. Becoming "properly" an existant is therefore only a "modification" of the primary impropriety of existence and this modification implies the assumption of one's own mortality. This is what happens in this singular "attunement" that is *Angst*, from which Heidegger says that it "individualizes and thus discloses *Dasein* as *solus ipse*."[6] But he immediately adds that this is an "existential solipsism" insofar as, instead of cutting off *Dasein* from the world and from the others, it brings it before itself as a being devoted to the world and being essentially dependent on it. Instead of seeing in solitude the "sovereignty" of the subject, as does subjective idealism, which Levinas seems here to follow, Heidegger sees in it an "authentic" experience of *Dasein*, which, as a finite being, can never be considered as an independent entity. Solitude, that is to say, the non-actual presence of the others, cannot, therefore, be opposed to the being with the others but should rather be understood as its privative experience, as it is, for example, in the case of mourning, which is in fact a being with the other since the dead person, precisely because she or he has left the world, is more present to us than ever before. The great silence of authentic solitude is in fact full of the voices of many others, which explains that, instead of being a state of "despair and abandonment," it can be, as says Levinas, "a freedom of beginning";[7] it can be creative, creation being never, as Levinas believes, the act of a sovereign subject, but this capacity that was called "inspiration" that allows a common "spirit" to express itself in us.

This kind of seclusion in a pretended "sovereignty" is what in Hölderlin's view defines the modern human being. In a letter to his brother dated January 1, 1799, he draws a rather dark picture of his compatriots in comparison to the ancients, the Greeks: "I believe that the most common virtues and shortcomings of the Germans boil down to a rather conceited domesticity. They are everywhere *glebae addicti*, and the majority is in some manner, literally or metaphorically, tied to its soil (. . .) Everyone is only at home where he has been born and can and will hardly move beyond that with his interests and concepts" whereas "among the ancients, where everyone belonged to the surrounding world with sense and soul, there is to be found much more inwardness in individual characters and situations."[8] This "inwardness," this *Innigkeit*, should not be misunderstood. It does not mean, for Hölderlin, the closed interiority of a "subject," but the fervent inwardness which characterizes the Greeks in so far as they remain intensively in relation with everything. This is what Hölderlin says again in the letter he writes after his return from Bordeaux to his friend Böhlendorff where he defines what characterizes the Greek people as "their way to welcome foreign natures and to communicate themselves to them"[9]—their proper character being "tenderness," the openness to the others, whereas the character of the German is "sobriety," the reserve proper to a closed individuality. The modern human being has lost the capacity of being open to the otherness and strangeness of what can be encountered in the world, and this is the reason why he suffers from loneliness, having no longer any intimate relation with the surrounding world—the price to pay to have wanted to become the "lord of beings" as Heidegger would say.[10] In the same manner Hölderlin explained to his brother in a letter dated June 4, 1799, that the mission of the human being, which is to develop and bring nature to its perfection, has been forgotten today, so that the task of philosophy, art, and religion consists now in leading the human being to never consider himself as "the master and lord" of nature and "in all his art and activities to bow with piety and modesty before the spirit of nature."[11]

But, as we have already seen, in opposition to the loneliness of the modern human being, there is an authentic solitude in which it becomes possible to hear again the voices of nature. This explains why the young Hölderlin could write in July 1795 to Schiller, for whom he felt a kind of veneration: "I am living a very solitary life and I believe that it does me good."[12] Hölderlin, who had spent the previous months in Iena, at that time the center of the German literary and philosophical life, where he met Schiller and Goethe and attended Fichte's lectures, was living again in Nürtingen, in his mother's house. This was his first experience of solitude, after the five years spent in the seminary of Tübingen in the companionship of Schelling, Hegel, Neuffer, and other friends and the year spent in Waltershausen and Iena as the tutor of Charlotte von Kalb's son. Since the beginning of 1795, having no success in his tutorship, he had been released of his duties and during the following months he lived in the house of his friend Sinclair in the neighborhood of Iena where he could dedicate all his time to work on his novel *Hyperion*, from which a first fragment had already appeared in November 1794 in *Thalia*, Schiller's review. This period of solitude was therefore welcome, since it allowed him to concentrate on his work in progress, far from the social obligations in which he had been previously engaged in Iena. But even in this time of respite and creative solitude Hölderlin does not seem to be completely happy, as a letter to his friend Neuffer from April 1795 shows: "This summer at least I will live completely independent and in peace. But such is the human being that he is always in need of something—this is also my case, and this something is you."[13] This shows clearly Hölderlin's ambivalent relation to solitude and his constant longing for friendship.

The months he spent in Nürtingen from May to December of the same year were not particularly fruitful. He had suddenly decided to leave Iena, perhaps because of the political disturbances among the students in the university, which led to Sinclair's dismissal, but also because he had no longer any means of living. Coming back home brought him no relief since it meant the end of independency and the necessity to find a new job as a tutor. He also had the feeling that there was no proper place for him in the high society. In another letter to Schiller written in September 1795, he described his present state of mind in the following manner: "I feel too often that I am not an exceptional man. I am stiff with cold in the winter all around me. The heavens are like iron, and I am like a stone."[14] But his situation changed completely once he was in Frankfort, where he had been offered the tutorship of Banquier Gontard's son. The two years he spent in Frankfort, from January 1796 to September 1798, were probably the happiest of his life, since he found there again friendship in the company of Hegel and reciprocal love with Suzette Gontard. But this period was also dedicated to poetry and philosophy. In a letter from February 1796 to his mentor Immanuel Niethammer, he describes his conditions of life: "The new circumstances in which I live now are the best ones imaginable. I have much leisure for my own work, and philosophy is once again my almost exclusive occupation."[15] In fact, Hölderlin's most important philosophical essays will be written later, but the proximity of Hegel, who in 1797 acquired a position as a tutor in Frankfurt where he remained during three years, gave him the decisive impulse. As proof of the "philosophical community" between Hegel and Hölderlin,[16] and also Schelling (who came to visit him in 1796), the unsigned manuscript of "The Oldest Systematic Program of German Idealism," written in Hegel's hand, but probably composed by all three, can be mentioned. Philosophy could not, however, remain Hölderlin's main preoccupation, as he recognizes in the same letter to Niethammer: "Philosophy is a tyrant, and I endure its force more than I subject myself to it by free choice."[17] What he really wants is to be a poet and write in a creative manner, as he explains in a letter to his brother dated June 2 in the same year: "I hope to work more this summer than before. The drive to create something out of ourselves, which will remain when we part, actually is what alone ties us to life."[18]

The main achievement of this period is in effect the final composition of *Hyperion*, of which the first volume appears in April 1797. The second volume, which he secretly dedicated to Suzette Gontard, was published only after he had left Frankfurt in October 1799. Hölderlin began to form the project of this novel during the years spent in the seminary of Tübingen, but it was only after he met Suzette Gontard that he was able to bring an end to it after several different drafts, from which seven at least have been preserved. *Hyperion or the Hermit in Greece*, its complete title, belongs, at least apparently, to the literary genre of the *Bildungsroman*, the novel of education. It tells the story of the hero's life, of his childhood spent in the midst of nature, his education under the direction of a mentor, his experience of friendship and love and the loss of both, and finally of his assumption of his finitude and death and his choice of a "hermit's life." The story is situated in modern Greece and his fundamental theme is the search for a way leading to this unity with nature whose symbol is ancient Greece, a unity which has been lost in modern times where the human being experiences separation with nature and a loss of the divine.

Already at the beginning of the novel, this fundamental thematic is clearly announced. The question for Hyperion is "to be one with everything living, to go back in blissful self-forgetfulness to the whole of nature."[19] Nature can be identified with the whole, because it is a divinized nature. As Hyperion explains, the world is not poor enough to oblige us to search for a God outside of it.[20] The culminating point in thinking is therefore the elimination of duality. This is what Hölderlin wants to suggest in quoting at the beginning of the second volume the famous passage from Sophocles' *Oedipus at Colonus*: "Not to be born surpasses all reckoning. The next best thing by far, when one has been born, is to go back as swiftly as possible whence one came."[21] Birth, that is, separation from the whole, is the beginning of suffering, and suffering can only be appeased through the return to unity. From there it becomes possible to describe the unfolding of the whole process. It begins with childhood understood as spontaneous unity with the world, followed by the stage of education with the birth of self-consciousness and opposition to the world and others, which is the first experience of solitude. Next is the moment of friendship with the encounter of Alabanda, which ends in failure and leads again to solitude, and finally comes the stage of love with the encounter of Diotima, who is the incarnation of the recovered unity with nature. Here the novel seems therefore to find its conclusion. But a real unity has to include in itself suffering and scission; a harmonious relation with the whole can only be accomplished through the assumption and endurance of separation. A long time was therefore needed in order for Hyperion to understand that the reunion with nature requires the confrontation with death and the loss of the beloved. This is what he explains to his friend Bellarmin at the end of the second volume: "Everything must suffer, is that not so? And the higher its nature, the more deeply it suffers. Holy Nature herself, does she not suffer? For a long time

I could not grasp that she, my divinity, could grieve and yet be blessed. But a happiness that does not suffer is mere sleep, and without death there is no life."[22]

After the death of Diotima, Hyperion went to Germany, but the narration of his life begins only after his return to Greece and the choice of a hermit's life as shows the first line of the novel: "Here in my beloved country my joy and grief revive."[23] But *Hyperion* had for Hölderlin, but unknown to him, the meaning of a prefiguration of what would be his own destiny. The story that was told in the second volume would precisely become the story of Hölderlin himself, doomed, like his hero, to the hermit's life he spent, during thirty-six years and until his death in the famous *Hölderlinsturm* in Tübingen.

Hölderlin had to leave Frankfurt in September 1798, probably after a quarrel with Gontard, and settled down in Homburg, a small town in the vicinity of Frankfurt, where he lived again in the company of Sinclair. This was the beginning of a period of relative solitude and hard work and thinking. He was seeing Sinclair almost every day and even some secret meetings with Suzette were arranged. During the year and a half he spent there, he wrote not only many letters to his mother, brother, sister, friends and to Suzette but also his most important poetological and philosophical essays and he worked hard on the different versions of his *Empedocles*. What was most important, however, was that he became aware of his true vocation and decided to sacrifice all professional ambitions to poetry. He explains it in this way to his friend Neuffer in a letter dated November 12, 1798: "The life in poems—this is what chiefly preoccupies now my mind and senses. I feel so deeply how far I am still to attain to it and yet I strive for it from all my heart (. . .) Alas! The world drove my spirit back in upon itself even when I was a child and I am still suffering the effects (. . .) I am too shy of what is coarse and commonplace in real life." But this is not a sufficient reason to give up poetry: "There is indeed a haven in which every injured poet of my kind can honorably find a refuge—philosophy. But I cannot abandon my first love, the hopes of my early youth and I would rather perish undeserving than leave the sweet home of the Muses from which I was driven away by mere accident."[24] Even to his mother, who was eager to see his son established in the stable social position of a parson, he does not hesitate to confess in a long letter dated from January 1799 that he has finally chosen to dedicate himself entirely to "this most innocent of all occupations," that is, poetry, since "all art requires the entire life of a man."[25] This decision was risky and in fact opened the door to a lasting solitude. However, during this period he tried his best to become independent as a poet and to insure himself a regular income by founding a monthly journal, *Iduna,* and becoming his editor and chief contributor. But this project could never be realized and in May 1800 he had once more to go back to Nürtingen. He then went to Stuttgart for a while to visit his friend Landhauer, but came back again in Nürtingen in order to look for another tutorship.

The two following years, from the end of 1800 to the beginning of 1803, were the most difficult of his life, but strangely enough they were also the most creative. During this period he wrote the odes, the elegies, and the hymns that later made him one of the greatest poets of Germany. Nevertheless, during the same time he had to live as a tutor, that is to say as a kind of domestic, at first in Switzerland, in Hauptwil, at the Gonzenbach's house where he remained only three months from mid-January to mid-April 1801. There he suffered bitterly from solitude, since, as he wrote to his friend Landauer in February, the people with whom he lives "take an interest in foreigners only to the extent that it does not impair their heart."[26] In the following letter from March, he relates even more clearly that "here there is no one I can speak to, no one I can wholly open myself to" and expressed his longing for friendship: "Tell me, is my loneliness a blessing or a curse? It lay in my nature and whatever moves I make to get out of it, be they ever so reasonable in every respect, all the more irresistibly I am forced back in. Oh for a day with you all, oh to shake hands again. My dear friend, if you go to Frankfurt, think of me. Will you? I hope I shall always be worthy of my friends."[27]

Having left Hauptwil, where a tutor was no longer needed, he shifted again between Nürtingen and Stuttgart until having arranged for a new tutorship in France. He left at the end of the year for Bordeaux, where once again he remained for only a little more than three months from the end of January to mid-May 1802 having traveled both ways more than one month each time, mostly walking. He described his journey in a letter written some months after his return to his friend Böhlendorff: "I have been meanwhile in France and have seen the sad, solitary earth, the shepherds of Southern France and individual beauties, men and women, who have grown up in the anxiety of patriotic doubt and hunger. The tremendous element, the fire of the sky, and the silence of the people, their life within nature, and their limitedness and satisfaction, has continually affected me, and as it is said of the heroes, so I may say that Apollo has struck me."[28] Apollo is for Hölderlin not only, as it was for Nietzsche, the God of art, but the God of the celestial fire, who can give death with his bow and can predict the future. To be struck by Apollo means therefore not only that Hölderlin experienced the light of the Southern France as similar to the light of Greece, but also that such an experience could be fatal. This is confirmed by another passage in a previous letter to Böhlendorff that was written just before his departure for Bordeaux: "I will have to keep my wits about me in France," since "I fear that I might end like the old Tantalus who received more from the God than he could take."[29] This can to some extent explain Hölderlin's state of confusion and agitation when he arrived at the beginning of June at his mother's house and, as writes Schwab, the author of the first Hölderlin biography, "of the most desperate mental derangement."[30] But he knew most probably already when he came back home that Suzette had died on June 22, since he had learned of Suzette's death in Stuttgart through a letter from Sinclair. After that, he was considered as a mental patient, and even Sinclair, who did not believe at first that he was becoming mad, and who took care of him in the following years, had finally to put him in a clinic in Tübingen in September 1806.

Nonetheless, during the four years from his return from Bordeaux until his internment, Hölderlin continued to work on some of his best poems, such as *Patmos* and *Friedenfeier*, and he also published his translations from Sophocles and the accompanying remarks. He knew now that he was made for solitude. In "The Titans," a poem most probably written in 1802, he proclaimed: *Ich aber bin allein*, "But I am alone,"[31] responding thus to the anxious question he asked in a later poem, "Remembrance," written in 1803: "But where are the friends? Where Bellarmin/ and his companions? Many a man/ is shy of going to the source."[32] Solitude is needed if the poet wants to go to the source in order to stand "where no mere master teaches" in nature's "light embrace," a nature there "miraculously omnipresent, God-like in power and beauty," as Hölderlin says in "As on a Holiday," a poem written in 1800 during his stay in Nürtingen.[33] He understood then that "a fire has been lit in the soul of poets" since "even when they seem to be alone," "they are always divining" the coming of the day and the awakening of nature. He finally grasped that in solitude only, "the thoughts of the communal spirit" "quietly come to rest in the poet's soul."[34]

After having been dismissed from the clinic in August 1807 as incurable, he was taken in charge of by Ernst Zimmer in the ancient tower of Tübingen. It is here that Hölderlin became finally free. For thirty-six years he continued to be a poet, writing each day or declaiming through the window in the open air. According to Zimmer, Hölderlin would sometimes receive visitors, among them young poets, but pretending to have no name, or strange names, for example Scardanelli. As if he was now, like Nietzsche also seemed to be many years later, delivered from the seclusion in his own ego and as if in radical solitude nobody is there any longer, but only the world as such, which can now come to word in the poem. This is what the beginning of a famous poem that was attributed to

Hölderlin by the poet Waiblinger who came to visit him in his tower conveys: "In lively blueness with its metal roof the steeple blossoms. Around it the crying of swallows hovers, most moving blueness surrounds it. The sun hangs high above it and colours the sheets of tin, but up above in the wind silently crows the weathercock."[35]

Notes

1   E. Levinas, *Time and the Other*, trans. R. Cohen (Pittsburgh: Duquesne University Press, 1997), 54.

2   Ibid., 42.

3   Ibid., 40.

4   Ibid., 55.

5   M. Heidegger, *Being and Time*, trans. J. Stambaugh (Albany: State University of New York Press, 1996), § 27, 118 [126].

6   Ibid., § 40, 176 [188].

7   Levinas, *Time and the Other*, 55.

8   F. Hölderlin, *Essays and Letters on Theory,* ed. and trans. Thomas Pfau (Albany: State University of New York Press, 1988), 136–37.

9   Ibid., 152 (translation modified).

10 M. Heidegger, "Letter on Humanism," in *Basic Writings*, ed. David Farrell Krell (San Francisco: HarperCollins, 1992), 245.

11 Hölderlin, *Werke und Briefen*, Band II (Frankfurt am Main: Insel, 1969), 899–900.

12 Ibid., 846.

13 Ibid., 844.

14 Ibid., 847. *Essays and Letters on Theory*, 340.

15 Hölderlin, *Essays and Letters on Theory*, 131.

16 See C. Jamme, « *Ein ungelehrtes Buch* ». *Die philosophische Gemeinschaft zwischen Hölderlin und Hegel in Frankfurt 1797–1800* (Bonn: Bouvier, 1983).

17 Hölderlin, *Essays and Letters on Theory,* 131.

18 Ibid., 134.

19 Hölderlin, *Werke und Briefen*, Band I (Frankfurt am Main: Insel, 1969), 297.

20 Ibid., 300.

21 Ibid., 376. Sophocle, *Oedipus at Colonus,* l. 1223 sq.

22 Ibid., 430. Translation in David Constantine, *Hölderlin* (Oxford: Clarendon Press, 1988), 349.

23 Ibid., 295. Translation in David Constantine, *Hölderlin*, 348.

24 Ibid., Band II, 880. Partial Translation in David Constantine, *Hölderlin*, 354–55.

25 Partial Translation in David Constantine, *Hölderlin*, 354.

26   Hölderlin, *Werke und Briefen,* Band II, 932.

27   Ibid., 934. Translation in David Constantine, *Hölderlin,* 364.

28   *Essays and Letters on Theory,* 152.

29   Ibid., 151.

30   Ibid., 380.

31   F. Hölderlin, *Poems and Fragments,* trans. Michael Hamburger (Cambridge: Cambridge University Press, 1980), 629.

32   Ibid., 491.

33   Ibid., 373.

34   Ibid., 375.

35   Hölderlin, *Poems and Fragments,* 601.

Part Four

Solitudes

12

Off the Beaten Track

David Wood

Much has been written about the writer's cabin. Among the most notable recent books on the topic are *Heidegger's Hut* by Adam Sharr and *A Place of My Own: The Architecture of Daydreams*, Michael Pollan's account of imagining and then actually constructing his own writing space. A standard internet search can quickly yield images of the writing rooms (cabins, huts, sheds) of legendary scriveners: Dylan Thomas, Virginia Woolf, Ludwig Wittgenstein, Roald Dahl, Carl Jung, Henry Thoreau, and—a writer of a markedly different sort—Ted Kaczynski, to name a few. And Jill Krementz's 1999 collection of photographs "The Writer's Desk" gives us tantalizing glimpses of writers sitting at their desks. But why the interest? Have these places somehow become secular sites of the sacred?

Who has not fantasized about the books they would write if only the right conditions could be found! I have carried around just such a dream, sparked by a weekend alone in an austere mountain cabin in the Austrian Alps when I was a boy. Rumination was unstoppable, and poetry just poured out.

For the most part, these buildings are small, plain, unprepossessing, and sparsely furnished. This poses a problem for my first hypothesis—that the fascination of these dwellings rests on the hope that we may glean something of the secret of the writer's genius from the creative space to which they habitually retreated. For we might well conclude from Wittgenstein's famously almost empty college room in Cambridge (in which he had a deck chair), and indeed from the plainness of so many of these huts, that far from giving expression to, or feeding in some revealing way, the otherwise inaccessible inner workings of the brilliant mind, they reflect a disdainful resistance to the importance of surroundings, an asceticism, an architectural tabula rasa. This would explain why some people work well on planes, in hotel rooms, library carrels, even monastic and indeed prison cells. (Boethius, Bunyan, Gramsci, and Negri all wrote significant works

A statue of Henry David Thoreau and a replica of his hut are on display at Walden Pond Reservation.
RhythmicQuietude at en.wikipedia [CC BY-SA 3.0 (https://creativecommons.org/licenses/by-sa/3.0)]

while imprisoned.) They are relieved of distraction. Sartre was famous for writing in the corner of Les Deux Magots—café privacy, where the white noise of conversation and cutlery damps down distracting input, fashioning a creative cocoon in the midst of the world.

It is not clear, when we look at Heidegger's writing scene—the wooden desk, with the ink blotter, the old chair—whether these items have some deep meaning, or whether they are the recessive background that makes possible a certain concentration. Most of the items visible in the images available to us are generic and without distinction. Perhaps that is important. The sad truth may be that while we (especially we writers) *hope* to learn something of the secret of the author from his or her workspace, we are often disappointed, just as meeting a famous person can be a letdown.

Photographs of writer's retreats fall into three broad categories: exteriors, interiors, and prospects (views from within), and each has a distinct significance. Exteriors give focus to the imaginative challenge: What was going on in that room? It seems a touch more decipherable than what was going on in her head. Interiors, especially those furnished as our own spaces might, with a desk and a chair, allow us to make comparisons imaginatively to transpose ourselves into that space, even as we mark the distance. But there are distinct details of the writer's room too, ones we can never assign to ourselves: the fat fountain pen on Freud's desk—now an anachronism, as well as a *cliché*. Or his row of Egyptian figurines? Were they vital parts of his creative process? But ultimately, it is the typical ordinariness of these interiors that is of real interest.

The third category of perspective—prospects, the view outside from within—offers a different sort of insight. Bertrand Russell's house, at Plas Penrhyn, near Portmeirion, Wales, is somewhat plain, but its distant view up the Glaslyn estuary to the slopes of Snowdon is spectacular. As it happens, we do not have many photos of the views from writers' cabins, and of them, Heidegger's is the prettiest, if not exactly sublime. From the dozens of such cabins that I have inspected—some personally, others in books or through Google—it is clear that most of these spaces look inward rather than outward. Desks are often in the center of the room, rather than at a window, as if the view of the outdoors was not at a premium. To the extent that some satisfaction is taken in being in nature, it is not so much having a view of nature as being part of it.

Perhaps the humble shack is precisely designed not to stand out more than necessary. Tree, rock, path, shack. And when perusing the image of the shack, we are offered a view of what can be seen from inside or from its immediate vicinity, there is no doubting the interpretive complexity that awaits us. We look to these images as satisfying a certain desire on the part of the writer—"a room of one's own"—a desire with which we can identify. It is tempting to suppose that the significance we give to the view is shared by the writer. This is behind the disappointment we may well feel at the visual modesty of so many of these sites. Russell's Sierra Club vista—with its views of Snowdon and the estuary—is truly an exception. More important, the aesthetic distance sustained by a beautiful view may actually be problematic. Heidegger said as much in his ruminations in "Why I Stay in the Provinces," in which he distanced himself from an aesthetic appreciation of the working landscapes of his South German peasants.

The possibility of exploring all three categories obviously gives an actual visit to the site a special appeal. The sign near Heidegger's hut that marks it as Heidegger family property, and that indicates that the family does not welcome tourists, must be dispiriting for those who trekked in expecting some sort of dwelling communion with the genius loci, if not the spirit of the master. And yet, unless the original has been preserved and made publicly available, photographs may be far the best access to a past that is no more.

Photographs that include the author can then be particularly valuable; Krementz's images give us tantalizing glimpses of writers sitting at their

Dylan Thomas's writing shed in Laugharne.
By Tony in Devon [CC BY-SA 4.0 (https://creativecommons.org/licenses/by-sa/4.0)],
from Wikimedia Commons

desks. But might they not also strain the imagination? A contemporary viewer inclined to imagining himself working in the same space might find the image of the writer doing so an obstacle. This is analogous to the privilege of radio over TV; TV kills the imagination that radio requires. Again, it is hard to know what to make of the onsite reconstruction of Thoreau's cabin at Walden Pond, or of the Newseum's exhibition of Ted Kaczynski's 10-by-12 Montana shack, each of which effects a serious displacement of the reality effect, the magic of touching the original. If I pick up Freud's pen, the very pen he held in his hand, does something flow from him to me? Am I not at least licensed to imagine a common ground between us, however structurally, culturally, historically mediated? Is not the same true of opening the very door that Nietzsche or Kaczynski, or Dahl opened, turning the same handle? Who could not be moved by the thought of touching even a fragment of the linen shroud that held the body of Christ, and still preserves his crucified image? Why reach out to touch the hem of a rock star? Is the famous writer's cabin a modern fetish?

It is not uncommon to mark one's reservation at the Arcadian settings so favored by these huts, as if marking the shape of distance that serious writing must take—distance from technology, from the modern, from the city. Is there not something politically anachronistic about the image of the water trough outside Heidegger's hut, where a spring unfailingly flows? Is anything like a progressive stance compatible with such atavistic images? Is there not a tacit repudiation of a different style of critique—the sort leveled by (say) the peripatetic eye of a Walter Benjamin at our urban Arcades? Politically perhaps Hannah Arendt had it right: "Flight from the world . . . can always be justified as long as reality is not ignored but acknowledged as the thing that must be escaped" (*Men in Dark Times*). More broadly, might it not be that the bland space of the cabin, like the yellow pad, or the laptop screen, is something of a neutral ground making room for the refiguration or transformation of the real—not a flight in the sense of repudiation of the real, rather relief from the pressure of its organizing principles?

One does not have to be a Thoreau or a Rousseau for one of these modest spaces to supply what is needed to write. Identification with nature is not required (if indeed it were possible); a certain harmony with nature is already broken by putting pen to paper. And would one really seek harmony with nature if one were privy to the ruthless struggles being played out under every rock? The roof of the cabin, the door, the window are all designed to keep nature at bay. The flat surface of the desk, the laptop screen, the artificial light all bear witness to the necessity to subordinate nature's spontaneous irregularity, to fashion a little Versailles.

Between world and word there is both a bridge and a chasm. Sometimes it seems that nothing could be more natural than speaking or writing. And yet we know that a manifesto, a book, even a well-turned, well-timed phrase can change the world. Writers are at times, as Pope decried, fools in dunce's caps. But they can also be magicians, conjuring other worlds, brave new possibilities. The cabin is one culturally powerful image of that semidetached space in which those creative discontinuities are spawned. It seems to hold a secret, but behind the first there hides another. If the first secret is that to write one needs a blank sheet of paper, or a blank screen, the second secret, the secret of the cabin, is that one does not strictly need a mountain or a shack at the end of a trail, off the grid. Rather, a table, a chair, somewhere simple, free of distraction. For some, even a cupboard in an office building no one is using that day will do. But bring your noise-cancelling headphones just in case.

Dedicated to my (living) friend John Llewelyn (David Wood's writers cabin).
Photo by David Wood

13

Landscapes of Solitude: Some Reflections on the Free Spirit

Jill Marsden

I'm happiest when most away
I can bear my soul from its home of clay
On a windy night when the moon is bright
And the eye can wander through worlds of light—
When I am not and none beside—
Nor earth nor sea nor cloudless sky—
But only spirit wandering wide
Through infinite immensity. (Emily Brontë)

The aloneness of creativity is quite unlike other solitudes. Time spent writing and thinking is time spent "away," in a kind of exile from the daily clamor of life. For the migrant spirit of Emily Brontë's poem, to be "most away" is to seek more than distance from the distractions of sociality. It is to slip out of existence for a while— to savor a kind of reprieve from a human location in things. "Wandering wide" the free spirit feels itself distributed through regions undetermined by the familiar co-ordinates of earth and sky. Night winds stir the starscape, tempting the wanderer with the promise of other suns. There is something both disarming and familiar about this freedom, as if in our creative solitude we reconnect with those domains guessed at and half-glimpsed in dreams. As David Krell notes, the "populations of the night ... probably do touch our work of the day, at least if there is anything at all creative about it" ("CS" 23). If the spirit happy to be "most away" carries something of the night into waking reality it also brings something of its uncertainty.

> No matter how joyous and exhilarating our solitudes may be, they are always haunted. We may feel at home in them, yet our being-at-home is riddled with uncanny, unhomelike sensations. ("CS" 23)

Paradoxically, there seems to be a relationship between this "exile" from the world and a particularity of place, at least this is so for the two figures whom I shall discuss here: Emily Brontë and Friedrich Nietzsche. In a way that is not at all dialectical, the experience of being "most away" seems to require a landscape or *Heimlichkeit* as its precondition. It is the aim of this essay to explore the relationship between these landscapes of solitude and creativity. For Brontë, the desolate moorland of her native Haworth not only supplies the setting for her only novel *Wuthering Heights*, it also sustains and inspires her poetic and literary flights. Similarly, for Nietzsche, the landscape of the Swiss Engadine stimulates his creative powers to such a degree it conducts him to the thought of the "eternal return of the same." In each case, the landscape is the means through which "uncanny, unhomelike sensations" are communicated. Landscapes of solitude, however, are not created by placing a lonesome figure in them, to either command the scene or to be dwarfed by its immensity. Such a "view" of solitude is precisely that—a "representation" within a frame. As will become apparent, for Emily Brontë and for Nietzsche, the landscape is *itself* solitary and its "voice" is not so much that of the outsider as that of the outside.

In a biographical sketch of her sister Emily, Charlotte Brontë emphasizes the profound affinity that Emily felt for the moorland wilderness that surrounded their family home, the parsonage at Haworth, West Yorkshire:

> My sister Emily loved the moors. Flowers brighter than the rose bloomed in the blackest of the heath for her; out of a sullen hollow in a livid hill-side her mind could make out an Eden. She found in the bleak solitude many and dear delights; and not the least and best loved was—liberty.[1]

The wild moors present an unimpeded vista of summits and hollows, an imperious, sparsely featured landscape stretching from modernity to prehistory in the sweep of an eye. In this uncultivated terrain, every outcrop of moss and turf, every thicket of bramble and stump of heath stands as a counterargument against civilization and its refinements. Characteristically taciturn and socially retiring, Emily Brontë favored this unpeopled landscape above any form of "society" and relished freedom from all its constraints. In her preface to the 1850 edition of *Wuthering Heights*, Charlotte pays tribute to the "rusticity" of *Wuthering Heights*, noting that the author was a "native and nursling of the moors."[2] Emily Brontë was formed and nourished by this "remote and unreclaimed region," imbibing its icy winds and exhaling the breath of its moist bracken and ochred heather.

[Emily] did not describe as one whose eye and taste alone found pleasure in the prospect; her native hills were far more to her than a spectacle; they were what she lived in, and by, as much as the wild birds, their tenants, or as the heather, their produce.[3]

One imagines Emily Brontë rolling back on this springy bed of moss and heather, her fingers brushing the knotted roots and crumbling earth in tiny cascades. This is a world evoked from the vantage point of one who, half-sleeping, glimpses "spires of bright green grass/ transparently in sunshine quivering." When she looks up it is to earth rather than to sky, to grassland illuminated in a soaring majesty of light. The austere beauty of this wasteland is evoked in her terse, unvarnished verse and the desire to make her bed in this "quiet earth" is the dark fantasy that pervades her single work of fiction.

It would be no exaggeration to say that the high winds and turbulent weather of the West Riding moors sustained Emily Brontë, supplying her body with the vital stuff of life. According to Charlotte Brontë:

Liberty was the breath of Emily's nostrils; without it, she perished. The change from her own home to a school, and from her own very noiseless, very secluded, but unrestricted and inartificial mode of life, to one of disciplined routine (though under the kindliest auspices), was what she failed in enduring. Her nature proved here too strong for her fortitude. Every morning when she woke, the vision of home and the moors rushed on her, and darkened and saddened the day that lay before her. Nobody knew what ailed her but me—I knew only too well. In this struggle her health was quickly broken: her white face, attenuated form, and failing strength, threatened rapid decline. I felt in my heart she would die, if she did not go home, and with this conviction obtained her recall.[4]

The three brief periods of absence from her beloved Haworth were dangerously depleting for Emily Brontë, as if at Cowan Bridge, Halifax and Brussels she was deprived of the very oxygen that fed her creative spirit. She struggled to breathe this communal air, she was unable to assimilate this alien atmosphere. No longer eating, weak and pale she courted death. And yet, returning to Haworth parsonage and moorland for good in 1843 she was able to resume a life that was so thoroughly invigorating, her brief excursions were consigned to healthy oblivion. It was as if time had left no mark on her, indeed it was as if she had never ventured beyond the parish. The irony was that Emily could only be "most away" when so fundamentally "at home."

For Nietzsche, too, the landscape of solitude was elemental rather than situational. In his beautiful text, *The Good European: Nietzsche's Work Sites in Word and Image* (compiled in collaboration with Donald L. Bates) David Krell notes how Nietzsche's thoughts are thoroughly embedded in the Alpine landscape of forest, lake and mountain. Somehow this high altitude found a way into Nietzsche's writing. Ideas jotted on scraps of paper when breathing the air of the heights impress the reader with their thrilling clarity as if crystallized from the ice-capped peaks and distilled from the biting air. It was in Sils Maria in Switzerland where Nietzsche spent several summers that many of his most celebrated works were composed. Most significantly it was here that Nietzsche experienced the "revelation" of the thought of eternal return as if for a moment the quiet mountains were able to show him something that resists manifestation in shape and form. Nietzsche relates in *Thus Spoke Zarathustra* that the thought of eternal return came to him when out walking in Sils Maria by the lake of Silvaplana. Stopping by a pyramidal boulder the thought suddenly came to him and was scribbled down on a piece of paper "6,000 feet beyond man and time." When he comes to relate this experience in his famous letter to Peter Gast (August 14, 1881) he emphasizes the emergence of this elusive "thought" within the Alpine landscape:

> The August sun is overhead, the year is slipping away, it is becoming more quiet and peaceful on the mountains and in the forests. On my horizon, thoughts have arisen such as I have never seen before—I will not speak of them, but will maintain my unshakeable calm. (KSB 6/112)

The excitement that Nietzsche reports at the emergence of unimagined thoughts on his horizon has an infectious pull on the reader, drawing us in to this vortex of intensity. Thoughts arise like mist from summits as if the shining of the sun, the slipping of time and the quietening of the mountains and forests were all elements contributing to a "vision" that words could only guess at. Nietzsche writes that he takes it as a reward that this year has shown him two things that belong to him and are "intensely intimate" to him—namely Gast's music and this landscape. Of the latter he remarks that it is "something *altogether different*" from Switzerland and Recoaro and that he would have to travel far afield to find something even approximate.[5] At all events when Nietzsche vows to retain "this Sils Maria" in his life it is as much an intensive geography of experience as it is a location of ideas.

It is of great interest that Pierre Klossowski[6] in his examination of Nietzsche's thought of eternal return should insist on describing the "revelation" of eternal return as the "Sils-Maria experience," prompting the reader to ask what it is about this particular place that made this encounter possible. David Krell cites Curt

Paul Janz's view that this landscape was all Nietzsche needed to "step beyond the everyday, the customary and habitual into a land of unaccustomed thoughts and insights."[7] Perhaps this is because such sublime scenery so readily evoked the extra-human dreamscape of the mythic. This elevation—"6,000 feet above man and time"—was like those high, wild, desolate moors, up above the whole world, the "very realms of silence." Krell notes that "solitude was what Nietzsche prized above all about the Oberengadin."[8] In a letter to Carl von Gersdorff, written from Sils Maria towards the end of June 1883, Nietzsche commends the Upper Engadine as a privileged site for creativity.

> Dear old friend, I am in the Upper-Engadine again for the third time and again I feel that here and nowhere else is my true home and breeding-ground. Oh how much lies hidden in me and wants to become word and form. There is no limit to the quiet, the altitude, the solitude I need around me in order to hear my inner voices. (KSB 6/386)

The Upper-Engadine is the fertile element within which Nietzsche's thoughts take root and grow. It is here that nascent ideas blossom into words, here that uncanny voices set the silence echoing. In the same letter to von Gersdorff, Nietzsche goes on to insist that the Sils Maria landscape is the dwelling place of his Muses: "Here is where my Muses live: as far back as *The Wanderer and his Shadow* I wrote that this region is 'related to me by blood, and by more than blood'" (KSB 6/387). With this assertion, Nietzsche acknowledges a physiological continuity with the Swiss landscape which complements Brontë's "nursling" connection to the Haworth moors. In the section of *The Wanderer and his Shadow* to which Nietzsche alludes (*Doppelgängerei der Natur*, sec. 338), this affinity is described in yet more intriguing terms. The passage begins with the startling assertion: "In many of nature's regions we rediscover ourselves [*endecken wir uns selber wieder*], with a pleasurable shudder: it is the most beautiful kind of *Doppelgänger*" (KSA 2/699). David Krell notes that here Nietzsche invokes "nature's *Doppelgäng erei*, that is to say, its uncanny pull on us at different times in different places—a pull that is somehow both human and alien, hence *double* in its effects."[9] This discovery of self (once again) has all the surety of *Heimlichkeit* and all the fright of uncanny displacement. In this passage, Nietzsche describes a kinship so intimate that it cancels out the distinctions by means of which self and other might be defined. To be affiliated by blood "and more than blood" is to share a common artery with the landscape. One may speak of eyes attuned to the "purest brilliance of light," skin which registers the moderate coolness of temperature, nerves which thrill at the peaks and plateaus so close to the "terrors of eternal snows" but these are no longer simply ways that "one" feels within a landscape. These are ways which the *landscape* feels.

Like Nietzsche, Emily Brontë's protagonist in *Wuthering Heights* (re)discovers herself in nature. In her delirium prior to her death Catherine Earnshaw longs to be outdoors: "I'm sure I should be myself were I once among the heather on those hills." (109). This longing to be "of the earth" (a macabre obsession of both Catherine and Heathcliff) is at the same time an expression of uncanny intimacy with death—with all that exceeds the singularity of the "one." Indeed, Catherine's refusal of a Christian model of finitude is simultaneously a movement towards the abyssal immanence of the unknown. Her assertion, "I *am* Heathcliff," is probably the best known line of *Wuthering Heights* and at one level may be interpreted as the most supreme affirmation of spiritual affinity ("whatever our souls are made of, his and mine are the same"). However, the phrase "I *am* Heathcliff" comes at the close of a long and impassioned speech by Catherine to Nelly Dean in which the account of "doubling" offered does not rely on a logic of reciprocal definition: "I cannot express it; but surely you and everybody have a notion that there is or should be an existence of yours beyond you" (71). This other existence is not equivalent to the existence of *an* other in any obvious sense. Catherine struggles to express a thought for which the logic of identity is plainly unsuited: "What were the use of my creation, if I were contained entirely here?" (71). The existence of yours beyond you cannot be named as other because Catherine does not experience it as wholly separate from her present state. The self that is not entirely "here," that is distributed somehow in the world, is a self that eludes the determinacy of figure and concept, the order of utility and rational things. In this profound assertion, Brontë's heroine articulates the uncanny sensation that one's sense of self is not simply contained in the space or located in the time of the "here" and "now": "he's more myself than I am." This is no invocation of an ethereal beyond but an immanent one. Her connection to Heathcliff is vitally and continuously close, felt from both without and within: "My great miseries in this world have been Heathcliff's miseries, and I watched and felt each from the beginning" (71).

Memorably, Catherine likens her love for Heathcliff to the "eternal rocks" beneath the woodland foliage. Her love for Heathcliff is equally Brontë's love for "heath" and "cliff." One recalls Charlotte Brontë's declaration that her sister Emily "loved" the moors. Love of this nature appears to exceed all that one might hope to receive from another person, a friend or lover. Emily Brontë had no friends and did not appear to require any. Desire of this order does not seek recognition by and in an other; it feels its own existence "beyond itself." In this respect, Catherine's "doubling" is not dissimilar to Nietzsche's doubling with the Sils Maria landscape—the sharing of a vital, inhuman pulse. For Nietzsche as for Brontë, landscape is a continuation of flesh, of lived experience, by other means. This constellation of stardust, sunlight, and rain that we differentiate as human is experienced in these solitary locations purely as life. Life without any definition or delineation is anegoic but not universal. It is an a-subjectivity achieved through extreme intimacy and is not to be commuted to some objective or neutral state. The sensations are uncanny because they are keenly and viscerally felt but are received involuntarily and inexorably as if a force of nature. As Catherine says of her love for Heathcliff, it is "a source of little visible delight but necessary" (71). This is the fundamental paradox which unites a sense of place with being "most away." In feeling one's existence beyond oneself, a union is attained which is so profound it is estranging. The artist must "lose" himself or herself in the landscape in order to write "from the impulse of nature."[10]

Freud notes the prominence of the phenomenon of the double in literary works treating the uncanny:

> Thus we have characters who are to be considered identical because they look alike. This relation is accentuated by mental processes leaping from one of these characters to another—by what we should call telepathy—so that the one possesses knowledge, feelings and experience in common with the other. Or it is marked by the fact that the subject identifies himself with someone else, so that he is in doubt as to which his self is, or substitutes the extraneous self for his own. In other words, there is a doubling, dividing and interchanging of the self. And finally, there is the constant recurrence of the same thing—the repetition of the same features or character traits or vicissitudes through several consecutive generations.[11]

Freud suggests that the quality of uncanniness associated with the double can be traced back to a "time when the ego had not yet marked itself off sharply from the external world and other people."[12] Indeed, in Freud's terms, an uncanny experience may stem from the revival of an infantile complex, imbuing us with a powerful sense of "magical thinking" or the omnipotence of thoughts.[13] These primitive ideas are the product of an infantile overaccentuation of psychical reality and may be effectively reproduced in fiction when "the distinction between imagination and reality is effaced."[14] As commentators have noted, part of the appeal of *Wuthering Heights* derives from its power to regress us to the lost state of childhood, "activating the child we have left for dead."[15] When reading this unnerving text we hover on the brink of a feeling that resists the shape of a recollection. Freud notes that the storyteller has the power to "keep us in the dark for a long time about the precise nature of the presuppositions on which the world he writes about is based," cunningly avoiding any definite information which would resolve the tension.[16] This is particularly true of Emily Brontë's novel which "has a peculiarly directive power over us,"[17] guiding the current of our emotions in such a way that we feel propelled to refuse the logic of reason in the "name of all that feels" (105).

In seeking to confide the secrets of her heart and soul to Nelly Dean, Catherine Earnshaw declares, ". . . if you will not mock at me, I'll explain it: I can't do it distinctly: but I'll give you a feeling of how I feel" (68). The dream that Catherine wants to tell to aid this process of affective transmission threatens to go unvoiced, so frightened is Nelly by these prefatory remarks: "I've dreamt in my life dreams that have stayed with me ever after, and changed my ideas: they've gone through and through me, like wine through water and altered the colour of my mind" (69). To be claimed by a dream, to be changed by it, is to resist any notion that the world of the mind is governed by the values of waking reality. The separation between waking reality and dream life is the property of reason but the lingering power of the dream suffuses the mind, changing its *sense* of reality. In one respect, the content of the dream is of little account for it is the bid to communicate a feeling rather than to relay an idea that so unnerves Catherine's interlocutor. However, there is something very significant about her dream narrative. Catherine tells Nelly that she had once dreamt that she was in heaven and now knows that she would be miserable there: "I was only going to say that heaven did not seem to be my home; and I broke my heart with weeping to come back to earth; and the angels were so angry that they flung me out into the middle of the heath on the top of Wuthering Heights; where I woke sobbing for joy" (69).

Catherine's dream is striking not simply because it asserts her longing for the heath as her true spiritual home but because she wakes from her dream *within the dream*. The transition from dreaming to waking implies a continuum of states via which the self gradually comes to its senses, but sometimes the process folds back on itself, deviating from any progressive course. This creates a qualitatively different third state in which the vagrant self "wanders wide." The power of *Wuthering Heights* as an uncanny text derives from its power to scour away the borderline between fantasy and reality, capturing the thrill of travelling between worlds. The Catherine who wanders the moors and tries to "get in" to Wuthering Heights in Lockwood's dream is terrifyingly real yet also most "away"—only "spirit wandering wide in infinite immensity."

It would be too swift to assume that creative solitudes spawn flights of fancy when the journeys in question are all too real. For Nietzsche, dreams are primary productive forces in which nature's art drives are "directly satisfied" without reference to "waking reality" or the intellectual depth or artistic culture of a single being (KSA 1/30). Dreams frequently refer to other dreams, stimulating a memory which belongs to a different landscape of experience. When Nietzsche writes that in many of nature's regions "we discover ourselves again" perhaps he is alluding to the discovery—forever for the first time—that others continue to think in us:

> I have *discovered* for myself that primeval human and animal kind continues in me to poetize, to love, to hate and to conclude: I suddenly woke up in the middle of this dream but only to the consciousness that I am still dreaming and that I *must* continue dreaming so as not to perish—just as a sleepwalker must go on sleeping in order not to fall down. (KSA 3/416–17)

To wake within a dream is not to negate the reality of the ebbing perceptions but to endorse their directive power all the stronger. The uncanny feeling that we are "possessed" by nature both familiar and foreign is affirmed on waking for it is never a matter of correcting our sensations. Lockwood's nightmare hovers over the narrative of *Wuthering Heights* as a placeless prophecy and has more "reality" than any other episode. This is true of all such nocturnal wanderings. It is imperative to resist the commonplaces of thought in favor of the "commonality of dreaming . . . and therewith the *continuation of the dream*" (KSA 3/417). Nelly Dean and Lockwood are right to be fearful of ghosts:

> There are spirits all around us, every moment of our life wants to say something to us, but we refuse to listen to these spirit-voices. We are afraid that when we are alone and quiet something will be whispered in our ear, and so we hate quietness and deafen ourselves with sociability. (KSA 1/379)

The risk is that a demon will whisper into our loneliest loneliness, will tell us another tale of time and eternity, will even show us the gateway to the outside.

We could never learn what thoughts ascended on Nietzsche's horizon that August in Sils Maria. As his copious notes on eternal return testify, the horizon is an unreachable place, constantly changing as it is approached. Klossowski notes Nietzsche's abortive attempts to initiate his friends into the thought of eternal return as if it were a doctrine of the understanding. However, Klossowski suggests that in his obsessive efforts to communicate the thought to his friends, the *mood* of the experience is cast like a spell by the ciphers of its utterance: "When

Nietzsche invited them to think with him, he was really inviting them to feel, and thus to feel his own prior emotion."[18] In fact, Nietzsche goes further than this by repeatedly taking visitors to the *place* of this emotion, to its *body*.[19] It is as if he retraces the contours of his uncanny experience, stepping back into the landscape of memory, seeking to catch the wave of a just unreachable dream.

The thought of eternal return is generated amidst these water-washed rocks, high mountain peaks, dark green lake and cerulean sky. Nietzsche obsessively revisits the scene to try and re-inhabit the physicality of the moment, "a memory outside my own limits" as Klossowski might say.[20] If the thought of eternal return belongs to this landscape perhaps we should look to the landscape in Nietzsche's "corpus" for sites of its epiphany. The descriptions of the Alpine environment that one encounters in Nietzsche's work are not only gorgeous and abundant they also testify to a desire to be "one" with the landscape, a dream in which "one" might disappear.

> *At Noon*—Whoever in his life has been granted an active and stormy morning finds that an odd craving for tranquility overtakes his soul at life's noontide, a craving that can last for many moons, many years. It grows quiet about him, the voices fade away and are now far off; the sun shines straight down upon him. On a concealed meadow in the forest he sees Great Pan sleeping; all the things of nature have gone to sleep with him, an expression of eternity on their faces—at least that is the way he thinks of it. He wants nothing, is troubled by nothing, his heart stands motionless, and only his eye still lives—it is a death with vigilant [*wachen*] eyes. (KSA 2/690)

Away from the clamor of the human world, in an oasis of divine enchantment, the wanderer experiences what it is to be "most away." Wanting nothing, a spirit untroubled by desire, the wanderer experiences his own "death" as a subject. The experience of *amor fati* eludes the categories of knowledge, perception and understanding, just as the revelation of the eternal return eludes what Klossowski calls the "gregarious code of signs." To experience death is to continue to dream. Illicit from the critical vantage point of reason, this experience of the "outside" is not so much about loss of identity as affirmation of an utter continuity with things.

Landscapes of solitude are not solitary because they are inhabited by a lonesome figure. However intense loneliness may be it has lack and a relationship to futurity as its constant companions. Loneliness is of "one" albeit a one suffering from its own sense of incompletion. By contrast, solitude is a plenum. Emily Brontë, like her literary creation, Catherine Earnshaw, was so profoundly attracted to solitude that her fierce isolation was no more alienating than the gathering storm clouds on the horizon of the moor. For Nietzsche too, despite the periodic need for company, solitude was prized as the most essential means of becoming attuned to otherness. Unlike loneliness, solitude is the power of being no-one.

Both Nietzsche and Emily Brontë found a way of getting "outside" and "most away" from the state of being human. Bataille says of Brontë that "she lived in a sort of silence which, it seemed, only literature could disrupt."[21] *Wuthering Heights* is a relentlessly dark portrayal of savage affects and "harshly manifested passions,"[22] a fierce vision nowhere countermanded by a redemptive morality. Bataille cites Jacques Blondel's claim that for Brontë "there is a desire to break with the world in order to embrace life in all its fullness and discover in artistic creativity that which is refused by reality."[23] This refusal of reality, a failure to accept the sacrificial contracts of the social order, is played out to intense effect in the narrative of *Wuthering Heights*. The ideal limits of life and death are violently rejected. Death will not separate Catherine and Heathcliff nor will it bring repose so long as it is possible to travel between worlds. For Brontë's protagonists, everything devolves on the question of getting through to the outside that the commonplaces of reality obscure and deny. Conversing with the spirit voice of Heathcliff, Catherine entreats him to follow her in death, for she will not lie there by herself: "Find a way, then!" (109).

In their creative solitudes, Nietzsche and Emily Brontë show that what we call "reality" is precisely a product of the imagination. The "truths" of life and death are compelling fictions and the irresistible force of their writing and thinking lies in their creation of other realities—landscapes which are fully real. The reader shares something of their excitement and their exile. Temporarily "swept away" by imaginary identities, one has no abiding sense of one's own. If not a haunting as such, this is at least a "possession" by other voices. In this way, something of the thrill of dream life is spirited into the day. It is this space which the reader travels, swept along by feelings "remembered" but never known. And so when Catherine, delirious and dying, entreats Heathcliff to follow her into death, the wordless hurt and ruined expectation is felt with the full force of painful knowing, as sharp as a memory and as vague as experience. And it is neither. Your "memory" of this creeping catastrophe, your helplessness and ebbing hope, is contemporaneous with your "experience." The feeling that Brontë evokes is born in the reading—as if you dreamt this already and were haunted by your failure to remember. This is the inverse of creativity, its mirror image. In your solitude you breathe the air of this place of lost dreams. And it is from here that you write.

Notes

1	Cited in Elizabeth Gaskell, *The Life of Charlotte Brontë* (Oxford: University of Oxford Press, 2009), 109.

2	Charlotte Brontë, "Editor's Preface to the New Edition of *Wuthering Heights*," cited in Emily Brontë, *Wuthering Heights* (London: Everyman, 1907 [1850]), xl.

3	Ibid.

4	Gaskell, *The Life of Charlotte Brontë*, 109.

5	See Nietzsche's letter cited in David Farrell Krell and Donald L. Bates, *The Good European: Nietzsche's Work Sites in Word and Image* (Chicago: University of Chicago Press, 1997), 149.

6	Pierre Klossowski, *Nietzsche and the Vicious Circle*, trans. Daniel W. Smith (London: Athlone, 1997).

7	Krell and Bates, *The Good European*, 157.

8	Ibid., 150.

9	Ibid.

10	Charlotte Brontë, "Biographical Notice of Ellis and Acton Bell," in Emily Brontë, *Wuthering Heights* (London: Everyman, 1907), xxxvii.

11	Sigmund Freud, "The Uncanny," trans. James Strachey (Middlesex: Pelican 1985), 356.

12	Ibid., 358.

13	Ibid., 362.

14	Ibid., 367.

15	Stevie Davis, *Emily Brontë: Heretic* (London: Women's Press, 1994), 39.

16	Freud, "The Uncanny," 374.

17	Ibid., 375.

18	Klossowski, *Nietzsche and the Vicious Circle*, 218.

19	One of Nietzsche's Swiss acquaintances, Resa von Schirnhofer, recalls how Nietzsche had taken her—as he did other visitors—to the Zarathustra stone on the shore of Lake Silvaplana where the thought of eternal return had come to him (cited in S. L. Gilman and D. J. Parent, *Conversations with Nietzsche: A Life in the Words of his Contemporaries* [Oxford: Oxford University Press, 1987], 161):

> He led me . . . as he led others of his visitors before and after, to the waterwashed boulder on the shore of Lake Silvaplana, the Zarathustra stone, that wonderful place of serious natural beauty, where the dark green lake, the nearby forest, the high mountains, the solemn silence join in weaving their magic.

20	Klossowski, *Nietzsche and the Vicious Circle*, 58.

21	Georges Bataille, *Literature and Evil*, trans. Alastair Hamilton (London: Marion Boyars, 1997), 15.

22 Brontë, "Editor's Preface," xxxix.

23 Cited in Bataille, *Literature and Evil* (London: Marion Boyars), 23.

References

Brontë, Charlotte. 1907. *Wuthering Heights.* London: Everyman.

Krell, David Farrell. "Creative Solitudes," in this book (cited as "CS").

KSA. *Friedrich Nietzsche Sämtliche Werke, Kritische Studienausgabe.* Edited by G. Colli and M. Montinari. 1967–1977 and 1988. Munich: dtv; Berlin: Walter de Gruyter.

KSB. *Friedrich Nietzsche Sämtliche Briefe: Kritische Studienausgabe.* Edited by G. Colli and M. Montinari. 1967–1977 and 1988. Munich: dtv; Berlin: Walter de Gruyter.

14

Cabin Solitudes

Dawne McCance

Some thirty years later, the work of Michael Olito, a Winnipeg installation and performance artist, still has a hold on me—although the pieces I find most compelling are nowhere to be found. In resistance to the idea of art as precious product for exhibition and sale, a "perfect plastic object" that "sit[s] forever in time" (Enright 14), Olito's work is all about the process of making art, or—fascinated by the surveying motif—of what he refers to as "siting" (Heath 22), something "almost akin to writing" (Enright 16). His works are studies in creative solitude. For Olito makes his art alone, graphing an open prairie landscape that is as vast as it is empty, remote, relentlessly flat, and for much of the year snow-covered, a strange version of what David Krell in this volume, citing Herman Melville, calls "the nakedest possible plain of writing." Yet even as his art-making explores the isolation, often loneliness, of life on this barren plain, Olito develops the theme of connection, suggesting that both "isolation and the desire to communicate" (Olito 8) belong inseparably to prairie solitude. In an early performance piece, *Island Link*, for example, Olito used a rope to draw a visual and marked (sight-site) line between two remote islands (Crow and Dog) that dot the enormous unbroken 24,500 sq. kilometers of the northern Lake Winnipeg, literally tying the islands together in what he described as an "attempt at communication" (Enright 16).

In August 2009, after returning to my cabin on Kendall Island in Canada's Lake of the Woods from Thera and the extraordinary Santorini Voice Symposium organized by David and Salomé Krell, I received an email from David expressing the wish that our cabins were closer together. For a while after that, I considered tying a rope between my cabin and his, perhaps the sort of golden-haired line that Melville's Ishmael favored, soft but also strong, a long distance connection between our two solitudes, something we could each hang onto, give a tug now and then. *What is an island?* Some might ask with David's Sankt Mechthild cabin in mind, but let me leave the question for now; we could knot the interlacing strands of our island link around the majestic Douglas fir just to the side of his outdoor writing table, while at my end, we could do our ropework around a much less stately, but sturdy, red pine. Rope, after all, offers as tangible a connection as email blips can provide, and as I have come to learn from living on an island, it enables both the connection and isolation essential to creative solitude: it holds my boat ready when I want to leave the island, and has it waiting at the landing when I make my solitary return.

The tin boat in question is far from a luxury craft. Left behind by the former cabin owner, fitted with an old Yamaha outboard, it doubles as a rowboat when the motor, as often happens, won't start. Yet by island standards, this simple motorboat makes for what my neighbor calls "a good rig." Wider, deeper, and longer than the other tin boats that dock at the landing, it drives well into wind and waves, at least for the distance from landing to cabin; out into the big lake it could not venture. Many times, particularly early or late in the season, I have arrived at the landing during a deluge to find the boat half-filled, heaving on its line in the wind, and close to capsizing. After an hour or more of bailing my boat and the others, loading gas tank, oars, supplies, and dogs; after crossing the water in driving rain, and making the last, steep and soaking, climb up the twenty-some stairs to the cabin, I have learned another lesson in the cost at which solitude comes. And whether I arrive in rain or shine, each time I open the door to the empty cabin, I am both immensely relieved to be back and overwhelmed by the realization that I am alone. After sunrise, when the color and movement of morning return, I will embrace my cabin solitude and settle into precious long days of writing. But for all I cherish those days, the uneasy, melancholy, awareness that tracks me through them is that, "I am alone."

"I am alone." With these words, Jacques Derrida opens the second (2002–03) year of his final seminar on *The Beast and the Sovereign*, translated by Geoffrey Bennington and released in 2011 by the University of Chicago Press. What might it mean to say that "I am alone," Derrida asks, or given that "the world" provides the protocol for this seminar, what might it mean to say that "I am alone in the world"?[1] On the opening page of the seminar, Derrida suggests that "I am alone" can signify sadness or joy, either one or the other or both simultaneously, as in my ambivalent experience of cabin solitude: both "'I am alone,' alas," and "'I am alone,' thank God, alone at last" (1). The statement "I am alone" wavers, he notes, between deploration and triumph—and to be sure, even as I lament arriving alone at the cabin, there is something triumphal for me in having taken flight, successfully if only temporarily, from the city and the university. My examples, however prosaic, hint at one of Derrida's central interests in this seminar: the "unstable differentiation" (98) between, on the one hand, the solitude that suffers its loneliness and the solitude that exults in being alone. "Insularophobia is also insularophilia," David Krell remarks in *Derrida and Our Animal Others* (63) of the second *Beast and the Sovereign* seminar, where "Derrida finds solitude to be an instance of double-bind and even of auto-immunity."[2] I want to suggest in what follows that the autoimmunity of solitude—of a sovereign solitude that "distinguishes, sets apart" (BS 99), cannot be shared, elevates its aloneness as exceptional—pertains first of all to man's self-positioning vis-à-vis what he terms "the animal." For as Derrida points out in "Violence Against Animals," the question of animality, not simply one question among others, "represents the limit upon which all the great questions are formed and determined" (62–63), the question of solitude surely included, the kind of solitude he broaches in his final seminar which, already in its title, brings sovereign and animal together.

In part, Derrida asks in this seminar whether "the profound solitude of Dasein" (Krell DA, 63) is akin to that of Daniel Defoe's Robinson Crusoe. Finding himself shipwrecked on the Island of Despair, without prospect of relief from his unsought isolation and fearful of being devoured by wild beasts, murdered by savages or dying from starvation, Robinson feels lonely and very much alone until, soon enough, endearing himself to his solitary condition, he assumes sovereignty over his island world, now eating the beasts he feared would eat him, and saving the skins of all the creatures he kills, each an "emblem" (BS 55) of his sovereignty. I am interested in Derrida's response to this question and in David Krell's reading of it, both of which I take to belong to an ongoing conversation between these two heirs of Heidegger. As Krell notes in *Derrida and Our Animal Others*, this conversation often centered on Heidegger and on his treatment of "the essence of animality" (106). And given that, for Heidegger, determination of the essence of animality depends on a prior definition of life, the touchstone of which, he says, is death, the problems of life and death, or of *lifedeath*, are inevitably at issue in the Derrida-Krell conversation.

Curiously, the second *Beast and the Sovereign* seminar makes no reference to Krell's *Daimon Life*, published ten years earlier with the dedication, "for jd for life." Not even the "Where Deathless Horses Weep" chapter is mentioned, despite its remarkable reading of Heidegger's 1929–30 lecture course on the very questions that preoccupy Derrida in his seminar. Yet, *Daimon Life* may well have been (how could it not have been?) generative for Derrida, his second *Beast and the*

Sovereign seminar in some ways a response to it, just as Krell's *Derrida and Our Animal Others*, continuing and refining his analyses in *Daimon Life*, responds to Derrida's engagement with Heidegger in *The Beast and the Sovereign*. Suffice it to say that when reading Heidegger, one would do well to keep both Krell and Derrida in hand, their work so often taking up the same crucial questions and in the process demonstrating that "deconstruction" involves, as Nicholas Royle puts it, not only "thinking about ghostliness, about how things are haunted—by difference, by otherness" (12), but also "making a difference, changing the ways we think and what we think, altering the world" (13). This is a case I hope to make in the following pages.

It strikes me as somehow uncanny that during approximately the same period of time, unbeknownst to each other, Krell and Derrida, both thinking about solitude and about the thinking of solitude bequeathed to us by the Western tradition, especially in the work of Heidegger, turned to two nonphilosophical texts, Krell to Henry David Thoreau's *Walden* and Derrida to Daniel Defoe's *Robinson Crusoe*. The latter is one of the two texts on which Derrida focuses in the second year (2002–03) of his *Beast and the Sovereign* seminar, while Thoreau's text is central to Krell's *Where's Walden? Conversations with Henry David Thoreau and Marlonbrando*, which was completed by at least 2004, when he sent me a copy of the as-yet unpublished manuscript.[3] Derrida points out in his seminar that *Robinson Crusoe* appeared in 1719 when Defoe was already fifty-nine and had published a good deal, including the 1710 *Essay Upon Public Credit* (BS 14). Yet, in what is not typical for a work of fiction, it is *Robinson Crusoe* that has enjoyed an extraordinary, and particularly political, reception history, from Joyce's fascination, "congratulating Defoe for emancipating English literature, for making it accede to a certain national sovereignty" (15), to Marx's critical interpretation of Robinson's "individualist and asocial isolationism, of insularism as a symptom of the development of capitalist society" (26). Derrida is careful to observe as well that Defoe's fiction has a "real, non-fictional" referent in the memoires of the Scottish seaman Alexander Selkirk (14). Not incidentally, in Chapter 2 of *Walden*, Thoreau cites two politically freighted lines from "The Solitude" section of William Cowper's "Verses Supposed to be Written by Alexander Selkirk," the same Scottish seaman upon whom Defoe based *Robinson Crusoe*: "I am monarch of all I *survey* / My right there is none to dispute" (214). This is perhaps but a minor detail linking the coincident reading choices of Derrida and Krell, but it is one that contributes nonetheless to an uncanny effect. In any case, should someone (and someone should) attempt a study that brings

Krell and Derrida together on the question of Dasein's solitude—more careful and comprehensive a study that I can offer here—Krell's reading of *Walden* will prove as indispensable to it as Derrida's engagement with *Robinson Crusoe*.

Although Krell's *Where's Walden?* differs in form from Derrida's seminar approach to *Robinson Crusoe*, it approaches *Walden* too as a classic portrayal of solitude—albeit of a solitude that, at first glance, appears as pure insularophilia. For Thoreau relishes the words, "I am alone." He *loves* to be alone, loves the solitude of his *Life in the Woods*, and like the Rousseau Derrida cites in the second *Beast and the Sovereign* seminar (65), he has met no other with whom to share his natural taste for solitude. "There can be no very black melancholy to him who lives in the midst of Nature and has his senses still," Thoreau writes in the "Solitude" chapter of *Walden* (263).[4] "I feel it wholesome to be alone the greater part of the time. To be in company, even with the best, is soon wearisome and dissipating. I love to be alone" (267). Overall, Krell reacts ambivalently to this rendering of solitude, to Thoreau's "bragging about his autonomy and economic independence: on the one hand, I cannot match his vaunted self-reliance, and on the other, I don't want to try" (4–5). Indeed, it is as if Thoreau loves solitude because it removes the burden of sharing—"I have never found the companion that was so companionable as solitude" (W 267)—whereas for Krell, solitude is double and contradictory: if he is alone in his cabin, "it is not always by choice, indeed most often not by choice" (WW 30). And while there alone, he "toil[s] from eight to six" (4), rather than indulging in Thoreau's idle and self-absorbed reverie: "Whereas I love to fill my morning with projects and purposefulness, Thoreau loves to warm the doorstep with his butt" (23).

This is not to say that Krell is without sympathy for some of Thoreau's sentiments. Both like to rise before first light (WW 22), and, while David surely has no equal here, both love their woodpiles (25). Both are friends of the forest. "In fact," Krell writes, "Thoreau is never more tender than when he accompanies a felled tree to its final resting place, and this seems right to me" (27). Admitting that "we see flashes of generosity throughout *Walden*, along with the famous extended, generously detailed *descriptions* of nature" (71), even passages in the "Solitude" chapter in which Thoreau declares himself to be " 'partly leaves and vegetable mold' " himself (71), Krell reminds us that "[t]he mold soon molders, however, and Thoreau finds even the vernal vegetation of the spring hillside *grotesque*" (71). Inevitably, Thoreau's musings on solitude catapult us back into "Higher Laws," Krell notes (74), remarking at one point that while "surely Thoreau's equal in solitude," Herman Melville "knew how to puncture the inflated solitude that is so full of itself that it counts for all the company in

the world" (88). "Inflated" is the key word here (from the Latin *inflare*: to cause to swell, become distended, puffed up; or, as in currency increases, to become unreasonably elevated), for what Krell pointedly resists is the "transcendental capital" that Thoreau makes out of almost everything (39). Even the "rippled, glassy, specular skywater" of Thoreau's Walden pond is infinitely "more transcendent and transcendentally spiritual" than the "earthwater" roundabout Krell's cabin in the *Kaltwasser*, "Cold Water," Woods of the Black Forest where, in the darkness cast by forest shadows, flowing stream water appears to be black (13). Much unlike Krell's, "Thoreau's trajectory is always ascensional, gliding every upward to the most rarefied ethers" (14).

This is my suggestion: that in his engagement with *Walden*, much as in Derrida's with *Robinson Crusoe*, Krell finds his "center of gravity" (BS 28) not just in Thoreau's self-absorbed "autobiography" or "Autopresentation" (31) of a solitary life in the woods, but more specifically in Thoreau's account of solitude's higher reaches, his text as "a theatre of solitary sovereignty, of the assertion of mastery (of self over slaves, over savages and over beasts, without speaking— because the point is precisely not to talk about them—without speaking of women)" (28). For example, Thoreau's patronizing accounts of the poor (the Irish poor in Walden), "run from pitying condescension to pitiless exploitation," and they belong, Krell contends, to "a 100% U.S.-American attitude, as ubiquitous today as it was in his time"—an attitude of "contempt spiced with violence" (WW 44). He goes on: "The Irish whom Thoreau meets are either shanty-town laborers working on the railroads or bog-trotters draining swamps. They ought to be placed in the chapter called 'Brute Neighbors,' except that [for Thoreau] the Irish haven't the dignity of animals" (44–45). So much for the Irish poor. As for African Americans, those men and women, slaves such as Brister Freeman, who formerly inhabited the woods around Walden Pond and of whom only folklore remains: I cannot possibly summarize Krell's reading of these pages of *Walden*, save to say he is "bemused and troubled" (162) with Thoreau's choice of words pertaining to men and women of color, and this despite his "grand and principled resistance to slavery, which is well-attested" (160; see also 158–162).

And what of animals, of Thoreau's sovereign solitude in relation to beasts— not just to the Irish poor, vanished slaves, or even the elderly for whom he has contempt (WW 126)—but the beasts to which he is admittedly allied, and thus to the "lower" brutish orders within himself? Here again, even where, as if often the case, Thoreau asserts his mastery "without speaking" it, higher laws win out: cleanliness over filth (that involved, for instance, in cleaning and eating fish rather than bread and potatoes); civilized over savage (vegetarians over meat-eaters, and those who have given off eating each other over savage cannibal tribes) and, especially, spirit over flesh. For notwithstanding Thoreau's once-savage instinct to devour a woodchuck raw or his experience of eating a fried rat with good relish, his "repugnance, if not squeamishness" about food, particularly about eating animals, has to do, Krell points out, with *flesh* (66)—not just theirs, but his: those gross appetites and coarse senses which he would subsume to "nonsensuous savors of the spirit that spurn the wormy reptile and the healthy hog with equal animus" (70). This is about upward and downward flows, Krell reminds his reader, citing Thoreau from the "Higher Laws" chapter to say that "'[h]e is blessed who is assured that the animal is dying out in him day by day, and the divine being established'" (70).

It is safe to say then, that despite his advocacy of vegetarianism, Thoreau's quintessentially Christian elevation of spirit over flesh spurns animal nature in favor of a purity that man *alone*, unless he is heathen, shares with God. His spirit/flesh hierarchy leaves intact what Derrida in the interview "'Eating Well,' or the Calculation of the Subject," refers to as the "sacrificial structure," the "eat-speak-interiorize" schema, that "is still today the order of the political, the State, right, or morality" (113–14). For Thoreau, "eating well" has to do with mastering the beast, which in turn comprises a kind of "eating" (assimilating) of the lower by the higher. All sensuality is at issue here; all purity is one, Thoreau explains, "whether a man eat, or drink, or cohabit, or sleep sensually" (W 240). Reading this passage, Krell puzzles: "Sleeping sensually? Alone in a cabin at Walden Pond? I do wish I had some sense of what this admonition means. For I have not yet been able to sleep intellectually, except during convocation and commencement exercises at the university" (WW 30). No doubt, there is more at stake in Thoreau's admonition than the fluffs and folds of Krell's featherbed, "made of the down of the angel's wings you wrap around the ones you love when they are far away" (30). Yet, aside from the term "cohabit," what is at stake remains unsaid: in *Walden* as in *Robinson Crusoe*, sexuality and sexual desire go without mention, and woman, if she would be involved in such, is absent from both texts. "That's sovereignty, that's solitary and exceptional sovereignty," Derrida exclaims. "No desire to come along and limit sovereignty, and if there were homosexual desire, it would go, symbolically and symptomatically, via the symbolics of young slaves and beasts" (BS 55). Because it cannot be divided, because it is solitary, alone, or it is not (8), sovereignty is silent on sex and sexual desire. "No trace of woman" (55). Not in Thoreau's text, and except for old holes in the ground where dwellings once stood, scarcely a trace of the African-Americans who once lived in the Walden woods.

Already less generous, and less nuanced, a reader of *Walden* than is David Krell, I dare not ask whether the sight of a hole in the ground where life once stirred, even of the abandoned hole of a well, might have occasioned in Thoreau, if not Robinson's terror of being swallowed alive or of sinking to the bottom, at least some apprehension about his own death—the death that Christianity vehemently associates with woman, the carnal (animal) flesh that drags man's spirit down. "Among the things that frighten Robinson, or his author, are women, who are absent from the account of the island. Woman is 'the absolute unsaid' of Defoe's novel, the primal English novel, the novel which helped to create the genre," Krell writes in *Derrida and Our Animal Others* (62). No doubt woman frightens Thoreau too, as does the beast for which he records both a hunger and a horror. Perhaps for this reason, desire, emotion, feelings, and longings are for the most part absent from *Walden*. If Thoreau went into the woods to mourn his dead brother John, "the 'private business' of Henry's mourning remains private," Krell observes. "In all of Walden, nary a word about brother John's demise; the editor alone raises the veil on the silent mourner" (WW 104). All and all, "Icy intellect is at work here, rather than any faculty of affect or passion" (167).

Still, in what seems to me another moment of generosity, Krell suggests that Thoreau struggles in *Walden* "with the *tragic* sense of life, which our civilization has lost" (105). A few pages later, in discussing the "Solitude" chapter of *Walden* where Thoreau likens thinking to a kind of theatre, Krell, drawing on Hölderlin, offers a stunning snapshot of tragic theatre, one that may have less to do with Thoreau's work, however, than it does with Krell's own, and not the least in *Where's Walden?* (109–13). Indeed, for this reader at least, it is precisely Krell's tragic vision that distinguishes his more *creative* solitude from that of both Thoreau and Defoe, and it is Krell's tragic sense of life that frees his solitude from any need to immunize the human against the beast, or to absolutize the mastery of the solitary self, man *alone* and/or his One and Sovereign God. There is nothing ascensional about Krell's trajectory—and this despite the fact that his cabin sits on the very top of a valley, with his office, a spot in the woods lushly carpeted in moss and amply furnished with rocks and pines, situated even higher. Such "angels" as deer sometimes visit him in this forest office: "I have always sensed that the only angels there ever were—apart from the crystalline variety—are animals, wild animals, so that there are still angels galore, even as an encroaching civilization systematically snuffs them out" (15). Animals as angels, not beasts, but make no mistake: Krell's sense of life—for instance, in the passages describing Oma bending over a stuck pig, capturing its blood in a yellow plastic bucket (107), or recounting Krell's experience of finding a monarch butterfly in December, nurturing him back to health, then releasing him to freedom and death (39–40)—is neither sentimental nor bleak. His inimitable humor no doubt helps: reacting to Thoreau's silencing of sexuality and sexual desire, Krell remarks that he "would trade all the transcendentals for a wink from a too liquid eye (She needn't be inebriated.)" (29). But my point is that Krell's philosophy of life (which has yet to be given its due reading), without bifurcating man from animal or spirit from flesh, positions him as kin, rather than master, of all he surveys: periwinkle and ivy; Douglas the Fir; the goats who are "his closest, ever-present, ever-cheering neighbors" (11), equal in every way to Frau Troglodyte and her troglodytic doggie (51); the animals who talk to Frau K. from behind her Schwarzwald *Hof* wall (130); and not the least, Marlonbrando.

"It all started with a November storm," Krell explains. "The wind wanted to blow the cabin off the hilltop clear to the next village, but the cabin demurred and held fast. I was enjoying my supper and a glass of *pinot noir* from nearby Alsace when a gray and white cat hopped up onto the windowsill" (16). Thus begins a series of conversations between Krell and this feral cat—at first a recalcitrant interlocutor but soon enough David's wise and knowing psychoanalyst, the one to whom he recounts his dreams, including those involving his mother and father, their deaths, and his irreparable mourning. Having twice met Marlonbrando myself, and having been held in the gaze of "his great golden eyes" (17), I can state unequivocally that he is no figment of Krell's imagination.[5] On the contrary. Marlonbrando, who is real, releases the vulnerability, passion, sometimes fear, often loneliness, that belong to Krell's experience of solitude. When Krell returns to the cabin after months away teaching in the United States, Marlonbrando is soon there: "It takes him a few minutes to notice—maybe five, maybe thirty—but he is remarkably quick to see that the Soft Touch is back" (209). And when, not without misgiving, David leaves the cabin to return to the States, he puts a share of his own breakfast into Marlonbrando's bowl, for: "He and I too are blood relations. By this time he incorporates so many others to whom I am related and indebted—Douglas the Fir, the Storm Beech, the kids, Rüdiger and the forester, the women who supply my milk and my herbs and my wisdom, such as it is, the hay harvesters and the hay itself, and all the living and the dead of valley and village. Marlonbrando will keep watch. He will welcome me back" (210).

As I write this (August 2012), I cannot but recall the last conversation I had with David Krell, about two weeks ago, which concerned "the difficult problem of death," in this case the death of Marlonbrando. He had been failing for some time, until one day he did not return to eat and drink from the bowls David set out for him.

But did Marlonbrando die, properly speaking, or in line with Heidegger's distinction between human dying (*Sterben*) and animal "perishing" (*Verenden*),

did he simply cease to live? The distinction, not incidental to Heidegger's 1929–30 lecture course, is "decisive and troubling" for Derrida, "along with everything that binds it to [Heidegger's] discourse" (BS 115), including his definition of *logos*, *logos apophantikos*, as a *power* that the animal lacks (242) and that deprives it of death *as* death. Derrida points out that, "in the dominant tradition of how the animal is treated by philosophy and culture in general, the difference between animal and human has always been defined according to the criterion of 'power' or 'faculty'" (243), what in *The Animal That Therefore I Am*[6] he refers to as a "*can-have* [pouvoir-avoir] of the *logos*"—that the human possesses but "the" so-called animal is said to lack (27). This is the traditional thesis that, Derrida says, Heidegger maintains: "At bottom, all these people, from Defoe to Lacan via Heidegger, belong to the same world in which the animal is cut from man by a multiple defect of power (speech, dying, signifier, truth and lie, etc.). What Robinson thinks of his parrot Poll is pretty much what Descartes, Kant, Heidegger, and Lacan, and so very many others, think of all animals incapable of a true responsible and responding speech, of a *logos semantikos* and a *logos apophantikos*" (BS 278).

Always attentive in his second *Beast and the Sovereign* seminar to the motif of "the path" both in *Robinson Crusoe* and in Heidegger's 1929–30 lecture course, Derrida makes it clear that throughout the seminar he follows a path of his own, indeed that "each of my choices and my perspectives depends broadly here, as I will never try to hide, on my history, my previous work, and my way of driving, driving on this road, on my drives, desires, and phantasms" (BS 206). Since, through much of his previous work, the question of "the animal" and of Heidegger's rendering of human/animal difference, has been pivotal for Derrida (I am thinking, among other texts, of the *Geschlecht* papers, *Of Spirit*, *Rogues*, "Violence Against Animals," *Aporias*, and *The Animal That Therefore I Am*), it is not surprising that, in the second year of the *Beast and the Sovereign* seminar, Heidegger's *Sterben/Verenden* hierarchy has everything to do with shaping Derrida's path (its leaps, detours, and circlings back). Indeed, in the second session of the seminar, having already engaged sections 1–15 of Heidegger's lecture course, Derrida chooses "to open" *The Fundamental Concepts of Metaphysics*[7] at its exact center, section 42, in which, setting out on a path of comparative interpretation, Heidegger presents three theses: (1) The stone is worldless; (2) The animal is poor in world; and (3) Man is world-forming (BS 57; FCM 177. In the latter text, man is lower case). From this halfway point on, Derrida observes, "Heidegger explicitly and systematically broaches the question of the animal, which is our theme here" (BS 57). And from this point on in his seminar, Derrida's path never takes him far from Heidegger's assertion of animal poverty, the lack that, among other things, would have deprived Marlonbrando of his own death.

Central to Derrida's reading of this animal impoverishment is his claim that what Heidegger calls *Benommenheit*, *benumbment* or *captivation*, belongs solely to the animal, and accounts for its world poverty. For Heidegger, Derrida argues, it is the *Benommenheit* of the animal that removes from it the possibility [*power*] of relating to the entity *as such*, of relating to the world *as such*, of relating to death *as* death (BS 63). And as he circles back from section 42 of Heidegger's course to sections 16 to 18, then sections 19 to 41, back again to sections 2 and 7, then ahead to sections 43, 44, 60, and 61, Derrida makes the point again and again, tying animal *benumbment* to other of the themes or threads of Heidegger's course, that of boredom for example: "The animal poor in world, in its *Benommenheit* (in its Dasein-less being-captivated) supposedly does not get bored," at least not in Dasein's deep sense (70). As well, at stake in the great question of the circle, Derrida notes, is not only the methodological approach to questioning that Heidegger justifies and assumes, "but also the circle of an animal encirclement (*Umring*), the 'self-encircling (*das Sichumringen*)' that characterizes the animal in the benumbment of its captivation (*Benommenheit*)" (94). And as to the question of life on which in the 1929–30 lecture course the question of animality depends, Derrida points out that in section 43, Heidegger takes the determination of death to be the key to the question of life, of "what makes life life" (113), such that the first criterion of life, of the "being-in-life of life," is the possibility of dying (114). Paradoxically, then, although it is living and alive, the animal, lacking access "to the open, the manifest (*offenbar*), the manifestness (*Offenbarkeit*) of beings *as such*" (116), cannot die, properly speaking. Some 120 pages later, Derrida observes, when he has progressed from section 43 to section 61, "in the middle of the elucidation of animality poor in world, enclosed as it is in the circle of its *Ringen* and its *Umring*, and of its *Benommenheit* (benumbment, captivation), Heidegger asks again the question of death, now calling it explicitly the "touchstone" (*Prüfstein*) of the entire enquiry, and comes to the assertion that only man dies, whereas the animal for its part does not die, but simply ceases to live" (115). In other words, methodically making his case, Derrida asserts in the second *Beast and the Sovereign*, as he has in some earlier works, that with his discourse on animal captivation (*Benommenheit*) and world poverty, Heidegger reinstates one of Western philosophy's fundamental hierarchical either/or oppositions, effectively elevating the power of man *alone* over his Dasein-less others, and thereby confirming a long tradition of thinking sovereignty and sovereign solitude. *Benommenheit*, then, is crucial to Derrida's reading of Heidegger on "the animal" question. As I am about to suggest, it is as well to Krell's—but with a difference that matters.

Along the path that he marks out for himself in reading the second year of *The Beast and the Sovereign* seminar, Krell, on the one hand, expresses reservations similar to Derrida's as to Heidegger's distinction between human death and animal perishing, suggesting that the distinction, with its attribution of power, *das Vermögen*, to human mortals, belongs to the phenomenological and ultimately metaphysical tradition from which Heidegger endeavored to set himself apart (DA 66). "Derrida agrees with Heidegger that the Cartesian *sum* has never been thought through," Krell remarks. "Yet to think it through requires a consideration of *life* to which Heidegger is unequal" (88). And as to one dimension of Heideggerian sovereignty, though I am moving far too quickly here, Krell comments more than once on Heidegger's self-assurance, his apparent confidence "that he can use animal life in his comparative metaphysics of world-relations in the way that Robinson Crusoe is confident in his task of subjecting the animals of his island. Heidegger, always prepared to reject the *homo rationalis*, never challenges the *homo robinsonniesis*" (73). On the other hand, however, Krell suggests that Derrida's second *Beast and the Sovereign* seminar leaves readers of Heidegger—readers intent on making a difference in the way we think about and treat animals—with work yet to do. "Derrida's principal complaint is that Heidegger is all-too confident that human comportment—toward its vision, language, world, and death—is separated from animal behaviors (in the plural) by an abyss of essence. Derrida's complaint will never, by any reading of Heidegger, be made superfluous. Yet there is reason to look once again at *Being and Time* in our common effort to overcome that putatively singular abyss, since there are passages in Heidegger's magnum opus that straddle both banks of the abyss" (110).

There is reason to look again at *Being and Time* – *again*, because Krell has previously offered the insight, for example in *Daimon Life*, that in his magnum opus, using "the very word" that in the 1929–30 lecture course will be used to designate *animal* behavior, Heidegger portrays Dasein too as benumbed, "both bedazzled by the world and stunned by anxiety" (*Daimon Life* 181). In chapter 4 of *Derrida and Our Animal Others*, after considering the etymology of the word "benumbment" (*Benommenheit, Benommensein*) and examining Heidegger's use of the word in six passages of *Being and Time*, Krell comes to the similar conclusion that "*Benommenheit* is *both* what dazes and distracts Dasein, causing it to be *lost* in the allurements of the world, *and* what stuns Dasein with its own uncanniness, in this way allowing Dasein to *find* itself as a proper self. Not only is a bedazzled Dasein not the dullest of Daseins, it is Dasein in its most proper, most appropriately human, moment. *Benommenheit* is the way of all mortals at their very best" (DA 111–12). Krell asks here whether this attribution of *Benommenheit* to Dasein is "only an accident of misapplied terminology," whether Heidegger has "quite suddenly grown sloppy in his use of words," or as another possibility "is something unraveling here, something like the simple oppositions of giving/taking, granting/depriving, finding/losing, living/dying, having/not-having? Would not such unraveling undo the entire fabric of fundamental ontology? And if the fabric of fundamental ontology frays, can it possibly serve as the basis for a 'comparative' ontology of life?" (112). Suggesting that the conversation between himself and Derrida is ongoing, Krell then writes: "It seems important to me that Derrida turn his attention to the matter of anxiety as benumbing, and benumbment as the *proper* of humankind" (112).

Why does Derrida "not mention" that "what Heidegger will call '*Benommenheit*,' the 'benumbment' or 'hebetude' of animal life" is "also precisely the condition of a Dasein that achieves insight into *its* mortality" (DA 84)? The matter seems to puzzle Krell, particularly when, in chapter 3 of *Derrida and Our Animal Others*, he turns from the second *Beast and the Sovereign* seminar to the Derrida papers from a 1997 Cerisy conference that are collected in *The Animal That Therefore I Am* and to a question that Derrida raises at the Cerisy conference but postpones treatment of: the question of whether the animal *has time*, or as Derrida quotes Heidegger from section 68b of *Being and Time*, whether the animal "is constituted by some kind of 'time' " (ATT 22). The second year of *The Beast and the Sovereign* seminar is where we might expect to find Derrida's further treatment of this postponed problem, Krell suggests, but not so, and this despite "the gravest challenges to Heidegger's fundamental ontology of Dasein" that Krell sees in the section of *Being and Time* (section 68b) that Derrida cites at Cerisy, including the problem of "*Benommenheit* as the very effect of ecstatic time on Dasein, the effect of ecstatic openness as a form of oblivion, *Vergessenheit*, or closure, *Verschliessen/Erschliessen*" (DA 93).

Not unrelated to this, in chapter 4 of *Derrida and Our Animal Others*, Krell refers to something else that Derrida misses, mentions but does not discuss in detail, in his second *Beast and the Sovereign* seminar, where his chosen path takes him from section 42 through sections 60, 61, and 62 of Heidegger's 1929–30 lecture course, but then bypasses section 63 (DA 107). Krell is surely disappointed that Derrida "nowhere" performs a close reading of section 63 of Heidegger's lecture course, where the touchstone of death is put to work. "For here Heidegger raises at least some of the objections that Derrida himself raises. If a close-reading of section 63 were to take place, I believe, Derrida would see that matters are the other way round: for Heidegger, the touchstone is a stumbling block against which life, human life *and* animal life, 'shatters' " (107). It is in section 63, Krell writes further, that "Heidegger allows the distinction between animal coming-to-an-end and human dying to be subsumed under the larger notion, that of 'shattering,' *Erschütterung*. For both the sphere of human life and the ring of animal behavior are in an essential way 'shattered' by death" (108). And he adds: "It would be worth tracing with great care throughout Heidegger's work the use of the words *Erschüttering* and the related *Scheitern*, 'shattering' and, of all things, a Crusoe-like 'shipwreck.' Those words, as far as I can see, are much more essential to the touchstone of all philosophy than the word *Walten*, 'dominion' " (108).

Does Derrida, in his reading of Heidegger's 1929–30 lecture course, make too much of this word, as Krell suggests? Is Derrida at times "too quick to hear in *Walten* the danger of 'preponderant violence' (2:74), *Gewaltsamkeit*, *Gewalttätigkeit*, in the sovereign dominion of *physis*" (DA 60)? I do not know, but what interests me, and what Derrida says "matters" to him (BS 279), is the excess he reads in *Walten*, the word appealing to "a sovereignty so sovereign that it *exceeds* the theological and political—and especially onto-theological—figures or determinations of sovereignty" (278, my emphasis); the excess of a sovereignty that "overruns any historical configuration of an onto-theological and therefore also theological-political type" (279). A few sentences later, Derrida adds: "*Walten* would be too sovereign still to be sovereign, in a sense, within the limits of the theological-political. And the excess of sovereignty would nullify the meaning of sovereignty" (279). Would the excess not then nullify the sovereign distinction between human death and animal perishing?

On this note, we must conclude that the conversation between Derrida and Krell is indeed very much ongoing, no books soon to be closed. What moves Krell to insist that Derrida return and continue the seminar on the beast and the sovereign, a return that Derrida himself anticipated and desired, is that the 2002–03 seminar neglects to comment on Heidegger's remarkable reference, in section 63 of *The Fundamental Concepts*, to Paul's epistle to the Romans. In this epistle (8.19-22), Paul refers to the anxious awaiting of *all* creatures—and the sighing or groaning of *all* creation—for the end of transiency and death. Heidegger refers to his own meditation on this suffering of all creatures, which Luther calls their anxiety, a "fabulating" (*fabeln*), and it seems unlikely that Derrida could have overlooked this allusion to his, one of Derrida's own favorite genres, the fable. As uncanny as Derrida's own overlooking of such a passage is Krell's own noticing of it, the only passage "in all of dreary Paul" that, he says, is worth contemplating (DA 119). Why is this fable concerning what Nietzsche called "the cosmic Jesus"—that is, the Jesus who saves not only human beings but also all creation, transforming every living creature into a "child of God" (see DA 117)—so important for Heidegger? Is it because the fable shows the violence of *Walten* to be the shaking and shattering of *all* life by death? Krell suggests that in section 63 of *The Fundamental Concepts* Heidegger no longer falls back on the spurious distinction between human dying and animal perishing; that in the end, both the sphere of human life and the ring of animal life are shattered by death. This is the fable that might bring Heidegger and Derrida and their readers, including Krell, back to the "fundamental attunement" (*Grundstimmung*) that unites them all, the tragic attunement I referred to earlier.

In the meantime, along the way, much could be said about what draws Derrida and Krell together and makes their conversation so important today. For one thing, both recognize that inheritance is never finished, that "past" tradition is always ahead of us, awaiting a response. As well, both are incomparable Heidegger scholars, given to delineating from within the work of this great thinker differences that can make a difference to the way the dominant ethical and political discourses frame "the animal" question. Finally, to put this in Krell's words, here spoken of Derrida (though entirely applicable to *Where's Walden?*), both "recognize the Earth's surface as a garden of infinite differences and differentiations, a garden not spoiled by any single sovereign division, which always amounts to an 'us' versus a 'them.' Especially where other animals are concerned" (DA 106). To add Derrida's words, articulated both through the three theses he posits in the first session of the second *Beast and the Sovereign* seminar and again over several pages in the tenth session, these infinite differences and differentiations cannot be subsumed into a totality like the "world" (*Welt*): "there is no world that is one: *the* world, *a* world" (BS 266). Rather, the differences between the world of humans and the world of animals, between the worlds of animals of different species and between the worlds of humans of different cultures, are and "will remain always unbridgeable" (BS 8).

And, still as to the way, you might well ask what my path has been in this essay, if not a series of fits and starts? Although I set out to write on my experience of cabin solitude, two of David Krell's texts (*Where's Walden?* and *Derrida and Our Animal Others*) along with Derrida's second *The Beast and the Sovereign* seminar, soon lured me into treacherous waters. Perhaps I should have stayed on my island. I flee the city for the island because it is a retreat, a version of what David in chapter 4 of *Derrida and Our Animal Others* refers to as "The Peaceable Kingdom," a place where species coexist, and where humans cannot so easily escape the presence of death in life: a dead fox, for instance, tightly curled against the cold under the landing shed stairs, uncovered as a warm spring sun melts the winter's snow. Was the lone fox lonely and anxious as she sought shelter— or surrendered to her death—under the makeshift stairs? Or are humans more alone still, caught up in phantasms of their solitary privilege over all else that lives, and even then, lonely and apprehensive as I often am in my cabin, needing something, even a rope, to hold onto, something that will connect us across our too-far-removed solitudes?

For although "there is no world," as Derrida writes, although "there are only islands" (BS 9), including David's and mine, this does not lessen our need to connect with and "to carry" each other. Quite the contrary. "*Die Welt ist fort, ich muss dich tragen,*" Derrida writes more than once in the second *Beast and the Sovereign* seminar, citing Paul Celan. "The world is gone, I must carry you." (e.g., 255). And today, against all odds, the "end of the world" dares us to think that a difference can be made, that humans and animals are not separated from one another, "like one island from another by an abyss beyond which no shore [*rive*] is even promised which would allow anything, however little, to happen [*arriver*], anything worthy of the word 'happen'" (266).

Notes

1 All subsequent references to Volume II of the English edition of *The Beast and the Sovereign* are abbreviated as BS.

2 Hereafter abbreviated as DA. All of my citations from this 2013 book are taken from the Spring 2012 manuscript copy that David sent me. I should also point out that the first two chapters of *Derrida and Our Animal Others* appear in two separate 2012 issues of *Research In Phenomenology*, vol. 42, no. 2–3.

3 Hereafter abbreviated as WW.

4 Hereafter abbreviated as W. For altogether unscholarly reasons—because it is beautiful and belonged to my father, a man of solitude who also loved his life in the woods—I am following the edition of Walden annotated by Philip Van Doren Stern.

5 In the opening pages of *The Animal That Therefore I Am*, Derrida, too, recounts his experience of being held in the eyes of a cat, his cat, a real cat, behind whose gaze "there remains a bottomlessness," an alterity that is "uninterpretable, unreadable, undecidable, abyssal and secret" (12).

6 Hereafter abbreviated as ATT.

7 Hereafter abbreviated as FCM.

References

Defoe, Daniel. 2001. *Robinson Crusoe*. Introduction by Virginia Woolf. New York: Modern Library.

Derrida, Jacques. 2011. *The Beast and the Sovereign, Volume II*. Translated by Geoffrey Bennington. Chicago: University of Chicago Press.

Derrida, Jacques. 2008. *The Animal That Therefore I Am*. Edited by Marie-Louise Mallet. Translated by David Wills. New York: Fordham University Press.

Derrida, Jacques. 2005. *Rogues: Two Essays on Reason*. Translated by Pascale-Anne Brault and Michael Naas. Stanford, CA: Stanford University Press.

Derrida, Jacques. 2004. "Violence Against Animals." In *For What Tomorrow: A Dialogue with Elizabeth Roudinesco*. Translated by Jeff Fort. Stanford, CA: Stanford University Press, 62–76.

Derrida, Jacques. 1993. *Aporias*. Translated by Thomas Dutoit. Stanford, CA: Stanford University Press.

Derrida, Jacques. 1993. "Heidegger's Ear: Philopolemology (*Geschlecht* IV)." Translated by John P. Leavey Jr. *Reading Heidegger: Commemorations.* Edited by John Sallis. Bloomington: Indiana University Press, 163–218.

Derrida, Jacques. 1991. "'Eating Well,' or the Calculation of the Subject: An Interview with Jacques Derrida." Translated by Peter Connor and Avital Ronnell. In *Who Comes After The Subject?* Edited by Eduardo Cadava, Peter Connor, and Jean-Luc Nancy. New York: Routledge, 96–119.

Derrida, Jacques. *Of Spirit: Heidegger and the Question.* 1989. Translated by Geoffrey Bennington and Rachel Bowlby. Chicago: University of Chicago Press.

Derrida, Jacques. 1987. "*Geschlecht* II: Heidegger's Hand." Translated by John P. Leavey, Jr. In *Deconstruction and Philosophy: The Texts of Jacques Derrida.* Edited by John Sallis. Chicago: University of Chicago Press, 161–96.

Derrida, Jacques. 1983. "*Geschlecht*: Sexual Difference, Ontological Difference." Translated by Ruben Berezdivin. *Research In Phenomenology* 13: 65–83.

Enright, Robert. "Letters from the Earth: An Interview with Mike Olito." *BorderCrossings*, vol. 4, no. 4 (Fall 1985): 10–17.

Heath, Terrence. "Drawing a Line: The Art of Michael Olito." *BorderCrossings*, vol. 5, no. 3 (May 1986): 22–23.

Heidegger, Martin. 1995. *The Fundamental Concepts of Metaphysics: World, Finitude, Solitude.* Translated by William McNeil and Nicholas Walker. Bloomington: Indiana University Press.

Heidegger, Martin. *Being and Time.* 1962. Translated by John Macquarrie and Edward Robinson. New York: Harper & Row.

Krell, David Farrell. 2013. *Derrida and Our Animal Others: Derrida's Final Seminar, The Beast and the Sovereign.* Bloomington: Indiana University Press.

Krell, David Farrell. 2004. *Where's Walden? Conversations with Henry David Thoreau and Marlonbrando.* Unpublished manuscript.

Krell, David Farrell. 1992. *Daimon Life: Heidegger and Life Philosophy.* Bloomington: Indiana University Press.

Olito, Michael. *Earth Dialogue Earth Sounds.* Catalogue. Winnipeg Art Gallery Exhibition, February 2–April 6, 1986.

Royle, Nicholas. 2005. "Blind Cinema." In Kirby Dick and Amy Zeiring- Kofman, *Screenplay and Essays on the Film Derrida.* New York: Routledge, 10–21.

Thoreau, Henry David. 1976. *Walden; or, Life in the Woods.* Edited, annotated, and introduced by Philip van Doren Stern. New York: Bramhall House.

15

The Abandonment of the Circus Horses

H. Peter Steeves

It is an utterly bourgeois exercise, no doubt, but there is a tradition of wondering what prized possession one would rescue from one's home if it were on fire and there were only a few moments to grab a couple of things on the way out. My copy of David Farrell Krell's *Daimon Life* (1992) is always on my list. Out of all of David's books it is, perhaps, my favorite. But even so, in this magical age of one-click-Amazon shopping, it's not the book *per se* for which I'd risk my life. Rather it is my copy of the book, one of only two on Earth that is, in Krell's own words, *completed*. I prize it for the handwritten corrections and notes throughout its more-than-350 pages—each little mark tracing his careful reading, keen eye, and desire to make everything right. As a scholar who is well known for being a close and careful reader of texts, David Farrell Krell's presence announces itself more than ever on the page in these notes— thoughts about his own thinking. When I have this text close to me, I read those annotations and I read the personal inscription on the title page that speaks of friendship, and I am reminded of all that can go right in philosophy, in thinking, in community. All true. But I prize this book, as well, because of the handwritten final page. There, filling the white space on page 319, is a story, a conclusion to a final story—one that closes with the words, "The book is now finished." I am, perhaps, one of only two people who knows how *Daimon Life* really ends.

Other than death—which, as Heidegger knew, isn't an ending at all since endings have to be experienced as such in order to be endings, and death, the unthinkable trajectory of Dasein, is the impossibility of reflecting on something, looking back, and taking anything as anything at all—every ending is actually an opening up. When a text concludes, it begins. It begins reflecting back on itself, reconstituting its meaning, and pulling us back with it, into it, to begin being again. The point is the particular question with which we are left when the text ends and the journey begins. For any careful reader of *Daimon Life*, the question, though unwritten, should have been obvious: And what became of Cristy?

The story of humanity—the story we tell ourselves to make ourselves human, all too human—all too often refuses to investigate the correct lingering mystery: "And what of the animal?" It takes a pointed, perhaps daimonic, mind to ask such a question as well as to know, as David knows, that the question is already ethical even as it is also the question of Being and thus already asking after a "unified field of disclosure."[1]

In 2011, Hungarian filmmaker Béla Tarr released *The Turin Horse*, a two-and-a-half hour black-and-white film he has claimed will be his last. As in most of the lives of humans and other animals, there is very little plot to the film. Food is eaten, water is fetched, life is lived—until it is not. The story describes these details of everyday living and dwelling with care, following a man, his daughter, and their horse. The film begins with the following introduction:

> In Turin on 3rd January, 1889, Friedrich Nietzsche steps out of the doorway of number six, Via Carlo Alberto. Not far from him, the driver of a hansom cab is having trouble with a stubborn horse. Despite all his urging, the horse refuses to move, whereupon the driver loses his patience and takes his whip to it. Nietzsche comes up to the throng and puts an end to the brutal scene, throwing his arms around the horse's neck, sobbing. His landlord takes him home, he lies motionless and silent for two days on a divan until he mutters the obligatory last words, and lives for another ten years, silent and demented, cared for by his mother and sisters. We do not know what happened to the horse.

At the conclusion of the famous and heartbreaking story of Nietzsche's breakdown, Tarr, that is, is left to begin again, to tell the story that demands to be told, to ask the question that demands asking. History will record how Nietzsche apparently lost his mind, how he lived for another decade, and how all of philosophy was changed. True. Yes. *But what of the horse?*

In the kitchen there was the tall, white chair, and now, in the middle of winter, it was cold even when the rest of the room was very warm. It was metal, and metal things were always cooler, even in the summer. Like the railings along the steps in front of the library and the thick, round poles holding the swings in the park.

Above the flame, Mother held a skillet with pork chops. Scott watched her cook for a moment then returned to looking around the room. Soon his uncle would come down and sit at the table, and his black eyes would not look up from his breakfast of pork chops, eggs, potatoes, mush, brown bread toast, and coffee. Scott could hear the shaving water drain from the basin upstairs.

Near the register in the corner of the kitchen a red cat sat half asleep underneath the metal chair. Scott thought about the weekend. He thought about Sunday, about Mildred. He walked across the room and reached down and felt the cat's ear, thin and wet. Nothing like his own. Or a pig's. He sat down on the floor and began to run his finger along the slope of the cat.

E. G. came into the kitchen and Mother put the plate with the toast on the table. E. G. dropped a spoonful of raspberry preserves on top of one slice, spread it around with the back of the spoon, and began to eat.

"I'm going to set traps around the barn when I come home for lunch."

Mother salted the pork chops and pushed them with a wooden spoon. She cracked two eggs and dropped them into the pan. They hissed back as they hit the fat.

"I don't think Scott should have his friends over for a while. We won't speak of it. There's no way to know who we can trust."

"It's ridiculous," said Mother.

"Hmph." E. G. collected the preserves from the corners of his mouth with his wormy tongue. "Those children have parents and know people. Someone who knew about the traps could make his way into the barn and burn the whole thing to the ground while we sleep. Is that what you want?"

"But it's just not necessary. It's so dramatic. What if there's an accident?" "There won't be any accident. I'll show you where each one is when I'm done. And Scott— you just keep from the barn until I say. Understand?"

Scott nodded and E. G. forced the last corner of toast into his mouth. Mother put the plate with the rest of his breakfast on the table. E. G. poked at the eggs on top of the meat, letting the ruptured yolks coat each pork chop in a yellow glaze.

At least she had responded to him. That was good. It was a stupid thing to be doing. There had been two fires in six weeks and that was a reason to set bear traps around the barn? It wasn't even a real barn. Not a proper one. It wasn't even red. And what would happen if the cat stepped in one of the traps instead of the barn-burner? Or a stray or some other animal? If he shows me where they are, thought Scott, I will sneak out at night and spring them with a stick.

Between his fingers the cat's ear was still thin and wet, and Scott thought of the pigs he had seen at the fair last summer that could race around a track when the man lifted the doors to their cage. They would smash their heads against the metal screen and cry to be released, and when they finished the race there was a butter cookie at the end of the track lying in the dirt for the winner. One by one they would round the last turn and jumble across the finish line, the winner sucking up his prize while the others sniffed the ground and pushed small piles of dirt with their thick noses as if expecting to uncover some undeserved reward.

E. G. finished his breakfast in silence. After he left, Mother made toast and an egg for Scott and washed the morning dishes. Scott did his Saturday chores and left just before noon with a kiss from his mother and a fresh change of clothes bundled into a pillowcase.

Horses have helped found cities since, perhaps, the days of the first city. When it comes to founding something, it's always about the horse who is a war horse, of course, of course. But there are other ways in which equine companions have helped pull together a polis.

The American circus and the American city grew up together, and both were built on the backs of American horses. Eighteenth-century riding schools gave birth to the American circus, and feats of equestrian daring and skill were the first circus acts, only later giving way to clowning, trapeze and wire-walking, and "exotic animal" taming. In the nineteenth century, the horse led the circus parade through town, announcing the show that was to come. By the turn of the next century, Ringling Brothers and Barnum and Bailey Circus had 1,400 horses employed between them—something like a multitude of cavalry regiments. When inspiration died and the circus animals abandoned the town, it was the horses that had them in tow.

We remember that Socrates, inspired while defending himself against his fellow citizens and accusers, referred to himself as a gadfly, or what is sometimes translated as "a horsefly."

> ἐὰν γάρ με ἀποκτείνητε, οὐ ῥᾳδίως ἄλλον τοιοῦτον εὑρήσετε, ἀτεχνῶς—εἰ καὶ γελοιότερον εἰπεῖν—προσκείμενον τῇ πόλει ὑπὸ τοῦ θεοῦ ὥσπερ ἵππῳ μεγάλῳ μὲν καὶ γενναίῳ, ὑπὸ μεγέθους δὲ νωθεστέρῳ καὶ δεομένῳ ἐγείρεσθαι ὑπὸ μύωπός τινος, οἷον δή μοι δοκεῖ ὁ θεὸς ἐμὲ τῇ πόλει προστεθηκέναι τοιοῦτόν τινα, ὃς ὑμᾶς ἐγείρων καὶ πείθων καὶ ὀνειδίζων ἕνα ἕκαστον οὐδὲν παύομαι τὴν ἡμέραν ὅλην πανταχοῦ προσκαθίζων.[2]

There's so much to interest us here that an entire civilization's philosophy could be started from these words. We might, for instance, wish to focus on that particular creature, the gadfly (μύωπός), and note that what Socrates is literally saying is that he is *myopic* and cannot see. The Greek μύωπός comes from μύειν ("to shut") and ὤψ ("eye"). How strange, then, that Socrates's most famous animal moniker is one that makes us conclude that either he is blind or he is driving the rest of Athens to the point of having to shut their eyes—not exactly, at least at first glance, what we would expect from someone who claims to see the light outside the cave. There is enough controversy, to be sure, in the gadfly, but if we focus instead on the beast that the gadfly is said to be annoying, we find the city of Athens in the curious guise of a horse.

This is not quite Hobbes's body-state fashioned on an artificial man. It is not quite Derridean political flesh founded on a healthy autoimmune system. This is the polis as daimon and equine. A horse-state that is about to kill its minor annoyance and send Socrates to his death. The size difference between Socrates and Athens, between the gadfly and the horse, is telling. But again, perhaps the deeper point is hiding in plain sight. Perhaps the problem with Athens is that it has a horse-body rather than a human-body, that it is beastly, monstrous, and far too large.

It is hard to find solitude of any kind in the metropolis, let alone a creative solitude. Some true philosophers take to the hills, to Black Forest cabins, to places farther away than the rest of us wish them. Some, upon reaching fifty, are reminded by their mothers that renouncing a promising career as a juvenile delinquent in order to become a sober philosopher instead should only ever be allowed if one commits to retaining the *joie de vivre* of a ten-year-old—otherwise it is far too dangerous and too costly. Such *joie*, however, is just the sort of thing that upsets the administrators and civilians, just the sort of thing that sets a nag to nipping.

Fearing a second swat, Aristotle fled Athens many years after Socrates was killed. Supposedly, he was not trying to save his own hide but instead merely did not want the city to "sin twice against philosophy." Nothing was as it should be—though one would think that Aristotle, of all people, pointing to the Earth rather than the heavens, would have known and understood that. Aristotle, at least, surely understood the problem of size. Concerning the extent of the polis, he wrote:

> [the] possibility of increase is not without limit, and what the limit of the state's expansion is can easily be seen from practical considerations . . . .[I]n order to decide questions of justice and in order to distribute offices according to merit it is necessary for the citizens to know each other's personal characters, since where this does not happen to be the case the business of electing officials and trying lawsuits is bound to go badly. Haphazard decision is unjust in both matters, and this must obviously prevail in an excessively numerous community. (*Politics* 1326b)

It would be unwise to ignore the importance of the relative size of the animals in Plato's metaphor. It is not merely that the gadfly is small and the horse is large, however. Nor is it merely that something so small can be constitutive of a larger beast (since it is the gadfly, after all, that causes the horse to act in a horse-like manner, buzzing around the horse so that the horse swishes her tail, twitches her ears, and generally acts like a horse; without the fly, that is, there would be no recognizable horse). Rather, in his gadfly speech, Socrates says that he has been divinely sent to nip at Athens because the city-state is like "a large thoroughbred, which is a bit sluggish because of its size." That is, it is the size of the overgrown polis-horse that is the source of the problem Socrates has been sent to address.

Plato will declare that there is an ideal size to the city. In book IV of the *Republic*, we learn only that the best size is one that is not too large or too small, but in *Laws* 737e we are told, precisely, that the ideal number is 5,040 citizens.[3] Aristotle will later make the more important, if less specific, claim: in order to decide questions of justice, citizens must actually know each other.[4] By the time of Socrates's death, Athens was far more populous than either philosopher would have recommended—perhaps on the order of thirty or forty times larger than Plato's ideal. It would follow that a trial in such a large city would be incapable of leading to justice. Rather than having direct experience of Socrates's actions, most of the jurors would have to go on hearsay. If it is correct to say that the self, for an Athenian, was constituted by what others said publicly about that person,[5] then Socrates is pointing out, by drawing attention to the size of the horse that is Athens, the fact that hearsay cannot lead to justice. More than this, though, the entire Athenian way of life, based on a sort of public hearsay constituting each citizen, was being criticized.

It is the nature of a horse to die if he never stops growing. And it is the nature of a gadfly to question all talk of nature and all talk of boundaries. This, too, is a point only made clear by putting Aristotle into conversation with Plato. We might imagine that the Greeks would have considered a fly to be the sort of creature that spontaneously generates. Socrates's origin, then, would be from nothing. The philosopher—and philosophy—arising from no-place, no-history, no-context. But in Aristotle's *History of Animals* we learn, and assume that it was widely believed, that the gadfly was not like other flies. "Some animals at first live in water," writes Aristotle, "and by and by change their shape and live out of water, as is the case with river worms, for out of these the gadfly develops."[6] Thus, in using the gadfly metaphor, Plato was casting Socrates as the sort of being that has left one home and taken up a very different place of residence in a very different form. The worm that slithers through water shifts into the fly that buzzes through the air. The philosopher is a liminal creature.[7] And if we think we know with certainty what a philosopher is by the end of Plato's text, we should remember that the lover of wisdom must move, modify, and change, living in the space between the water and the ether—neither of which is the Earth, the place of humans.

This liminal philosopher-beast does not merely annoy the horse-state. Rather, according to Aristotle, the gadfly uses his mouth as a weapon.

> This is plainly to be seen in flies and bees and all such animals, and likewise in some of the Testacea. In the Purpurae, for instance, so strong is this part that it enables them to bore holes through the hard covering of shell-fish, of the spiral snails, for example, that are used as bait to catch them. So also the gadflies and cattle-flies can pierce through the skin of man, and some of them even through the skins of other animals. Such, then, in these animals is the nature of the tongue, which is thus as it were the counterpart of the elephant's nostril. For as in the elephant the nostril is used as a weapon, so in these animals the tongue serves as a sting.[8]

If Aristotle reports to us commonly held beliefs about animals, then Plato's audience would know that when Socrates compares himself to a gadfly and swears that he only means to buzz and bother, the truth of the matter is that he is using his words—his *logos*, his speech, his humanity-by-way-of-animality—as a weapon to pierce, cut, and attack the horse that is Athens. Socrates's tongue bore holes in his listeners. It is little wonder that so few converted and took up the project of the examined life.

Conversions are always dangerous business, and convertors always perilous citizens. When Socrates heard his daimon speaking to him, he took it to be a gift from the gods, warning him and guiding him, making him "replete with knowledge." More than four centuries later, due southeast across the Mediterranean Sea, Saul of Tarsus was on the road to Damascus when he heard a divine voice as well. To be fair, the men traveling with Saul heard the voice, too, but Saul himself both heard and saw this daimon. Saul was headed to a new city in hopes of finding more Christians to kill—a vocation at which he had so far excelled as a zealous Pharisee—when suddenly Jesus appeared to him, blinding him, and Saul fell from his horse. Fully participating in logos, Saul heard Jesus and understood the words. And the knowledge of Jesus's divinity made him myopic. In the middle of the sandy road, he squirmed on the ground, overcome, as his men and his horse were startled but could not fully understand what was happening. At least this is how history has come to remember the event. Saul's horse, in fact, is very nearly the main subject in Caravaggio's depiction of this scene in his magnificent *Conversion on the Way to Damascus* (1601). The horse's beautiful painted haunches and raised right-front hoof take up more than half of the canvas, front and center, while Saul wallows in agony on the path below. Everywhere, such darkness and such light.

This is the birth of the greatest Apostle of Christ. It is a story every Christian, perhaps every Westerner, knows. The traveling companions end up taking the blinded Saul the rest of the way to Damascus, where he stays, rests, and starts to come to grips with his new faith as well as his redirected missionary zeal. Saul will soon start going by the name Paul: a new man is born. He'll become the cornerstone of a world religion, of a world that has just recently started counting time from the year zero. His converts will begin multiplying across the face of the Earth—across all of God's footstool—and come to play a major role in the world's history over the next two millennia. He will author more than half of the books of the New Testament, and be the subject of as many Acts of the Apostles. Saul enters Damascus a new man, and Damascus comes to be a new city because of it. This much we know, as we know the rest of Saul's ending and Paul's new beginning, though the Bible never speaks of Paul's death, his perishing, his meeting his maker years after the road to Damascus.

True. Good. Yes. But what of the horse?

In the summer, the walk downtown was much shorter. E. G.'s house, though it had a barn, was not really a farmhouse, and it sat on the edge of town—right where the change from country to town took place. Along the way, Scott thought about how much he missed the summer. E. G. said that dark winters mold men.

As he approached the Sigma Theatre, Scott felt in his pocket to make sure he had brought along the change for the picture. Jake should already be there, waiting before going inside. What did he say was playing? It didn't matter, of course, as long as she would be there. Mildred. It was a name to be pronounced slowly. Scott had said it to himself a thousand times over the last week, and now he would watch as she sat at the piano, silently repeating the syllables in her presence.

The front of the Sigma had a large case with pictures in it, and finding himself alone, Scott pressed his face against the glass and studied the photographs. Strangers. Movie stars. Soft faces, distant and expressionless. The window began to fog and Scott wiped the glass with his coat sleeve then opened his mouth and squeezed a slow and steady flow of air from his chest, watching it collect again around the swipe he had made. That was one of the tricks. He put his hand to his mouth and felt the warm air pass around his fingers. As he exhaled more forcefully the air became cold and less pleasant. That was how he could control the temperature of his breath. Still, it was a strange trick. The air got warm deep in his lungs and stayed that way when coaxed out. Even in the middle of winter his breath could be warmed in his body. *That was being warm-blooded. A warm-blooded creature. He wondered if the temperature of his breath was ever 98.6 and why it cooled so quickly when he blew faster.*

To save time, Scott went to the booth and bought two tickets with the money he and Mother had collected—pennies mostly, from the days when E. G. would take a nap on the couch and his large pockets would seed the cushions. E. G. was paying for the movie, and tonight he had agreed to let Scott spend the night at Jake's and go with his family to their church in the morning. *It was all falling together. He was in control. It was getting late. The music before the movie would start soon.*

Jake had seemed surprised days before when Scott admitted his love for the piano player. *She was at least twenty—so old—and Scott didn't even know her name.* Still, the next afternoon the boys waited in the alley behind the Sigma for the matinee to finish, and Scott pointed her out as she left the theater. "Oh, that's Mildred," smiled Jake. "She plays at our church."

Scott felt a slap on his back, and he emptied his lungs in a sharp, coughing pain. Jake smiled and raised an eyebrow, and the boys disappeared into the theatre. They were seated by a thin man with a flashlight who smelled like butter. As his eyes widened, Scott began to make out the form of the piano at the front of the theater where Mildred sat playing. *This is home*, he thought. *This is our home and everything is good and always has been good and always will be.*

Der Kluge Hans was not only a clever horse but a good horse as well. Perhaps he bit and stomped a bit when forced to undergo hour upon hour of testing at the hands of his impatient inquisitors. But such spiritedness was at least partially constitutive of his goodness.

In the early 1900s, Clever Hans became world famous for being able to answer mathematical problems by tapping out the solutions with his feet. Wilhelm von Osten, a math teacher in the gymnasium, was Hans's trainer and owner; and von Osten would speak to Hans (in German, of course), explaining the question having to do with basic addition, subtraction, or even complex problems involving multiplication, division, and fraction work in general, and, after a moment of quiet calculation, Hans would begin hoofing at the ground until he had counted out the correct numerical response. "Subtract 5 from 8," von Osten might say. "Now multiply by 4. Then divide that answer by half." *Tap, tap, tap, tap, tap, tap* came the response. Hans was correct about 90 percent of the time.

Because all of Europe, and even the United States, was obsessed with Hans, the German National Board of Education created The Hans Commission to study this apparent miracle: an animal that was not *weltarm*. The commission included a circus owner, military men, zookeepers, veterinarians, and school teachers; and it was chaired by Professor Carl Stumpf, who had been influenced by Franz Brentano in his mixing of philosophy and psychology in order to study, in a proto-phenomenological way, the manner in which experience takes place so as to discover its necessary and universal structures. Stumpf would go on to meet and influence Husserl who would go on to meet and influence Heidegger who would go on to meet and influence David Krell. David, it turns out, is part of an unbroken line—hand to hand to hand to hand to hoof—with Clever Hans.

In 1904, the commission submitted its report. Von Osten was not cheating. No evidence could be found of fraud; no tricks seemed to be involved. Amazed at the result, Stumpf asked his volunteer assistant in Berlin, Oskar Pfungst, to continue to investigate the matter independently. It would take three more years, but after going straight to the horse's mouth and running thousands of tests himself, Pfungst came up with similar findings. Varying his methodology here and there, he discovered, however, a telltale statistic. Hans's success rate was, indeed, close to 90 percent when he was asked a question the answer to which his trainer—or at least most others in the audience—knew the correct answer. But when no one near Hans knew the right answer to the question, Hans's rate dropped to 6 percent. This huge discrepancy needed explanation, and so Pfungst began working on various hypotheses. There was still no evidence that anyone was cheating. The owner and the audiences brought into the lab seemed to be sincere and honest. But Pfungst constructed a likely story that could explain it all away—a story involving body posture. Perhaps, reasoned Pfungst, von Osten and others were giving subtle cues to Hans even if they didn't mean to be doing so. When Hans began to tap his hoof, for instance, everyone would look down at the floor. As Hans got to the correct answer, people in the audience would "almost imperceptibly" look up again or relax their muscles in anticipation of Hans's stopping. Hans, argued Pfungst, was simply able to read the complex body language of the audience and perform a simple task: start tapping his hoof when people looked downward or tensed up, and stop tapping when people looked up or relaxed. Pfungst published his theory and "The Clever Hans Effect" was born, changing the way most experimental behavioral research is done involving animals (including humans). If the researcher can involuntarily give cues even when he or she wishes to suppress them, it was soon accepted practice that most subjects were tested in isolation, with minimal to no interaction between the subjects and the researcher. Von Osten was unconvinced, finding the story merely a story, and not a convincing one at that.

It is unclear if Pfungst was correct. Though celebrated as a high point in rigorous adherence to a modern scientific methodology, the truth of the matter is that Pfungst could never prove that the cues were responsible for Hans's behavior. Appealing to *imperceptible* body comportment that unconsciously appears even against one's will and outside of one's ability to notice doesn't exactly make for the strongest empiricism. Pfungst constructed a narrative. It's a narrative that explains a lot. It explains why Hans has a high success rate at math problems when he can see people who know the correct answer, and otherwise does not. But it is, in the end, a story. A piece of fiction. And we either accept it as helpful in understanding our experience of the world or we don't. It's like magic, really. The skeptic who wishes to "explain away" a handkerchief that floats around the magician's head, bobs back and forth, in and out of pockets, and seems to be alive, often appeals to hidden wires, translucent and imperceptible bits of fishing line, mirrors, or obscured assistants pulling all of the strings. In other words, the skeptic—somewhat ironically—appeals to that which cannot be seen, is not being seen, is beyond all seeing. There might be very good reasons to accept such a story, but if we think it is something *fundamentally* different from other explanatory stories—that it is not a story but is instead *the truth*—then we have fooled ourselves. Or perhaps we have always already fooled ourselves if we think that stories and philosophies and truths are ever separate things.

More than this, though, if Pfungst was correct and Hans merely learned to manage these micro-microscopic cues and figure out when to start and stop tapping his hoof based on them, it is utterly unclear in what sense this is not still deeply and profoundly clever. It is unclear, that is, what the word "merely" is doing in that last sentence.

And yet even more than this, too, it is further unclear how we are doing something so completely different when we humans communicate with each other and do math as well. My own von Osten was named Mrs. MacDonald. In the first grade she taught me that $8 - 5 = 3$. I learned the rules in hopes of gaining her approval, her love, and very likely a piece of candy. If you would have asked me a few years later in middle school *why* 3 was the right answer—why 5 from 8 is necessarily and universally equal to anything—I would have looked at you dimly and perhaps twitched my ear or resettled on my haunches in silence. Because I trained in analytic philosophy in graduate school, reading Plato, but then Frege, Gödel, Russell, and Whitehead, and because I continued my training later by reading Husserl and Heidegger, I could talk today until I was hoarse about what math means and why it means and how and why it seems to work. But I am not sure that this is anything more than a bit of higher *dressage*. If I can do calculus on my own, now, it is because I have internalized Mrs. MacDonald and all of the von Ostens that came after her in my life. Their still voices are in my head—or perhaps more accurately, their imperceptibly tensing and relaxing bodies watch over me like ghosts. And I tap my hoof and stop even when it seems I am the only one watching myself. Call this a trick. Call it a more advanced trick than any horse has ever done. Call it *nous*. Call us all in from the field, together.

David, in chapter 3 of *Daimon Life*, quotes Heidegger who has just quoted St. Paul. "In the end," writes Heidegger, "one does not really need Christian faith in order to understand something of those words that Paul (in 8 Romans 19) writes concerning the ἀποχαραδοχία τῆς χτίσεως, the creatures' and all creation's longing gaze [*von dem sehnsüchtigen Ausspähen der Geschöpfe und der Schöpfung*]; for the ways of creation, as the Book of Esra (IV, 7, 12) also says, have in this eon become narrow, mournful, and arduous [*schmal, traurig und mühselig*]." David then adds a gloss to the word *traurig*: "'Sad, sorrowful,' we would normally say. Here I would render it more literally as 'full of mourning.'"[9] The question is: If animals cannot die—if they merely perish as Heidegger would demand—then what does it mean to imagine a mourning animal? What does it mean, David wonders, to think about Homer's description of the immortal horses, "Achilles's deathless steeds,"[10] who stand over the body of the fallen Patroklos and weep?

Taking Heidegger to task for his inability to think outside a tradition that has, for so long, maintained a hierarchy in which humans are always above animals, David reminds his reader of Aquinas's reasons for celebrating the uprightness of *Homo erectus*, the fact that we, unlike so many animals, have hands at the end of our arms and walk on two legs. "Were man to scurry about on all fours," explains David, explaining Aquinas, ". . . his hands would be pedestrian utensils, his *utilitas manuum* lost forever . . . [And] if his hands were feet, man would have to seize food with his mouth, his head would be oblong, his snout extending far beyond the neck and torso . . . . All this, to be sure, would impede the speech of living language . . . ."[11] How could Heidegger hear Hans speak with his hooves, with *mere* pedestrian utensils? How could Heidegger believe that there was anything there thinking, anything there living, anything there ready to calculate or to die?

Von Osten continued to tour with Hans after Pfungst's report came out, drawing large crowds across Europe. Hans's oblong face appeared along with his story in the *New York Times*. He was beloved even when "debunked." Von Osten died suddenly in 1909, though, at which point Clever Hans was sold. History records Hans having several owners over the next few years until, eventually, he was conscripted into the German cavalry in World War I. By 1916, there is no record of what happened to Hans or if he mourned those around him or counted his dead. In the years that followed, Oskar Pfungst never earned his degree and published little after his time with Hans. He eventually took up a minor lecturing position with the University of Frankfurt and died in 1933. Carl Stumpf retired from the University of Berlin in 1921 and, because his approach had gone out of vogue and was not being elaborated on by the next generation of students and researchers, left little in terms of a scholarly legacy, dying bitterly in 1936.

Yes, yes. We know how their story ends; we mourn their passing. But what of the horse?

At the Hodgins's farm, Scott ate a long dinner, talked with Jake's mother, ignored Jake's sister, and, eventually, helped Jake's father pull a cot up from the basement and set it up in Jake's room. He tried to sleep. In the corner of the room, there was a spider sliding down from the ceiling. Scott watched her and listened to the sounds of the house. They were different. Jake's family was asleep. He could sense that. He could sense that he and the spider were the only ones awake in the house. And after a couple of hours of silence and dark, he could see and hear everything. They had become easy prey. In bed and trusting, the Hodgins family was no match. That's how E. G. would have it. Under cover of the night, slipping bear traps around their beds because you never know. Why had he given in? If you go to church then by God you'll be Presbyterian! And then, without warning, he had given permission. Maybe he thought it best to have Scott away tonight: some horrible plan to catch an innocent soul—best to do it all alone. But with his mother still there? That wasn't alone. It was almost alone. It didn't matter. Tomorrow would be the day to talk to Mildred. Everything was under control.

In the early morning, Mrs. Hodgins cut an apple and gave half each to her son and to Scott while Jake's sister gummed at a cracker. There was coffee and some sort of roll with white icing for the adults. After church, Jake had said, there would be a big meal for the entire family. The entire family. Us. Outside it was still dark.

When they arrived to the church, Jake's family moved toward the middle rows of pews. Scott had hoped they would be closer to the front. Lagging behind had at least made him the last to enter the long bench, and he sat on the aisle with a clear view of the piano. He took a hymnal and looked up the songs that were scheduled on the chalkboard, just as Jake had described. He thought he knew one of them. He had heard his mother sing those words when she was washing dishes, and now when Mildred played, he would sing it the loudest. He turned to studying the room. The stand where the minister would likely be was made of cherry. Probably cherry.

And a purple cloth fell across it like a blanket, hanging thin and sad down both sides. Behind the stand was a large circular window with wooden beams forming a cross and dividing the window into four unequal sections. The glass was thick and foggy, and the weak winter morning—still struggling to begin—was unable to force its way into the dark church. A row of square windows along the west wall of the church did little to help. Jake had said that Mildred would be sitting in the first pew when she wasn't playing, but Scott couldn't see her. There were other people that he knew, though. It was funny to see them all together. People who didn't belong together. People that you'd never think of in the same thought, sitting side by side.

When Mildred appeared and sat down at the piano, Scott straightened up and pulled at the sleeve on his left arm, stretching a shirt long outgrown. In front of the piano, she seemed somehow translucent—as if the weak light in the room could pass through her and exit more brilliantly, cast prism-like on the keys and pedals. The music expanded as she played, filling the silence, seeping into the walls, burrowing into the pews and ceiling beams. Scott could feel it as much as hear it, and he tensed his muscles as if bracing against a wind. He didn't want to cry, but he wanted to do something like crying.

The music finished and Scott saw the expression on Mildred's body change, her head lowering and her arms flowing to her sides in a hush. Through the back of her white dress he could sense her shoulder blades sleeping like the nubs of wings. In the stillness, as Reverend Brownson began to speak and the last remnant of music had tunneled and hidden itself away, Mildred turned to look out at the congregation and was met with Scott's burning stare.

David will remind us again how all of creation is "full of mourning" in *The Tragic Absolute* (2005). In a chapter entitled, "God's Footstool," the same passage from Heidegger that appeared in *Daimon Life*—the passage that references St. Paul and tells us that the ways of creation have become *schmal, traurig, und mühselig*—is once again analyzed, this time with an eye toward Paul's relationship to Schelling and the question of whether or not other creatures "languish with us."[12] They do, David wants to affirm, going on to claim that Heidegger comes close "—not as close as Schelling, but still very close—to expanding the notion of anxiety to include animal life, which, like human life, is invaded by death."[13] Three sentences below this, David quotes Joyce's *Ulysses* at a point where Stephen Dedalus is thinking about the languishing of the living world all around him; and the beauty of such fading, suffering, and neglect is so utterly convincing that we cannot help but conclude that we are all, indeed, in this together.

But let us turn for a moment to *Ulysses* at a different point. Later, in Bloom's final major hallucination in the Circe section of the novel, he encounters Madame Bella Cohen, the owner of the brothel in which he and Stephen find themselves, and imagines switching genders with her. She becomes Mr. Bello, and Bloom becomes the prostitute who is ridden like a horse and subjected to a series of cruel debaucheries:

> BELLO: (With bobbed hair, purple gills, fit moustache rings round his shaven mouth, in mountaineer's puttees, green silverbuttoned coat, sport skirt and alpine hat with moorcock's feather, his hands stuck deep in his breeches pockets, places his heel on her neck and grinds it in) Footstool! Feel my entire weight. Bow, bondslave, before the throne of your despot's glorious heels so glistening in their proud erectness.
>
> BLOOM: (Enthralled, bleats) I promise never to disobey.[14]

When it is difficult to tell the difference between a horse, a footstool, and a woman, there is always something driving such confusion, some troubling ontological as well as political and ethical power that is in play. In "God's Footstool," David tells us stories of horse-people and lascivious Centaurs, mixed forms of life "like the divine"—a point he drives home with a careful and nuanced etymological analysis of the German word for animal, *Tier*, by way of Nietzsche's phrase *Thierwerdung*, which David argues points to the "*Tyr-werdung* of God, the very becoming-god of god, . . . [such that] the distinction between God and animal dissolves altogether . . . ."[15]

These sorts of confusions abound when sex comes into play, especially when the focus is male sexuality which seems so often caught up in defining itself precisely in terms of its misogyny (i.e., what it hates but purports to love; what it is not) and thus power. *Ulysses* is, arguably, the greatest novel. *Don Quixote* was, arguably, the first novel. And as early as *Quixote* there are questions of confused identity at work driving the narrative. Don Quixote himself, of course, is up for grabs, and so, too, is his literary double, his old and worn out horse, Rocinante. Unlike Nietzsche, when Don Quixote lost his mind he kept his equine companion close by, and though Rocinante's name is itself a complex puzzle (literally meaning "he who was a low-quality horse before" but also acting as an etymologically complicated pun on "rationality/reasoning") such that the moniker calls into question the horse's vitality, Rocinante comes alive when faced with lure of sex. In chapter XV, then, the horse is let loose in a field to graze, but spying a herd of Galician ponies he rushes energetically toward the mares only to have them bite and kick him without mercy. The mares' owners fall on Rocinante as well, beating him with stakes, and the episode does not end well for Quixote, Sancho, or Rocinante. After the horse's amorous advances and resultant beating, there are many more adventures that Quixote will have before coming to realize who he truly is, and thus dying, at the end of the novel. It should not surprise us at this point, though, that we never learn the fate of his valiant horse.

Little Hans—who was, perhaps, less than especially clever, though that seems an unfair and perhaps even cruel thing to say about a five-year-old boy—became one of Freud's most famous case studies. We know Hans's fate. We know of Hans's childhood obsession with his (and his father's) "widdler." And we know that Hans's phobia concerning horses was diagnosed by Freud to be a confusion. Unable to face his true fear of being castrated by his father, Hans was said to transfer the fear onto something representing his father: horses, especially white horses with black bits and blinders (which represented Hans's father who was pale, had a dark mustache, and wore glasses). Hans, that is, molded his world so that he couldn't tell the difference between his father and a horse. Freud's Oedipus Complex theory was already worked out at this time, already in Freud's past. It would be more than a decade until his notion of death drives (*Todestriebe*) would bring *Thanatos* to challenge *Eros*. One wonders, looking back, if the later-Freud would have made more of Little Hans's initial report of his fear, a report long before the details of bits and blinders and biting came to the fore. Initially, Hans claimed that he was afraid that horses would fall down in the street and make a noise with their feet. It was only later that he suggested he was afraid of a particular kind of horse, and apparently afraid of being bitten. Hans had witnessed a horse die from exhaustion while trying to pull a bus-carriage laden with humans. The horse, in the throes of death, collapsed on the cobblestones, his hooves rattling and clattering against the paving rocks in violent spasm while the boy looked on. While Freud would no doubt be the first to describe such pangs as orgasmic, it seems just as likely that Little Hans was spooked by the sound of a horse *dying* rather than *perishing*, the sound of true languishing and finality, the sound of what it means to be "invaded by death."

David tells us that Schelling never saw God's footstool—a vanished statue that Schelling nevertheless describes in the 1811 version of *The Ages of the World*. The problem of how one gives an account of what one has never seen is, according to David, the problem of Schelling's "The Past."[16] Of course, David means that it is, as well, the problem of *the past*, the problem of history. As it is a problem for Freud, who diagnosed Little Hans without even seeing him at first. As it is a problem for every map that contains on it a utopia, the only sorts of maps, it turns out, the lascivious Oscar Wilde cared to consult. In his analysis of Raphael's painting, *The Vision of Ezekiel* (1514–18)—the likeliest candidate for the painting to which Schelling is referring when he speaks of God's footstool in the work of Raphael—David remarks that the "right foot of the Lord is reposing on one of the pinions of the winged ox or bull (Luke), an image that conflates heaven and earth, throne and footstool."[17] With conversions, there is always confusion. With iconography, there are always conflations. But how could anyone mistake earth for heaven, the place of languishing for the place of joy? Isn't heaven a place beyond, while here and now we are merely waiting for the riders of the apocalypse, torturing each other in the meantime?

Chivalry, that most sexist of virtues, begins with the quixotic knight, with, literally, *horse soldiery*. It turns out that there is no mention in the Bible of Saul riding a horse on his way to Damascus, yet most of us, looking back at a past we have never seen, would declare otherwise. Another apocryphal (and less than chivalrous) story involving a fictional horse is often told about the death of Catherine the Great. Having plotted a coup against her husband, Peter III, and then, most likely, dispatching an assassin to kill him, Catherine found herself the Empress of Russia at the Christ-ascending age of thirty-three. Never one to hide her joy of sex and her desire for young lovers sometimes a third her age, Catherine soon found herself the object of misogynistic rumors. At a time when women were thought to be inferior in every way to men—a time not necessarily in our past—Catherine shaped Europe, wielded power adeptly, made her enemies into footstools, and never apologized for who she was or what she desired.

In the end, there is very little to separate a good story from good philosophy— or a bad story from bad philosophy. One should rightly be confused in trying to do the separation, but not so in making the judgment.

Catherine died from a stroke at the age of sixty-seven while sitting on the toilet. But that is not the story we all know, or want to know. It is not the story that swept Europe days after her death in November of 1796. Catherine, it is said, was in her royal bed, her servants at the ready attempting to do the impossible, trying to satiate her insatiable libido by lowering a fully erect stallion onto the naked Empress by means of a system of ropes and pulleys. Unable to handle the weight and violent kicking of the beast, the servants panicked on all sides as the ropes frayed and snapped and the half-ton animal fell onto the waiting Catherine, crushing her. Catherine, it is said, died instantly on her back. Her will read, "Lay out my corpse dressed in white, with a golden crown on my head, and on it inscribe my Christian name. Mourning dress is to be worn for six months, and no longer: the shorter the better."[18] In the end, the Russians dressed her in silver. The Europeans associated her Christian name with lust. And all of creation languished in mourning for another 121 years.

Da, da. But what of the horse?

"The question, my friends, is not one of preparation. We are not thinking today of elemental fury, eternal damnation, or the plight of the tortured soul cast into the fires of hell. We are not speaking of heavenly mansions, mystical euphoria, or the blissful spirit judged worthy of sitting near God like a trusted dog content to sleep at the foot of his master. We are not here this morning to prepare, that is, but to create. We are not here to ask, but to do.

"We open our fellowship together as Christ opens the Gospel of Mark, declaring that 'the time is fulfilled and the kingdom of God is at hand.' The kingdom of God is at hand! Do you hear this truth resounding? This is the kingdom of God. This town and this congregation. This world and this time. The kingdom of God is upon us but we are blind. We live as if our duty were anticipation, but God puts it to us to hear these words, to feel these words: ours is the kingdom!

"The message of our Lord Jesus Christ is that the future is here now. We need not wait for heaven, for it is all around us. The prophetic word calls us to be the people living in the future—to be the people accepting of such a vision and thus abandon the past to make the present into the future. This word creates, and so do we, for if we were but to live as if this were already heaven, we would see that we are already correct. The power through which that creation is channeled is, and always has been, love. 'What is the greatest commandment?' Christ is asked. 'Love,' comes the response. Love your God and love each other. The two are inseparable, and there is no greater commandment than this. It is love, friends. Love that opens our eyes to the kingdom already spread upon the Earth. Love that forges a world in which such a kingdom can already be seen to exist. And so we begin. Let us pray . . . ."

It was then that the first person heard the screaming and turned his attention to the world without. For a moment, the sound was just a shrill background noise, barely distinguishable from the wind. But as it grew louder and more distinct, it became clearer. Somewhere, a woman was screaming that there was a fire.

The church had been built on Beeler Road, a secluded stretch of dirt held together in the summer by rows of wheat and corn for at least two miles on every side. Now in the brown winter sea it stood alone, apart from the half-dozen or so houses dropped liked anchors in the open fields. The men who owned the land stood, realizing the implications of the screaming and the possibility of their barns' burning at that very moment.

Scott rose from his seat and looked for Mildred, but before his eyes could settle, a strange glow coming through the circular window behind the minister captured his attention and his will. With an erratic motion, it grew closer until it filled the window and cast an orange and hazy light into the church. A thundering followed it. Scott watched as the glow turned and passed along the bank of windows on the west side of the church, burning close to the ground and rumbling. Through the thick panes he could see the outline of a horse encased in flames, and he rushed to the glass, following the creature with his eyes until the blurry image was extinguished by the horizon.

Notes

1 Cf. David Farrell Krell, *Daimon Life: Heidegger and Life-Philosophy* (Bloomington: Indiana University Press, 1992), 316.

2 Plato, *The Apology* 30d-e. Editor's note: "It is literally true (even if it sounds rather comical) that [the] God has specially appointed me to this city, as though it were a large thoroughbred horse which because of its great size is inclined to be lazy and needs the stimulation of some stinging fly. It seems to me that [the] God has

attached me to this city to perform the office of such a fly; and all day long never ceasing I never cease to settle here, there, and everywhere, rousing, persuading, reproving every one of you." (Hugh Tredennick translation)

3   This has something to do with the mathematical specialness of the number more than any practical question. As befitting Plato, the nature of the formal number is more important than that number of physical bodies living in proximity to each other. The figure of 5,040 has something to do with the way in which 5,040 is perfectly divisible by 2; the resulting number is perfectly divisible by 3; the resulting number is perfectly divisible by 4; etc., up to 7—though Plato strangely mentions 10 as the cutoff. Aristotle will gently criticize this (Cf. *Politics* 1265a 30ff), as will many others over the years. I cannot, quite honestly, crack the "Da Vinci Code" mentality here, though something in the neighborhood of 5,000 does, indeed, seem like an appropriate cutoff for a community—one with a hope of being self-sufficient without also being alienating.

4   Aristotle, *Politics*, book VII, chapter IV.

5   I argue for this point in "The Dog on the Fly," *Plato's Animals*, ed. Michael Naas and Jeremy Bell (Bloomington: Indiana University Press, 2015): 96–111.

6   Cf. Aristotle, *History of Animals*, Book 1, Part 1.

7   So, too, is the horse a liminal creature, never fully domesticated and never fully wild. In this way, perhaps the horse and the gadfly both speak to the true nature of all things: always in the process of becoming rather than caught up in static being.

8   Aristotle, *The Parts of Animals II*, 661a12

9   Krell, *Daimon Life*, 130–31.

10   Ibid., 104.

11   Ibid., 123.

12   David Farrell Krell, *The Tragic Absolute: German Idealism and the Languishing of God* (Bloomington: Indiana University Press, 2005): 168–69.

13   Krell, *The Tragic Absolute*, 169.

14   James Joyce, *Ulysses* (London: Wordsworth Press, 2010), 464.

15   Krell, *The Tragic Absolute*, 170.

16   Ibid., 149.

17   Ibid., 160.

18   Simon Dixon, *Catherine the Great* (New York: Ecco/HarperCollins, 2009), 314.

Subject Index

Author Index